Subsidizing Democracy

Subsidizing Democracy

*How Public Funding Changes Elections
and How It Can Work in the Future*

Michael G. Miller

Cornell University Press

Ithaca and London

First published 2014 by Cornell University Press
Printed in the United States of America

Library of Congress Cataloging-in-Publication Data

Miller, Michael Gerald, author.
   Subsidizing democracy : how public funding changes elections and how it can work in the future / Michael G. Miller.
      pages cm
   Includes bibliographical references and index.
   ISBN 978-0-8014-5227-7 (cloth : alk. paper)
   1. Campaign funds—United States. 2. Political campaigns—United States. 3. Elections—United States. 4. United States—Politics and government—21st century. I. Title.
   JK1991.M65   2014
   324.7′8—dc23   2013021192

Cornell University Press strives to use environmentally responsible suppliers and materials to the fullest extent possible in the publishing of its books. Such materials include vegetable-based, low-VOC inks and acid-free papers that are recycled, totally chlorine-free, or partly composed of nonwood fibers. For further information, visit our website at www.cornellpress.cornell.edu.

Cloth printing   10   9   8   7   6   5   4   3   2   1

For Laura

CONTENTS

ACKNOWLEDGMENTS

This book began as a research project in the Department of Government at Cornell University, and though I swore to never think about it again when I finished, here we are. I am extremely pleased that the book has returned "home" to Cornell University Press for its publication, since the Cornell community was so important to its development. Suffice it to say that this book was a long time in the making, and I have accordingly incurred a long list of people who were integral in producing it. Nonetheless, it goes without saying that while the people named below made the project possible, the responsibility for all errors or omissions, should they present themselves herein, rests solely with me.

I know that it is customary for reasons of convention or style to acknowledge one's professional debts first and familial debts second, but I cannot in good conscience follow that template. I went to graduate school at the urging of my best friend and spouse, Laura Miller, who recognized that the academic life was the only one that would give me a sense of proper place. Without her constant support and willingness to uproot our family (three times), none of this would have been possible. My children, Carli, Landon, and Ava, have also borne some cost along the way. Most of these words were written with a child under my chair, and I fear that I have said the woeful phrase "just a second" a few too many times during the process. I thank them for their patience. Finally, my mother, JoAnn Miller, and father, Gary Miller, have been unwavering in their support of this and all my endeavors, and their willingness to indulge my intellectual curiosity from a young age placed me on this path. For my family's separate and collective sacrifices on my behalf, I am endlessly grateful.

Walter R. Mebane Jr. deserves to be at the top of the list as well. I went to Cornell to work with Walter because I believed that his scholarship was the finest example of rigorous quantitative political science on substantive topics that mattered. The intervening years have not only deepened this belief but have also yielded crucial lessons about the huge investment that a good mentor is willing to make in his students. Walter ably guided the project from pilot to completion, reading and rereading chapter drafts, and it seemed he was always a step ahead of me. It still seems that way. This book would not have happened without Walter's guidance. I owe him a bottomless debt that I will most assuredly pay forward, and I am proud to call him my friend. I am also deeply grateful to others at Cornell, each of whom provided crucial guidance: Theodore J. Lowi, Suzanne Mettler, Peter Enns, and Christopher Anderson. I also thank Sherry Martin, who helped to shape the project at its formative stages during two graduate seminars, as well as my fellow Cornell graduate students for friendship, support, and commiseration throughout the writing process.

The National Science Foundation was kind enough to fund the bulk of this project via a Dissertation Improvement Grant (SES-0819060), and where necessary, the Department of Government (via the personal generosity of Professors Mebane and Lowi) and the Department of American Studies at Cornell took up the financial slack. Judy Virgilio and Jackie Pastore were instrumental in helping to prepare the NSF grant application, which Laurie Coon ably administered. It is not a stretch to say that this project would never have been possible without the generosity of these benefactors, particularly the NSF. Their funding allowed for the fieldwork and data collection described herein, much of which was aided by what came to be called "Team America," a dedicated group of undergraduate research assistants at Cornell who worked tirelessly on data collection in 2007 and/or 2008: Erin Nuzzo, Tom Hudson, Zach Newkirk, Rebecca Dittrich, Chris Martin, Ben Gitlin, and Rob Morissey.

Parts of Chapter 7 originally appeared as an article in the July 2008 issue of *PS: Political Science and Politics,* and I thank Cambridge University Press for allowing it to reappear here. The Graduate School and the Department of Government also funded travel to a number of conferences at which this research was presented, critiqued, and subsequently improved. Various components of this book or its pilot study appeared at meetings of the American, Great Plains, Midwestern, New England, Northeastern, and Southern Political Science Associations. In their capacity as discussants, Clifford Brown, Dino Christenson, Dean Spiliotes, Christopher Larimer, and Kevin Wagner were most helpful.

Others who had neither institutional nor service obligations read parts of the book and offered critical advice at various stages (even though some no doubt will not recall doing so today). For going above and beyond, I thank Dan Butler, Bhavna Devani, Conor Dowling, Peter Francia, Danny Hayes, Paul Herrnson, Luke Keele, Ray La Raja, Kenneth Mayer, Seth Masket, Costas Panagopolous, Robert Shapiro, and Sophia Wallace. Finally, my friends Nick and Angie Behm allowed me to turn their Phoenix house into a base of operations during Arizona fieldwork in early 2007; I probably earned my nickname "Dupree" in those two weeks. I thank them for opening their home, and apologize for my cooking.

The state agencies of Arizona, Connecticut, and Maine were most helpful when I needed data or clarification, but two individuals deserve special recognition. Mike Becker at the Arizona Clean Elections Commission collected and provided special data at my request, and Kristin Sullivan in the Connecticut Office of Legislative Research navigated a tricky state bureaucracy to track down elusive precinct returns from that state.

My colleagues and students in the Department of Political Science and the Institute for Legal, Legislative, and Policy Studies at the University of Illinois, Springfield, were both a source of support and a sounding board as the project developed into this book. Richard Gilman-Opalsky, Christopher Mooney, Jason Pierceson, David Racine, and John Transue offered advice in this phase; they, along with the rest of the Department of Political Science at UIS, have also been strong professional mentors and good colleagues. I also appreciate the patience of my students, all of whom listened (often as a captive audience) to new ideas as they developed, and some of whom also provided assistance in data cleaning and manuscript formatting. Jennifer Carter, Jessica Luigs, and Meagan Musgrave deserve special recognition here. Both the UIS College of Public Affairs and Administration and the Institute for Legal, Legislative, and Policy Studies contributed by defraying the publication costs of the book, and I am thankful for their support.

Finally, I wish to thank the editors, staff, and faculty board at Cornell University Press, as well as two anonymous reviewers whose work greatly improved the project. Michael McGandy believed in the project early and has proven to be a brilliant editor. His guidance has been invaluable, and he is absolutely the most important contributor to this project whom I have never met in person. I hope to change that soon. Sarah Grossman, Ange Romeo-Hall, and Kim Vivier guided the manuscript to final form. They deserve commendation for their patience. I also thank Dina Dineva for indexing the book.

The old saying goes, "Choose work you love and you will never work a day in your life." Because of the investments made in me by the people named above, I have yet to put in a day's work on this project. Thank you all.

Subsidizing Democracy

Introduction

On June 30, 2011, comedian Stephen Colbert launched a satirical assault on the campaign finance environment in the United States. Standing on the front steps of the Federal Election Commission building, Colbert announced that he had received approval to use his television show on Comedy Central as a vehicle to "raise unlimited monies" for his Colbert Super PAC and to "use the monies to determine the winners of the 2012 elections."[1] Of course, Colbert's true intent was to mock the campaign finance regulations resulting from a series of federal court decisions, but his effort displayed marked financial success: Colbert Super PAC subsequently raised more than $1 million for comedic use in the 2012 presidential primary election cycle alone (Wilson 2012), and spent roughly $20,000 on a sixty-second television ad in the South Carolina Republican primary that accused Mitt Romney of being a serial killer.[2]

This claim was a tongue-in-cheek allusion to the controversial *Citizens United v. FEC* case in early 2010. Because the Supreme Court's decision in that case granted speech rights—and therefore the right to spend money to communicate a political message—to corporations, Colbert Super PAC reasoned in its ad that dismantling corporate organizations (as Romney had facilitated in his business career) was tantamount to murder. In a more serious reaction, President Barack Obama directly rebuked the Supreme Court in his State of the Union Address a week after the decision, saying it "will open the floodgates for special interests ... to spend without limit in our elections."[3]

The total effects of the opinion are not yet clear, but *Citizens United* and related federal court decisions have undeniably changed elections since 2010 via the creation of super PACs, which are able to accept donations of unlimited size from corporations and/or individuals so long as they do not coordinate their activities with any campaign. Super PAC spending infused more than $640 million into the political system in the 2012 election, during which President Obama reversed his previous opposition to super PACs and was aided by more than $60 million of independent expenditures from one pro-Obama super PAC alone.[4] The implicit message is that the large, unregulated contributions flowing through super PACs are a necessary tool in the new campaign finance landscape.

At the same time, uncompetitive elections are the norm in the United States. In a typical election season, only about 10 percent of challengers stand a reasonable chance of defeating a sitting member of Congress, and similarly daunting odds face challengers running for most state legislatures. According to the nonpartisan Campaign Finance Institute, the 305 congressional incumbents who won in 2008 (the last non–super PAC election) with more than 60 percent of the vote outspent their challengers by an average of more than $800,000.[5] Political action committees—the direct contributory arm of "special interest" organizations—fueled much of that difference, accounting for 46 percent of incumbent funding in 2008, compared with only 15 percent for challengers.[6] The simple truth is that PACs invest in winners, and incumbents are the safer bet.

When incumbents regularly win expensive campaigns funded by interest organizations, it is not difficult to understand why many people might come to believe that their political system is slanted toward the rich and powerful. The 2012 elections for Congress and the presidency came with a price tag of just under $6 billion, while total fundraising in state elections topped $2 billion.[7] Much of that money was raised in the Wild West of the unregulated super PAC environment, where any person or corporation can give as much as they like, sometimes anonymously. This money does not necessarily purchase effective government, however. Congressional approval ratings today are at an all-time low, and there is a perceptible belief among Americans that their government does not listen to them. Since about 1980, fully three-quarters of Americans polled by the Gallup organization have agreed that the country would be better off if government "followed the views of the public more closely."[8]

Simply put, in American politics the majority of legislators at both the state and federal level can bank on keeping their jobs for as long as they want, due in large part to their inherent advantages in name recognition and funding. As a result, strong potential challengers often stay away, recognizing that they will be at a financial disadvantage. The weaker challengers who do emerge find themselves outspent and outgunned, expending considerable time and effort on fundraising that more often than not fails to place them on par with incumbents. The most visible result of this story is the generally uncompetitive environment, but more cynical observers may also question whether incumbents—supported by the same large contributors every election—are always acting with their districts in mind. To be sure, the campaign finance system is not the sole ailment of American democracy. However, for those who view political money as a potentially corrupting force, who desire more competitive races, or who see increasingly expensive elections as effectively barring entry for many qualified potential politicians, the campaign finance environment in most of the United States must seem a bleak place indeed.

Since the early 1970s, one effort to move away from these circumstances has centered on offering candidates what Sorauf (1992, 131) termed "the fifth source" of political money: supplementing contributions from individuals, parties, groups, and the candidates themselves with money directly from the public coffers. Public election funding programs, in which money moves from the government to political organizations for the purpose of financing campaigns, began in 1976 with the presidential public funding program. The presidential system provides optional subsidies to candidates in both the major-party primary and the general presidential election in exchange for the acceptance of spending limits. Since that time, public funding programs have expanded in both geography and generosity. A few states started offering small subsidies to candidates in the 1980s, but by the next decade Arizona, Connecticut, and Maine were providing candidates for all state offices with subsidies sufficiently large to cover the *entirety* of their campaign costs. These measures, generally referred to as "Clean Elections" laws, are intended to deliver sweeping reform that improves both elections and representation.

Advocates of public election funding have long argued that it holds great potential to cure many perceived ailments of American elections. In combining direct campaign subsidies—designed to replace private contributions—with spending limits, reformers hold that public funding can curb the growth of campaign spending, foster more competitive elections, and reduce the role of contributors in influencing public policy. These are bold goals that, if achieved, would mark a fundamental departure from the dynamics of most American elections. It is therefore not surprising that public funding has proven to be remarkably popular at all levels of American government and is currently used in some form for presidential, gubernatorial, state legislative, regulatory, judicial, and municipal elections across the country.

Since the passage of broad state-level public funding programs, the burning question has been, Do they work? Unfortunately, this is not always an easy question to answer. For one, there is often no clear, universal definition of a successful policy. This problem generally stems from ambiguous or hard-to-quantify program objectives, which in turn do not facilitate precise research questions. For instance, the preamble to Arizona's public funding law states that it "will improve the integrity of Arizona state government by diminishing the influence of special-interest money, will encourage citizen participation in the political process, and will promote freedom of speech under the U.S. and Arizona Constitutions." These goals are all consistent with those of high-minded reform, but it is quite difficult to say for certain what influence, if any, special interest money has on the legislative process (for a discussion, see Witko 2006). Thus, the search for program success can often be reduced to "You know it when you see it."

Well-done, theoretically motivated analysis must also confront imprecise measures, even when it does not directly engage the stated policy outcomes. For instance, if public funding is supposed to make elections more "competitive," does that mean that fewer incumbents run unopposed, that they are less likely to win, or that they win with smaller margins? If it is expected to draw more candidates into the system, should we be concerned with attributes of the candidates such as race, gender, income, or previous political experience, or do any warm bodies suffice? These questions have no self-evident answer, and they underscore the difficulties associated with providing a singular answer to whether public funding is effective policy.

Nonetheless, political scientists, policy analysts, and other interested parties have examined public funding from various angles, and their efforts have nearly always focused on readily observable outcomes. Given that campaign contributions and expenditures are publicly disclosed, and that money yields a clearly measured variable, much of this work has sought to determine whether public funding alters campaign spending. Here, as in other areas, the size of the subsidy appears to matter a great deal: small subsidies do not change spending levels all that much whereas larger ones do.

For example, although partial subsidies have shown some promise in slowing spending inflation in Wisconsin (Mayer and Wood 1995), they have proven ineffective in New York City municipal elections (Kraus 2011, 2006) and Minnesota state campaigns (Schultz 2002). An early study of Minnesota found that public funds helped private contributors to gain an aggregate dollar advantage over PACs (Jones and Borris 1985). However, Schultz (2002) found that Minnesota's partial public subsidies have not actually reduced the spending of PACs, which simply channeled their money through soft money and lobbyists.

A different picture emerges in fully funded, "Clean Elections" states. For instance, the Government Accountability Office (GAO) found in 2010 that spending in fully funded Maine House and Senate elections decreased and held steady, respectively, compared with the two elections before public funding implementation (GAO 2010, 53), while spending overall increased in Arizona after 2000 (GAO 2010, 59). My own research (Miller 2011a) notes that the increased spending in Arizona is driven mainly by increased spending by challengers, who are generally in a much better financial position in publicly funded years. Indeed, the 2010 GAO report determined that the financial gaps between challengers and incumbents are smaller in both Maine and Arizona in the Clean Elections era (GAO 2010, 56, 62).

Much previous research has focused in addition on the question of electoral competition, since candidate lists and vote totals are also readily available. These studies have largely examined three areas: whether public funding changes the demographic composition of the candidate pool, whether more candidates are likely to run in fully funded environments, and whether victory margins are narrower when public funding is present. Several studies have examined patterns of candidate participation in publicly funded elections. For example, Werner and Mayer (2007) found that Democratic challengers are more likely to accept public funding in Arizona and Maine. That same study determined that women in Maine and Arizona House (but not Senate) races are significantly more likely to accept public money than men, but the makeup of neither the overall candidate pool nor the legislative bodies is different after Clean Elections. Finally, a 2008 report by the National Association of Latino Elected and Appointed Officials found little evidence of increased numbers of Latino candidates after the implementation of Clean Elections (NALEO 2008).

In terms of sheer candidate numbers, the GAO's report did not find overall that Clean Elections has increased the average number of candidates in state legislative elections, that it has raised the likelihood that third-party or independent candidates will emerge, or that it has changed the likelihood that a given election will be contested by more candidates than there are available seats in a district (GAO 2010, 49, 41). However, some of my previous work (Miller 2011a) suggests that Arizona and Maine incumbents in both chambers are more likely to face a general election challenger in years when Clean Elections funding is available. Taken together, then, existing findings are mixed with regard to whether full public funding encourages more candidates to run on the whole, but candidates appear to be more likely to run against an incumbent, when the odds of victory are seemingly longest.

When candidates do emerge to challenge an incumbent, there is a consistent body of evidence suggesting that those who accept full funding run more effective campaigns. Incumbents on average do not appear to be less likely to lose in publicly funded environments (GAO 2010, 35), but their opponents appear to enjoy some benefits that would be unimaginable for challengers in privately financed elections. For instance, candidates who run with Clean Elections subsidies devote significantly less time to raising money (Francia and Herrnson 2003) than their privately funded counterparts. Moreover, previous research that I conducted during the 2006 election (Miller 2011b) suggests that they also devote more time to interacting with the voting public. While the increased visibility of campaigns does not seem to spur turnout (Milyo et al. 2011), analysis of competition in fully funded environments has repeatedly shown that incumbent victory margins are reduced when candidates accept public funding (Mayer et al. 2006; Werner and Mayer 2007; Malhotra 2008).

Unfortunately for reformers, however, previous analysis found little competitive change in partially subsidized elections (e.g., Jones and Borris 1985; Mayer and Wood 1995; Malbin and Gais 1998, 136; but see Donnay and Ramsden 1995). Thus, evidence to date suggests that the size of the subsidy is crucial to the efficacy of public funding as policy: the availability of full funding (but not partial funding) appears to encourage the entry of some candidates, to alter some of the activities that they perform, and to bolster their vote totals on Election Day. This bodes well for Clean Elections programs that offer full funding to legislative candidates. However, in the search for the effects of public election funding on American democracy, a great deal still remains unknown.

Although it has made considerable progress toward evaluating certain observable effects of public funding as policy, political science has not fully examined the potential for public funding to change how campaigns are waged. As a result, we know a fair amount about the beginning of the story, when a candidate accepts public funding, and the end, when financial reports are filed and votes are counted, but very little about what happens in between. It seems rather easy, given conventional wisdom about money in politics, to simply assume that subsidized challengers control more money and that the expenditure of their money alone is causing any changes that analysts can observe. Yet this story seems grossly incomplete. If victory margins are lower or if voters are more likely to participate when a publicly funded candidate runs, then presumably the candidate *did* something to make it so.

In short, research to date tells us little about how public election funding affects the process of campaigning. Few existing studies consider the likely behavior and/or state of mind of the people in the systems themselves. Regardless of whether they are enacted with clearly stated policy goals, public election funding programs are implicitly designed to provide certain candidates with opportunities that may not have otherwise existed, to change the activities that candidates perform over the course of a campaign, and to compel both candidates and voters to orient differently to politics. Public funding therefore possesses an immense potential to alter the strategic framework in which campaigns are conducted and to transform the things that candidates think, feel, and do.

If candidates adjust their behavior in response to the different incentives that publicly funded systems provide, it seems safe to assume that public funding brings about fundamental changes in elections. Specifically, public funding is likely to affect the number of candidates running and to deemphasize the importance of political experience and/or connections, since donors are less important when candidates are subsidized. Moreover, subsidies shape candidates' ability to spread their message, not only in providing them more money to buy advertising and materials but also in diminishing the amount of time they spend fundraising, which allows them to focus on other areas. The end result could be an environment in which there are more candidates, who are spending more time interacting with voters, under the "air cover" of substantial campaign subsidies. Given the obvious implications for increased voter engagement and participation in this scenario, it is crucial to discover whether and how public election funding changes the conduct of American elections.

That is the goal of this book. Rather than evaluate whether public funding changes the funding levels or results in a given election, I focus on how publicly funded campaigns are undertaken and how we should expect subsidies to alter the strategy, behavior, and emotions of candidates and voters alike. These traits of legislative campaigns are often quite difficult to discern because learning them requires in-depth knowledge of individual candidates. Most of what goes on behind the scenes in a candidate's "war room" is therefore never known to the researcher. I overcome this problem by asking legislative candidates directly what they did during the campaign, what their reasons were for doing things, and how they felt about them.

In a series of interviews with Arizona candidates collected on the ground in the wake of the 2006 election, as well as a large-scale candidate survey conducted in eighteen states during the 2008 election cycle, I probed the minds of legislative candidates, searching for how public funding changes their behavior and mindset. These data, described in greater detail in Appendix 1, allow unprecedented insight into the candidate mind. In tandem, the data permit an in-depth examination of how the introduction of public funding alters the electoral environment, facilitating broad conclusions about the manner in which "subsidized democracy" differs from privately funded elections. Quotations from candidates throughout the book are from the transcribed interviews.

Understanding candidate motivation and behavior in publicly funded systems is crucial to evaluating those systems' capacity to change electoral competition, financial parity, and candidate participation. Indeed, absent a relatively complete picture of how candidates and voters behave in publicly funded elections, it is impossible to evaluate the policies in anything approaching a holistic fashion. Analyzing election statistics tells us what changed in the publicly funded era, but studying the strategy and actions of candidates yields answers about *how* and *why* those changes came about. I therefore focus throughout the book on the ability of public funding to affect the choices that candidates make at various stages of the campaign, and how those decisions manifest themselves in the behavior and/or attributes of legislative candidates.

In the following pages, I describe a theoretical framework in which public funding significantly shapes not only how costly candidates will perceive a campaign to be, but also how likely they think they are to win. Since public funding alters the cost-benefit dynamics among candidates, the theory suggests that such funding is likely to affect the strategic choices that candidates make before and during an election campaign. I therefore examine the impact of public election financing through the eyes of candidates, paying particular attention to how their incentives, strategy, and behavior are likely to change when subsidies are available. In short, I argue that the effects of public funding are likely to manifest themselves in altered strategic decision making throughout the course of a campaign, from the entry decision to the final hours, and that behavioral changes among candidates result in a fundamentally different political environment.

One of the most important changes is how candidates use their time. I argue that in traditionally financed elections, there is a space between what candidates *must* do if they want to win and what candidates *want* to do. Time is a finite resource, and while raising funds often requires a tenacious dedication, campaign spending itself does not determine victory (Brown 2013). So although they feel intense pressure to raise funds, I assume that most candidates prefer to maximize the amount of time they spend interacting with citizens. This book demonstrates that in providing candidates with all the money they need to run a competitive race, Clean Elections funding (but not partial funding) not only eliminates the time costs of fundraising but also fosters greater interaction between candidates and voters.

If fully funded candidates are spending more time interacting with voters, then it seems reasonable to expect more people to vote when those candidates are present. In other words, assuming that heightened interaction raises voters' information or salience levels regarding a given contest, then voters should be better able to confidently express a preference at the polls. Indeed, I find in this book that in both house and senate elections for all three fully funded states, fewer people appear to be "rolling off"—that is, voting for contests at the top of the ballot and leaving the remainder blank—when at least one candidate ran with public funding in the first election for which public funding was available. Thus, the book makes a strong argument that public funding allows candidates more flexibility with regard to how they use their time, which in turn affects mass voting behavior.

I also explore the notion of candidate "quality" in publicly funded elections. I find that while candidates are no more likely to possess political experience in publicly funded systems, public funding diminishes the utility of previous experience as a determinant of who will possess sufficient resources to wage a strong campaign. One reason for this is that election subsidies disrupt the "market forces" of traditional campaign finance, in which strong candidates supposedly attract the most donations. In funding all candidates well, regardless of attributes, full funding essentially manufactures "quality" candidates with the resources sufficient to win. It therefore appears that one way in which public funding enhances electoral competition is by giving sufficient campaign resources to candidates who would otherwise have been ill-equipped to make a serious run.

Given the ability of public funding to circumvent traditional market forces, I also consider whether candidates with very conservative ideologies would be less likely to accept public funding, and the extent to which ideologically based reluctance affects electoral competition in a partisan fashion. I find that personal ideology is indeed a crucial determinant of whether candidates choose to run as a "Clean" candidate: more conservative candidates are less likely to accept subsidies in Clean Elections states. This effect manifests itself in a partisan fashion, with Republicans being less likely to participate than Democrats. Consequently, Democratic incumbents are significantly less likely to face a fully funded challenger than their Republican counterparts.

The findings reported here have import well beyond the study of state legislative elections in any given year. The U.S. Supreme Court's 2011 decision in *Arizona Free Enterprise Club's Freedom Club PAC v. Bennett* and *McComish v. Bennett* (which this book describes in detail in Chapter 7) will certainly shape the design of future public funding systems, but public financing survived judicial scrutiny in that case and remains a powerful tool in the regulatory environment. While the next generation of public funding systems will necessarily evolve to keep pace with judicial precedent, future programs will no doubt share some features of those currently in place. Thus, understanding how candidates alter their behavior—and the ramifications for politics—is important not only for gauging the efficacy of present and past systems but also for fully considering the likely effects of proposed policies going forward.

A candidate-centric approach, in which a given program's incentives and costs are carefully considered, is therefore crucial because it will allow us to move beyond retrospective evaluations of existing public funding. Knowing whether a program worked in the past is helpful in framing future policy, but not as much as having a clear understanding of *why* it worked. Every public funding system is unique, and while future reforms are likely to resemble existing ones, they will almost certainly break new ground. Thus, it is my hope that shedding light on candidate behavior will allow us to say much more about how future reforms are likely to affect American elections.

1

Why Public Funding?

In American politics, money matters. As the role of political money has changed over time, campaign finance reforms have tried to keep pace. Regulations have been constructed to restore fairness, opportunity, and integrity to American elections. Fair elections are essential to any democratic system, but so is the absence of unreasonable restrictions on political speech. Even before the advent of mass media, money expanded the ability of political parties and individual candidates to communicate with voters. That said, elections in America today are expensive, and the high price of running is often a barrier to entry for prospective candidates. Policies that seek to regulate the flow of money in politics must therefore straddle a fine line as the freedom of those with the means to project their voices collides with the need for broad democratic dialogue.

Many jurisdictions in the United States have attempted to resolve this tension by implementing voluntary systems of public election finance. Public funding systems are variously constructed, but the reasons cited for their creation are almost always the same: to control the growth of spending, to diminish the role of "special interest" contributors looking for political favors, to enhance electoral competition, and to improve representation. Whether these goals are attainable, or whether they should be pursued, is debatable. Yet the use of public dollars in American politics has steadily expanded in the past quarter-century. Given the development of often expensive policy under conditions of such uncertainty, it is a worthwhile exercise to consider the objectives of public financing in America and how it shapes the behavior of candidates and voters. Before considering the effects of public funding on campaigns, we must first examine where the programs come from and what we already know about their effects.

The Roots of Regulation

Money has always played a crucial role in American elections. Indeed, candidates leveraging campaign cash predate both the federal Constitution and modern political parties. "Treating" political supporters to alcoholic beverages on Election Day was common practice in the colonies as early as the seventeenth century; it was rooted in English tradition and was generally seen as good candidate manners (Mutch 2001). As party organizations established themselves in the early to mid-1800s, they consolidated control of campaign finances, spreading "walking around" money on Election Day as an enticement to vote with premade party tickets; such blatant bribery was sufficiently worrisome that all states had enacted legislation banning the practice by middle of the nineteenth century (Bensel 2004, 58). Despite this step, voter bribery remained a relatively common phenomenon throughout much of the nineteenth century, and it was not until the widespread adoption of the secret Australian ballot in the late 1800s that party attempts to put preprinted tickets in the hands of whiskey-softened supporters were thwarted (Mutch 2001).

As the parties spent money on ticket printing and voter compensation, they tapped funding streams that flowed from members in government. During the era of civil service patronage, from the Jackson administration until the early 1880s, parties exploited their position within government to raise funds from political appointees, who kicked back a portion of their wages (Corrado 2005). In the first act of federal campaign finance reform in U.S. history, Congress added a provision to the Naval Appropriations

Act of 1867 banning government employees from soliciting political contributions of naval workers. The practice of party extortion was dealt a more serious blow with the passage of the Pendleton Act in 1883, which ended the spoils system and eliminated the assessments levied by parties on patronage appointees. State governments soon followed suit (Gross and Goidel 2003).

As patronage evaporated, parties turned elsewhere for financial support. Large business interests and wealthy individuals of the Gilded Age soon supplanted rank-and-file patronage appointees as the primary source of party funds, often donating vast sums (Corrado 2005). The election of 1896 marked a watershed of elite involvement in political campaigns, as new Republican chairman Mark Hanna created a funding system in which business interests appropriated a fixed percentage of their revenue to help the Republican cause. Many Republican candidates for federal office that year ran with the explicit promise that businesses would be more profitable under Republican guidance, and most business leaders believed them (Corrado 2005).

While corporations were pouring money into the political system at the end of the nineteenth century, the Progressive movement and the era of journalistic muckraking brought increased attention to the role of elite interests in government. As a result, by the turn of the century many Americans began to more closely scrutinize the role of big business in influencing campaigns. Indeed, in his 1907 State of the Union message, President Theodore Roosevelt called for regulatory legislation that would not only ban corporate political contributions but also provide public election subsidies "ample enough to meet the necessity for thorough organization and machinery." Congress did not take up the latter issue, but it passed campaign finance regulations that same year in the Tillman Act, named for Senator Benjamin Tillman (D-SC).

The Tillman Act outlawed political contributions from corporations and financial institutions and was the first in a string of bills passed over the next sixty years that aimed to diminish the influence of moneyed interests. The Federal Corrupt Practices Act of 1910 (also known as the Publicity Act) and its amendments of 1911 and 1925 established spending caps on congressional races and mandated disclosure of financial information. In a series of laws beginning with the amended Hatch Act of 1940 and ending with the Taft-Hartley Act of 1947, Congress also established a

$5,000 individual contribution limit to federal candidates and committees and banned direct contributions from labor unions.

On the whole, campaign finance regulation in many states has historically been less stringent than the rules gradually implemented at the federal level. According to the Campaign Finance Institute (2011), as of 2011, twelve states allowed unlimited individual contributions to candidates, and corporate contributions have been banned in only twenty-one. Moreover, in Missouri, Oregon, Utah, and Virginia, there remains no limit on direct corporate funding. The regulation of labor union money is even less widespread in the states: contributions from labor unions were proscribed in only fifteen states and were unlimited in seven.

Particularly in federal politics, the regulations of the early twentieth century often went unenforced, and campaign finance was dominated by the exploitation of legal loopholes. Despite the fact that campaigns were legally required to submit financial disclosures, there was no bureaucratic agency responsible for overseeing implementation, leaving Congress as the only regulatory authority. Financial reports were therefore rarely available for public examination, were sometimes not even collected, and even when clearly noncompliant, were generally ignored by the Justice Department (Corrado 2005). Meanwhile, corporations and labor interests were beginning to find ways around strict contribution prohibitions. When Congress outlawed direct contributions from labor unions, the Congress of Industrial Organizations formed a political action committee (PAC) in 1943. Members of the CIO voluntarily contributed personal funds to the union's PAC, which bundled them into larger sums for dispersal to campaigns. Thus, the PAC allowed its members to maintain great financial influence with favored candidates while preserving the legal individual source of contributions. Since the creation of the CIO PAC, political action committees have become a mainstay of American campaign finance.

While PACs were exploring new territory in the second half of the twentieth century, campaign dynamics were in flux. As the century progressed, campaign methods evolved with changing forms of mass media. Candidates became more visible, gradually supplanting parties as the dominant force in American elections. The preeminence of candidates was solidified with the emergence of television, first used as a campaign tool in 1952. The election of 1960 saw a charismatic candidate in John F. Kennedy, whose victory in the presidential race is often attributed to his successful use of television. Even before Kennedy, it had become clear that the campaigns of the last half of the twentieth century would be waged on the airwaves. Television advertising costs for political contests exploded during the late 1950s and early 1960s, pulling the overall cost of federal campaigns steadily upward.

Concerned about the high price tag of his election, Kennedy appointed an independent commission to investigate presidential campaign finance, apparently out of concern that expensive campaigns created a higher likelihood of public perceptions of corruption (Corrado 2005). While no major changes were adopted, meaningful campaign finance reform was increasingly part of the legislative conversation throughout the 1960s. Indeed, Oregon senator Richard Neuberger had introduced the "Teddy Roosevelt bill" in 1956, which would have provided major parties—but not candidates—with public subsidies based on the size of the electorate in previous years (Garrett 2011). Neuberger's allusion to Roosevelt was a recognition of the latter's proposal for public funding to parties in his 1907 message to Congress. Roosevelt had claimed that while the Tillman Act and then-proposed disclosure laws were good first steps at regulation, "there is always danger in laws of this kind, which from their very nature are difficult of enforcement; the danger being lest they be obeyed only by the honest, and disobeyed by the unscrupulous, so as to act only as a penalty upon honest men" (Roosevelt 1907). He had therefore proposed the creation of public funding for congressional elections, funneled to candidates through their party, provided that the latter also agreed to individual contribution limits: "The need for collecting large campaign funds would vanish if Congress provided an appropriation for the proper and legitimate expenses of each of the great national parties, an appropriation ample enough to meet the necessity for thorough organization and machinery, which requires a large expenditure of money. Then the stipulation should be made that no party receiving campaign funds from the Treasury should accept more than a fixed amount from any individual subscriber or donor; and the necessary publicity for receipts and expenditures could without difficulty be provided" (Roosevelt 1907).

As its name implies, Neuberger's bill worked in much the same way: in exchange for large subsidies ranging from roughly $42.5 million to $93.5 million in 2012 dollars, parties would agree not to accept contributions exceeding $100 from individuals, or about $850 in 2012 terms (Garrett 2011).

Although Neuberger's bill never received a floor vote, it was the first of several attempts that Congress made over time to provide public funding to elections for that body. Indeed, since 1973, ten congressional public funding bills have passed in at least one chamber of Congress; in 1992 a significant public funding bill was passed by both houses but vetoed by President George H. W. Bush (Garrett 2011).

Congress has not yet successfully created public funding for its own elections, but it established a significant program for presidential candidates in 1971, via the passage of both the Federal Election Campaign Act (FECA) and the Revenue Act. As amended in 1974, the FECA created a voluntary public funding system for presidential elections, including partial matching funds in primaries and full funding with spending caps in the general election. Per the Revenue Act, the program was funded by income tax check-offs that allowed citizens to designate a tax dollar for the purpose of funding the presidential race. The FECA also mandated contribution and spending limits in congressional elections, largely in response to Watergate-era perceptions that special interests had gained unfair leverage in expensive, media-driven campaigns. Thus, the FECA was designed to curb both campaign spending and the influence of any single contributor while preserving system transparency in all federal elections.

Subsequent litigation on several facets of the FECA set hard rules on campaign finance regulation that remain relevant today. In *Buckley v. Valeo* (424 U.S. 1 1976) the FECA was contested on the grounds that mandatory spending and contribution caps restricted the speech of candidates and their supporters. In a *per curiam* opinion, the Supreme Court upheld the presidential public financing programs because participation is voluntary. The Court also found that the main element of speech in a political contribution is the expression of support: "A contribution serves as a general expression of support for the candidate and his views, but does not communicate the underlying basis for the support. The quantity of communication by the contributor does not increase perceptibly with the size of his contribution, since the expression rests solely on the undifferentiated, symbolic act of contributing" (424 U.S. 1 1976).

This logic allowed the Court to uphold the constitutionality of contribution limitations while striking down forced spending limits. In short, the Court differentiated between a contribution, which is an expression of support of someone else, and campaign expenditure, which communicates a political message to the public. Since in a media-driven environment, campaign spending equates to campaign speech, the Court found that restrictions on candidate spending amount to "direct and substantial restraints on the quantity of political speech" and are therefore unreasonable restrictions of First Amendment rights (424 U.S. 1 1976).

For reformers who see money as a nefarious element in American politics, the *Buckley* decision has forced creativity in efforts to expand public funding to the states. Because spending limits cannot be imposed on candidates, states looking to reduce the role of money in politics must provide candidates with a reason to accept restrictions on their campaign spending. Public funding programs seem to be a natural vehicle to this end: not only do subsidies serve as an incentive for candidates to participate, but they also directly address several problems beyond cost inflation. Indeed, critics of the prevailing campaign finance system often cite public funding as a panacea of sorts, with the potential to alleviate one or all of at least four major deficiencies in American elections: high average costs, low average competition, the appearance of corruption, and the burden that fundraising places on campaigns.

Paramount among these is the failure of existing regulation to curb the growth of campaign costs. Since 1980, overall expenditure levels have grown markedly in both federal and state races (e.g., Jacobson 2009). Access to deeper, more established resource networks is but one component of the advantage that nearly all incumbents enjoy over challengers, and expensive races allow incumbents to construct a financial fortress that makes them seem unassailable (see Jacobson 2009). Faced with such a financial disadvantage, many potential challengers likely conclude that facing an incumbent is a quixotic pursuit.

This trend contributes to the second problem: uncompetitive American elections. When incumbents are met with a challenge, they consistently win by wide margins. Particularly for new candidates with little or no established funding network, raising sufficient funds is inherently problematic as they face the familiar paradox: to appear viable to the individuals and groups necessary for funding a serious campaign, candidates must have money; but to raise money, they must appear viable (see Jacobson 1980). Inexperienced challengers find it difficult to convince skeptical donors and are unable to keep pace financially with resource-laden incumbents.

Moreover, there is substantial evidence suggesting that while money alone does not necessarily equate to votes, its absence essentially eliminates a challenger from contention (e.g., Herrnson 2011; Malbin and Gais 1998, 145; Cassie and Breaux 1998). Thus, the absence of high-quality candidates perpetuates a wide spending gap between incumbents and challengers at both the federal (e.g., Jacobson 2009) and state (e.g., Cassie and Breaux 1998) level. Given these circumstances, it is no surprise that when incumbents run, they have an excellent chance of winning (e.g., Herrnson 2011).

Third, reformers claim that the gaudy sums required for political campaigning invite opportunistic behavior on the part of external actors seeking to influence public policy. With limited resources, federal PACs seek to achieve this goal by betting on candidates likely to win and to hold key legislative positions. In both federal and state elections, incumbents, party leadership, and powerful members of the rank and file benefited disproportionately from PAC donations in the 1990s (Cassie and Thompson 1998; Thompson et al. 1994; Thielemann and Dixon 1994). Recent evidence suggests that PACs tend to contribute late in the election to congressional candidates who have already demonstrated fundraising success (McGhee and La Raja 2008). Alexander (2005) and Brown (2013), who found that PAC and external (nonself) contributions, respectively, are associated with better-performing candidates, suggest that such a strategy is paying off in federal elections.

The strategic behavior of many PACs is intended to maximize the odds that the groups they represent receive a return on their investment, leading some reformers to conclude that PAC money is dangerous because of the possibility for a quid pro quo exchange between contributor and legislator. Scholarly analysis in this area has reached mixed conclusions. Some have found evidence that PAC donations influence member participation or votes (e.g., Witko 2006; Fellowes and Wolf 2004; Hall and Wayman 1990). Others, however, have found no relationship (Wawro 2001; Bronars and Lott 1997; Grenzke 1989). Hoffman (2005) finds that PAC money has heightened influence in nonprofessionalized state legislatures, in which members have fewer resources to provide a resistance buffer. In a comprehensive study of state legislatures, Powell (2012) finds that legislators with ambition for higher office, as well as those in better-paid and larger assemblies, are more likely to be influenced by campaign contributions.

When it comes to vote-buying by interest groups, however, academic evidence may be less important than the widespread public *perception* that elite influence-peddling is rampant in American politics (Magleby and Patterson 1994; Wertheimer and Manes 1994; Sabato 1989). Indeed, in rendering the *Buckley* decision, the Supreme Court found contribution limits acceptable not only "in preventing corruption" but also in avoiding "the appearance of corruption" (424 U.S. 1 1976). Advocates of public funding reason that even if there is no overt exchange of contributions for legislative votes, in reducing the role of business, labor, and other interest contributions in election campaigns, public money addresses the *appearance* of such nefarious relationships, thus increasing public confidence in democratic institutions.

Fourth, for many prospective candidates, even raising amounts necessary for a $20,000 state legislative campaign requires tenacious dedication, the assembly of a fundraising organization, and a large amount of time. For all but the most resolute, it is a daunting prospect made worse by the fact that most candidates view fundraising as a loathsome chore (Jacobson 1987). This fact alone no doubt keeps many challengers out of politics altogether, but for those who do enter, the necessity of fundraising detracts from time that could be spent interacting with voters, creating an opportunity cost in terms of improving stature against better-known incumbents (see Francia and Herrnson 2003). For officeholders, raising money has become such an onerous task that some have argued it threatens to erode the quality of governance (Epstein and Zemsky 1995; Blasi 1994; Nelson and Magleby 1990).

For reformers seeking to solve these problems, public election financing seems like a logical answer. Candidates opt into programs that include spending limits because they receive a subsidy in exchange. By providing challengers with more money while requiring candidates to spend less overall, public funding programs promise to close spending gaps between challengers and incumbents, reducing the overall cost of elections. Moreover, subsidies diminish candidates' reliance on so-called special interest contributions, making it less likely that interest groups will gain undue influence over legislative activities. Finally, candidates recognize that subsidies allow them to avoid the dreaded task of fundraising, which facilitates greater control over the remainder of their campaign time.

Public Funding in the States

As with campaign finance regulation at the federal level, the decade after the Watergate scandal proved to be an active period for reform in the states. The construct of public funding programs is as diverse as the politics of the states themselves, nearly half of which currently employ public funding in some form (Panagopoulos 2011). For instance, citizens in ten states are able to indirectly provide funding to parties, diverting money using check-offs or add-ons on their income tax returns. Ten states also allow citizens to deduct political contributions from their state tax burden to encourage donations. Other states maintain funds for the sole purpose of directly supporting candidates. When they participate, candidates agree to abide by spending limits, but aside from that commonality the subsidy amount and the scope of eligible candidates vary dramatically. For example, Florida, Maryland, and Michigan restrict the availability of partial subsidies to gubernatorial candidates. West Virginia and New Mexico provide full public funding, but only for candidates for the state judiciary and public regulatory board, respectively.

In the 2008 election six states—Arizona, Connecticut, Maine, Hawaii, Minnesota, and Wisconsin—provided direct subsidies to state legislative candidates. Each of these states required candidates to abide by spending limits, but the extent to which they funded candidates allows the publicly funded states to be classified into two groups: *partial* and *full*. Partial funding programs set the maximum subsidy payment at some percentage of the spending limit, but always less than half. Candidates in states offering full funding receive subsidies approximately equal to spending limits. The practical difference between the two types is that fully funded candidates need not raise additional money once they qualify for the program whereas partially funded candidates must raise the difference between the subsidy and the spending limit from private sources. I report the key features of each state's public funding laws in Table 1.1.

Hawaii, Minnesota, and Wisconsin offered partial funding to legislative candidates in the 2008 election. In Hawaii, public funding is paid for with a two-dollar income tax check-off and is also supported in part by the state's general fund. In order to be eligible for public money, state house candidates must raise $1,500 to show viability. The state's tax laws are designed to ease the fundraising process for participating

TABLE 1.1. Summary of Public Funding Regulations in 2008 Elections, State House Races

	Hawaii	Minnesota	Wisconsin
Qualification	raise $1,500	raise $1,500 in amounts < $50	raise $1,725 in amounts < $100
Total spending limit	approx. $32,000	$31,400	$17,250
Max. subsidy	15% of spending limit	50% of spending limit	45% of spending limit
Max. matching funds	NA	NA	NA
	Arizona	Connecticut	Maine
Qualification	220 $5 donations	$5,000 from 150 district residents	50 $5 donations
Total spending limit	$35,673	$41,000	$6,148
Max. subsidy	$31,673	$35,000	$5,648
Max. matching funds	3X subsidy	2X subsidy	2X subsidy

Note: Hawaii's spending limit is $1.40 for each voter in a district. Minnesota and Wisconsin spending limits apply only if all candidates in a given race accept them. In Arizona, Connecticut, and Maine candidates are allowed to raise $5,000, $6,000, and $500, respectively, before qualifying. Once they accept public funding, they may raise no additional money.

candidates: while contributions to any state campaign are tax-deductible up to $250, individuals may deduct up to $1,000 when they contribute to candidates who participate in the public funding program. The individual candidate deduction limit is in effect regardless of the candidate's acceptance of spending limits. However, a contributor can donate the $250 to four separate candidates, taking a deduction for each, if they all agree to limit spending.

Once they meet the eligibility benchmark, Hawaii's state house candidates receive a one-time matching payment equal to the $1,500 entry threshold and then receive dollar-for-dollar matching funds up to the maximum subsidy amount, which is 15 percent of their expenditure limit. That limit is based on a population formula; candidates may spend $1.40 for every eligible voter in their election. In 2008 the average expenditure limit for each primary and general election was $16,050. Perhaps due to the small subsidy size, few candidates accept public funding in Hawaii legislative elections: in 2008 only six candidates participated.[1]

Wisconsin candidates qualified for subsidies from the check-off-supported Wisconsin Election Campaign Fund by winning their primary and successfully soliciting $1,725 in individual contributions of less than $100. In 2008 participating candidates for the state house agreed not to spend more than $17,250 over the course of their campaign. Spending limitations applied only if all candidates in a given race agreed to abide by them. Participating candidates were given equal grants regardless of district population. The grant amount was dependent on the monetary level of the fund, and it therefore varied with the number of participating candidates and the generosity of Wisconsin's taxpayers. Candidates' grant amounts were reduced for every dollar they received from PAC sources, and in no instance was a candidate able to accept grants amounting to more than 45 percent of the spending limit.

Wisconsin's program was repealed in 2011 as the state made a number of cuts to balance its budget. The elimination of the WECF was an easy fiscal target. Neither the one-dollar tax check-off amount nor the spending limits had been adjusted for inflation since the mid-1980s, rendering them anachronistic and unable to meet the spending needs of a legislative candidate two decades later. It is therefore not surprising that as in Hawaii, participation rates in Wisconsin were fairly low for most of the late 1990s and early 2000s. Indeed, twenty-six candidates accepted public money statewide during 2008, and of those, none faced spending limits that would have been triggered by facing an opponent who also took WECF money (Nichols 2009).

Minnesota maintains a fund supported by a five-dollar income tax check-off. The check-off itself is more complex than in many states; taxpayers can check a box to divert five dollars to either of the major parties or to a general political campaign fund. Payments from the party fund are directed to candidates proportionally, based on the amount of money that was checked off from citizens in their districts. Payments from the general fund are dispersed equally to candidates for various state offices. The total payments may never exceed half the candidate's spending limit, and payments from both funds are disbursed after the primary to nominees contesting the general election. In 2008 most participating house candidates limited their expenditures to $31,400. Like Wisconsin, Minnesota releases publicly funded candidates from spending limitations when they face an opponent who does not abide by them. However, Minnesota is the only state to account for the inevitable existence of disadvantages that political neophytes face, adjusting its spending limit upward by 10 percent for first-time candidates and boosting the limitation by approximately $6,000 for candidates with closely contested primaries in which they won by a vote ratio of fewer than two to one.

The flexibility of spending limits is a powerful inducement to accept public funding, but Minnesota has historically taken additional steps to ensure that its program remains viable. First, rather than rely solely on the check-off for revenue, Minnesota has traditionally augmented those receipts with an additional diversion of $1.25 million from the state's general fund. In addition, from 1991 to 2008 the state reimbursed individual contributors up to $50 via the Public Contribution Refund Program (PCR) if they donated to a candidate who participated in the public funding program (the reimbursement program was terminated in 2009 due to budget constraints). That component of the law was intended to realize lower spending levels while facilitating easier candidate fundraising: candidates were able to ask contributors for a "loan" that the state treasury typically repaid to donors within six weeks.

In the early 2000s Arizona, Connecticut, and Maine implemented full funding systems designed to pay for all (or at least most) of participating candidates' campaign expenses. The successful passage of these laws is part of a larger national movement called "Clean Money, Clean Elections"; accordingly, the laws are generally called "Clean Elections" programs. This name is no accident; since the programs are often passed by voter referendum, advocates characterize them as furthering "clean" government in an effort to attract support from citizens who may otherwise pay little attention to campaign finance reform. One Arizona legislator communicated this quite clearly, remarking, "The name of the law helped to get it passed in the first place...who's not for clean elections?"

The Clean Elections programs in each state display some shared characteristics (hereafter I use the terms "Clean Elections" and "full funding" interchangeably). First, candidates qualify for full public funding by raising a small amount of money, often from a predetermined number of individual contributors. Once they prove their viability in this fashion, Clean Elections candidates receive public subsidies sufficient to wage an *entire* primary and/or general contest. In return, participating candidates agree to raise no additional money and to abide by spending limits equal to their subsidy amounts. To encourage participation, the original structure of the programs allowed candidates running against those who opt out of the program to receive limited matching funds for their opponents' expenditures above the spending limit. The matching funds provisions were intended to guarantee financial parity for participating candidates in all but the most exceptional of circumstances.[2]

Despite these broad similarities, regulations in each state create a unique environment. Maine was the first to move toward widely available full funding for both executive and legislative candidates. The Maine Clean Elections Act (MCEA) was placed on the ballot by voter initiative in 1996 and passed with 56 percent of the vote; subsidies first became available to candidates in 2000. To qualify in 2008, Maine House candidates solicited fifty contributions of five dollars, after which they received subsidies of $1,504 for the primary and $4,144 for the general election when those races were contested.[3] These amounts are equivalent to the average expenditure of candidates for the two previous primary and general elections. Candidates for the Maine House may raise and spend $500 in seed money before qualifying for the program. Through 2008 Maine provided matching funds grants in excess of the initial subsidy for participating candidates who faced opposing campaigns or independent groups spending above the initial subsidy amount, matching up to two times the original subsidy. Maine's program is supported by a combination of allocations from the state's general fund and a three-dollar income tax check-off.

In 1998 Arizona voters approved the Citizens Clean Elections Act. Unlike in Maine, Clean Elections in Arizona resulted from a sizable political scandal. In the 1990s seven state legislators and ten others were charged with a range of crimes, including bribery, money laundering, and obstruction, as part of the "AzScam" scandal in which legislators were caught accepting bribes in exchange for providing support for legalizing casinos in the state. Eventually, ten legislators resigned or were removed from office, and a number were sent to prison. The blow to public confidence in the wake of the scandal almost certainly led to successful passage of Clean Elections in Arizona, which received only 51 percent of the vote. Arizona began offering Clean Elections subsidies to candidates during the 2000 elections.

In 2008 Arizona's legislation provided participating candidates with a subsidy of $19,382 for the general election and $12,921 for the primary, so long as they were able to demonstrate their viability by successfully soliciting at least 220 contributions of exactly five dollars. The subsidy amounts are adjusted for inflation from the original total level of $25,000 in the 2000 election. During the qualifying phases, candidates may privately raise a relatively small amount (less than $4,000) of seed money, but if they ultimately accept public financing, they agree to forgo any additional sources of finance and to spend only the sum of the subsidy. Through the 2008 election, if participants in the program found themselves outspent by traditionally funded opponents or independent groups, Arizona matched the difference up to three times the subsidy amount, making its matching funds provisions slightly more generous than those in Maine. Arizona funds its system with the five-dollar qualifications that participating candidates raise, plus a 10 percent assessment on civil penalties and criminal fines in the state.

Connecticut was a late joiner to the Clean Elections club. Its Citizens' Election Program (CEP) is the only functioning large-scale full funding scheme for legislative elections passed by legislative act. Like the one in Arizona, the Connecticut law was passed in response to a highly visible financial scandal. Governor John Rowland resigned in 2004 in response to allegations that he had received more than $100,000 in gifts and kickbacks from state contractors; he eventually pleaded guilty to a federal bribery charge. In response, the Democratic-controlled Connecticut General Assembly worked with Rowland's successor, Republican Jodi Rell, to pass a Clean Elections–style full funding bill in 2005. Connecticut's system became active for the first time during the 2008 legislative election.

Connecticut's program, funded by the sale of unclaimed or abandoned assets, is the most complicated of the Clean Elections laws. In comparison to the qualifying thresholds in Arizona and Maine, Connecticut's bar is set high; state house candidates must raise at least $5,000 from a minimum of 150 contributors who reside inside their district. The subsidy structure also differs from those of Arizona and Maine; payment amounts in Connecticut are more variable and depend on the context of the race. The subsidy amount for the primary depends on the party's strength in the district; where the percentage of a party's registered voters exceeds that of the other party by 20 points, the district is considered to be "party-dominant" and the primary is acknowledged to be the de facto election. Recognizing that primary fields in party-dominant districts are likely to be more crowded, the state allocates $25,000 to primary candidates of the dominant party and $10,000 for all others. General election subsidy amounts are also dependent on the conditions of the race: candidates facing major-party opposition in the general election are eligible for further grants of $25,000 for that campaign, while those facing either minor-party or no opposition receive $15,000 and $7,500, respectively.

To calculate spending limits, Connecticut divides the election into three phases. In the qualifying period when they are raising the initial $5,000, candidates are permitted to spend that entire amount plus up to $1,000 of their personal funds, for an aggregate initial spending limit of $6,000. Spending limits in the primary and general elections are equivalent to the candidate's grant amount in each plus any unspent money remaining from the qualifying phase. Thus, for a major-party candidate in a competitive district, the overall spending limitation can be calculated as the sum of the primary and general grants plus the initial $6,000, or a total of $41,000.

Connecticut also provided matching funds allocations to participating candidates whose traditionally funded opponents exceeded the spending limit in 2008. Like Maine, Connecticut matched expenditures of opponents and opposing groups up to twice the total spending limit. However, rather than provide matching grants for every opponent expenditure above the spending ceiling, the state released four lump-sum grants equivalent to 25 percent of the spending limit. These grants were triggered when opponent spending exceeded 100, 125, 150, and 175 percent of the spending limit. With this money in hand, candidates were then restricted to matching only what their opponents had spent. Connecticut suspended the matching funds provisions of its law in 2010 in anticipation of a federal court injunction.

While each state's program is different, the common element is that participating candidates in Arizona, Connecticut, and Maine who meet uniform qualifying requirements are entitled to public subsidies that fund their entire campaign. Once they qualify, participating candidates in these states raise no money from private sources. Moreover, through the 2008 election, all three states in theory guaranteed an even playing field via matching grants that were triggered when an opponent exceeded the spending limit. Thus, nearly all the publicly funded candidates I surveyed in Arizona, Connecticut, and Maine assumed that they would compete at approximate financial parity.

Conclusion

The expenditure of money to influence elections is a well-established practice in American politics, as old as elections themselves. Nevertheless, political contributions have long been viewed as a nefarious and corrupting force. At the same time, money is often cited as the predominant reason for any number of democratic ailments—either because it exists in excess or because some candidates are consistently unable to raise enough of it to wage a strong campaign. Political money has therefore come to be viewed like water: it is necessary to sustain the political environment, but it will always flow, and can be a destructive force if left totally unchecked.

Campaign finance regulations are usually constructed to combat corruption, whether actual or perceived. Bans on corporate giving, limitations on donation size, and mandatory donor disclosure all ensure greater transparency and are intended to obstruct unscrupulous machinations. Yet unless a campaign planned to fund itself solely with large corporate donations, these policies do not change the process of campaigning very much. Like other campaign finance regulations, the primary intent of public election funding is to reduce corruption, since the direct provision of campaign subsidies reduces (or eliminates) the role of private donors who may want something in return. It is not a coincidence that Arizona and Connecticut passed their laws in the wake of historic financial scandals.

Given the salubrious potential of subsidies, it should not be unexpected that they have become a popular regulatory tool at all levels of American government: each election year, states collectively spend millions of dollars to subsidize candidates for political office. However, unlike other policies, public funding holds great potential to change the status quo in most American elections. Somewhat surprisingly, then, there is much about public election funding that remains unexplored. It is tempting to look for changes in victory margins or campaign treasuries as a way to evaluate public funding, and such examinations are valuable. However, changes to the macrodemocracy would presumably be observable only because a bevy of actors in the political system responded to new incentives in a publicly funded environment and changed their behavior accordingly. How public funding alters candidates' strategic choices is therefore a good place to start when we consider the impact of public election funding as policy.

2

Strategic Candidates and Public Funding

In our search for the effects of public funding, the first step is to recognize that participation is likely to change the strategic considerations that candidates make since it dramatically affects the costs—in several areas—that they must pay to wage a viable campaign. The recognition of this dynamic is important because an altered cost-benefit calculus will almost certainly affect what candidates think and do during the course of an election. Indeed, if public funding leads to broader shifts in electoral competition or interest group influence, these changes are likely to be the result of altered strategy and candidate behavior. Or as one Arizona legislator noted, "When people think of Clean Elections, they're thinking of it as keeping out special interests and…leveling the playing field. But I think if there's a nuance that the general public misses, it's the campaign strategy that comes into Clean Elections."

Broadly, candidates who opt out of public funding are most likely to do so if they have ideological objections to the program or relatively low fundraising costs in a traditionally funded campaign. Those who choose to participate in public funding programs do so when they determine either that accepting subsidies will lower their fundraising costs or that public funding will enhance their chances of victory. Significantly, these terms will be most affected for candidates lacking political experience and correspondent access to funding networks. Thus, it is reasonable to expect the campaigns of publicly funded candidates to be very different from those of their traditionally financed counterparts.

Clean Elections candidates in particular should find themselves in a better financial position than they otherwise would have been. Equally as important, the acceptance of full funding allows them to solve a crucial problem that exists for candidates in traditionally financed elections: the struggle to allocate time between raising money and turning out votes via personal interaction with citizens. Compared with even partially funded programs, the effects of Clean Elections funding on the decisions of strategic candidates should be stark, as fully funded programs hold vast potential to affect not only the financial dynamics of a race but also the manner in which candidates use their time.

Why Take Public Funding?

When we consider the strategic decisions that candidates make when they weigh whether to accept Clean Elections subsidies, the calculus of candidate entry provides a useful starting point. Black's (1972) classic formal entry model portrays prospective candidates as strategic actors whose entry decision is a function of campaign utility. Simply put, Black's model predicts that if the candidate judges the benefits of an office combined with the probability of winning it as exceeding the costs of running, she will run. Subsequent research has incorporated and extended Black's calculus; most has focused on the "probability of victory" component of Black's model, and has found that strategic candidates are less likely to enter when the chances of winning are low (e.g., Lazarus 2008; Maestas et al. 2006; Maisel and Stone 1997). Additional work has considered the effect of the marginal benefit of a higher office as it relates to progressive political ambition (Stone et al. 2004).

Campaign costs have received comparatively little attention in the discussion of the entry calculus. In a notable exception, Dowling (2011), who studied gubernatorial elections, expanded the cost component of Black's model, differentiating between "personal" and "institutional" costs of running. Dowling suggested that the availability of public funding should reduce costs and encourage candidate entry, but he found evidence that public funding encouraged the entry of only incumbent-party candidates in open-seat contests. Dowling's detection of such limited effects could be a result of the generally high level of quality typical of a major-party gubernatorial candidate; it seems reasonable to assume that many of the candidates in Dowling's study had a great deal of political experience, and that their perceived "institutional" costs may have been relatively low due to easier access to donor bases and networks.

I argue that for candidates contemplating an entry-level election, and particularly for those who lack political experience, public funding poses a greater potential to affect the utility calculus. As races become more expensive, candidates must pay higher costs in both money and time. For instance, Steen (2006, 11) found that the average "potentially competitive" non-incumbent congressional candidate in the 1992–2000 elections spent over $180,000 of her own money. Even with substantial contributions from their personal wealth, most candidates must also assemble sophisticated funding operations and devote considerable effort to "dialing for dollars" if they hope to remain financially competitive. The demands of funding a campaign are so substantial that fundraising often exists as a distinct sub-operation. Indeed, some scholars view a political campaign as actually containing two separate campaigns running concurrently: one for money and another for votes (Herrnson 2011).

The monetary costs of running for state legislative office usually do not approach those of running for Congress, but they are still a substantial hurdle for most potential candidates. For instance, the average cost of a 2008 campaign for the California Assembly—the most professionalized of all state houses—was about $360,000.[1] In the less professionalized Arizona and Connecticut houses, average costs for lower-house campaigns were about $41,000 and $18,500, respectively. In Maine, which has a part-time assembly, the figure was slightly less than $5,000. Even this sum is more than many citizens could comfortably spend, and stringent state contribution limits can lead to considerable fundraising time costs because a large number of donors must be contacted to raise necessary funds. For instance, the per-cycle individual contribution limit to any single legislative candidate in Connecticut and Maine was $250 in 2008. In Arizona it was $400.

In short, should they decide to run, inexperienced candidates in "traditional" systems of campaign finance, in which no public subsidies are available, must either spend their own money or devote substantial time to raising it from donors. Within this framework, and bearing in mind both Herrnson's distinction between the "two campaigns" and Dowling's recognition of the complexities associated with calculating costs, I argue that the true cost of running reflects the "two campaigns" framework. Candidates therefore consider two types of costs: those of funding the campaign and those of mobilizing voters. In the former area, candidates will incur personal financial costs if they spend their own money on the campaign. In addition, they must spend time and other resources to persuade prospective donors to contribute. When it comes to mobilization, candidates must expend time and energy on activities such as walking door-to-door, phoning, attending meetings, and the like. Thus, "campaign costs" are actually made up of the candidate's monetary costs, the time and effort spent fundraising, and the time and effort spent mobilizing the vote. For many candidates, public funding holds the potential to reduce the cost of both fundraising and mobilization.

This disaggregation of campaign costs clarifies the potential for public election financing to affect candidates' utility calculus. It allows us to consider five specific decisions that candidates must make as they weigh whether to accept election subsidies: how public funding affects the costs of raising sufficient funds, the effort associated with qualifying for public funding programs, the consistency of public funding with a candidate's political ideology, the candidate's estimated probability of victory, and the candidate's desire to avoid entanglements with contributors.

I first consider funding costs. Suppose a challenger is weighing whether to enter an election campaign against an incumbent legislator in a state that offers public subsidies. The candidate has three choices: run a traditionally financed campaign with private donations, run a publicly funded campaign, or do not run. The rational candidate will choose the path that imparts the highest net utility, weighing the costs and benefits of not running against those of running a traditionally financed campaign, using Black's (1972) calculus. However, the candidate must also calculate the utility of a publicly funded campaign, which is a slightly more complex endeavor. One reason for the additional complexity is that subsidies impart substantial changes to campaign costs.

In the states offering partial subsidies, participating candidates must typically raise about three-quarters of their funding from traditional sources such as individual contributions. For example, if a candidate has a target fundraising figure of $30,000 and receives a subsidy of $8,000, she will presumably incur lower funding costs (in terms of both money and time) in raising the additional $22,000 than if she were raising the entire $30,000 from private donors. However, since they must still raise the amount between the subsidy and the goal, partially funded candidates will likely have a day-to-day campaign experience that is little different from that of candidates accepting solely private funding: in both circumstances candidates must devote a large amount of time and effort to identifying and persuading contributors. Thus, while funding costs are lower for partially funded candidates, their costs of the "campaign for money" remain real and perceptible.

In contrast, candidates in states offering full funding recognize that the public subsidies essentially fund an entire campaign with a single financial allocation. Once they accept the grants, candidates spend none of their own money during the election and also agree not to solicit additional funds from private sources; thus, their fundraising costs during the election diminish to almost nothing. As one Arizona legislator I interviewed in 2007 put it, "Clean Elections just facilitated things for me, because the thing that so many aspiring politicians say is that raising money is an awful thing to do." One of his colleagues provided a more personal perspective, reflecting on how Clean Elections affected her orientation to funding the campaign: "I had never run for office before, and I certainly would not have run for office if I had had to go to my blue-collar friends as someone who had never run for office, saying, 'Give me fifty bucks.' I would not have made that step."

This anecdotal testimony is supported by previous scholarship confirming that the receipt of full subsidies effectively eliminates fundraising from the list of tasks that candidates perform (Francia and Herrnson 2003; Miller 2011b), and thus Clean Elections candidates can ignore the "campaign for money" once they qualify for public funding. The prospective candidate would realize that she would incur no fundraising costs if she accepted full public election subsidies, as Dowling (2011) suggests.

However, while the costs of raising funds are lower in publicly funded systems, participation is not a costless endeavor. In Clean Elections systems, candidates must qualify for subsidies by raising a relatively small amount of money from individual contributions. Arizona and Maine house candidates demonstrate their viability by successfully soliciting contributions of exactly five dollars from individuals (at least 220 in Arizona and at least 50 in Maine). In Connecticut, state house candidates must raise at least $5,000 from a minimum of 150 contributors who reside in their district. In the partially funded states, candidates become eligible by raising a set amount from small contributors (Hawaii), by winning their party's nomination for the general election (Minnesota), or by some combination of both (Wisconsin).

Particularly in the fully funded states, qualification requirements are designed to be sufficiently onerous to prevent marginal candidates from receiving public funding, but not so stringent as to deter participation. Candidates in Arizona almost universally acknowledged that raising "seed money" or "fives" was not a simple task; "difficult" and "tough" were commonly used to describe the process. For instance, one first-time candidate who ran with public funding said, "The most difficult thing with Clean Elections is getting those five-dollar contributions." Another neophyte said, "[Raising] 250 five-dollar contributions, if you think that's easy, you ought to try it. It's tough, it's really tough." Another offered a succinct comment: "You really have to work your butt off to get those five dollars. It really isn't easy."

Still, raising a small number of five-dollar contributions is certainly easier than funding an entire campaign with private contributions, particularly for challengers. Most candidates recognized that, as challenging as qualification was, fundraising would have been more difficult had they run as a traditional (privately financed) candidate. When asked why he chose to run with public funding as opposed to private contributions, one challenger said, "With Clean Elections I just needed to go qualify, which takes work, but I felt that that was much more doable than raising the money [from contributors]." Another challenger compared the anxiety associated with soliciting five dollars to the emotional toll of asking for substantially larger sums as a traditional candidate: "Five dollars is a fair amount to ask of people. I don't want to knock on my neighbor's door and ask for a hundred dollars." Even a state senator who had been in the legislature for multiple terms saw the effort associated with qualification as less than the work associated with private fundraising: "I'm not a good fundraiser; I don't like asking people for contributions. I don't mind hitting up my friends for five bucks, so it's not hard. [Running traditionally], that's kind of tough. If [donors] want to give me money, they can give me money, but I'm not going to do a lot of soliciting."

Many of the candidates I interviewed reduced the qualification costs by working through the party structure. One senate candidate was thankful to run in a district spanning multiple counties, which allowed him to attend several county-level party meetings for the purpose of soliciting qualifying contributions. "Fortunately, a lot of [my qualifying contributions] came from the Democratic Party meetings. I mean, I got about half of it from two different meetings, and that was really nice, but then at the end, it was like, 'O.K., we've got to get another 20 or so,' and it's just knocking on doors." Another candidate, this one running in a Democratic house primary, used the party's voter identification system and made qualification part of his early efforts to identify supporters in face-to-face canvassing. "For me, if I'm talking to Democrats, they like [Clean Elections], and it wasn't that hard to raise the money. It was harder for me to ask than it was for them to give me the five dollars. It's only five bucks. That's what made that nice."

This kind of testimony indicates that prospective candidates recognize that the act of qualification imparts some costs. However, it is worth noting that while meeting Connecticut's qualification requirement in particular is no easy task, the cost of raising the $32,000, $35,000, and $5,600 initial subsidy amounts for a combined primary/general election in Arizona, Connecticut, and Maine, respectively, from private donors vastly exceeds the costs paid to qualify. In the partially funded states the subsidy size is smaller but the qualification requirements are less specialized. For instance, raising $1,500 or winning one's primary are presumably things that a viable candidate would do even in the absence of public funding; thus, they likely seem less burdensome than raising "fives." Indeed, in Minnesota, where candidates qualify simply by winning a primary, the costs of qualification are practically invisible. So with the possible exception of Minnesota, I assume that participation in public funding requires candidates to incur some perceptible up-front costs of qualification.

One final factor alters the cost calculus for challengers: their own political ideology. Specifically, should they decide to participate in public funding programs, conservative candidates must reconcile the acceptance of government funds with a political ideology that generally places a high value both on the free market and on diminished government spending.

Alternatively, in some districts candidates may fear that the acceptance of subsidies will provoke a backlash from a conservative electorate. If present, this fear exists despite the fact that the general public pays little attention to campaign finance law (Primo 2002). Even in New Jersey, which has been running Clean Elections pilot programs in some districts since 2005, approximately 80 percent of residents in districts where candidates may receive public funding consistently report no knowledge of the program, despite a focused public policy experiment that garnered substantial news coverage (Woolley and Vercellotti 2007). Nonetheless, conservative candidates who participate in public funding potentially balance the benefits of a higher probability of victory with the fact that acceptance of public subsidies may be at odds with the political views of either the candidate or the district. Liberal challengers must make no such trade-off.

The size of the subsidy no doubt affects the extent to which conservative candidates will perceive an ideological cost to participating. For instance, it may be easier for a very conservative candidate to justify accepting a 15 percent subsidy in Hawaii than it is for one in Arizona, where the subsidy may constitute the entire campaign war chest. Thus, ideological costs are a function of both how large the subsidy is and how conservative the candidate is. As either factor grows, the potential for ideological costs increases.

The increase in campaign costs stemming from qualification or ideology in publicly funded elections is potentially offset by the fact that most candidates contemplating an incumbent challenge will determine that participation increases their chances of winning. Incumbents win most of the time when they run (Herrnson 2011). One major problem for new candidates with little or no established funding network is that prospective donors understand that incumbents are a safer bet. Thus, inexperienced challengers find it difficult to convince skeptical donors and are unable to keep pace financially with resource-laden incumbents (Jacobson 1980).

The matching funds provisions of Clean Elections (as originally constructed) promised an even financial playing field for all who opted in. Indeed, challengers who accept public subsidies generally find themselves in a considerably better financial position than those who run traditionally funded campaigns (Miller 2011a), and since the implementation of public funding in both Arizona and Maine legislative elections, challengers spend at levels approximately equal to incumbents (GAO 2010, 55, 61). In the eyes of most participating candidates, accepting full funding diminishes the importance of money in the campaign, so that, as one Arizona House candidate said, "We can have this race be decided by who has the best ideas, and not who has the most money." In short, there is reason to believe that most challengers will perceive Clean Elections as improving their capability to run *well*.

The disparity between fundraising costs in privately and publicly funded systems should be particularly large for inexperienced candidates, who would likely face funding difficulties in a traditional financing system. In exchange for some effort spent qualifying, any candidate—regardless of connections or comfort with fundraising—can obtain financial resources for a campaign. Moreover, in the case of states offering full funding, candidates are reasonably assured that they will be able to raise all the funds they need to run a credible race. One Republican candidate who ran in a decidedly Democratic Arizona district summed this sentiment well, noting that participation in Clean Elections afforded him the ability to compete: "Without Clean Elections, you can have the best ideas, but if you don't have the money, you don't have a chance. So [Clean Elections] takes another step toward leveling the playing field. [In this district] we don't have the demographics, so it's harder for a Republican to compete, but you know, I might have the best ideas, and with Clean Elections I have access to $30,000, and that can go a long way."

Given this testimony, it seems reasonable to expect that increased financial parity will lead to heightened electoral competition (Jacobson 1990), particularly in states where elections are especially uncompetitive (Mayer and Werner 2007). Previous research has found some evidence that full funding (Mayer et al. 2006; Werner and Mayer 2007; Malhotra 2008) but not partial funding (Jones and Borris 1985; Mayer and Wood 1995) enhances competition. However, it is important to emphasize that the candidate just quoted entered the race despite the fact that while Clean Elections funding would allow him to mount a much stronger campaign than he would have otherwise, he would still probably lose the election. One Republican incumbent lamented this arrangement, arguing that the state is "making a $30,000 investment on a candidate who's in a district where he's not going to win, and you're spending $30,000 just so he can have a voice."

Uncompetitive districts are not unusual in American politics, but in most safe districts in traditionally funded elections a challenger's probability of victory seems exceedingly low relative to the costs of running, and challengers are more likely to stay out of the race (Pritchard 1992; Hogan 2004). In raising the perceived probability of victory while reducing the costs, public election funding, and full funding in particular, would seem to shift the calculus the most for inexperienced candidates in apparently unwinnable districts, providing some hope where none existed otherwise.

Regardless of whether public funding is available, strategic candidates emerging in competitive districts may view their chances as reasonably high to begin with. Public funding may help somewhat in close districts, but strong candidates in competitive conditions are more likely to possess attributes that make them both good fundraisers and competent field organizers. They are therefore less likely to view public election funding as a necessary condition of running a strong campaign. The same is true of incumbents, who possess institutional advantages that reduce the importance of accepting public funding.

Every bit of funding helps, but the candidates who could raise little money without subsidies will be most aided by public funding. Thus, while most candidates (especially non-incumbent candidates) will perceive participation as likely to enhance their chances of victory, I argue that candidates are ironically likely to perceive the performance bonus as highest in districts that are the most unwinnable, or when they lack political experience and/or access to donor networks. In the words of an Arizona legislator, "Clean Elections does alter the opportunity for Joe Smith, coming off the street, to run, more than a former councilman or something."

There is also another benefit to participating. As noted in the previous chapter, political scientists have found conflicting evidence regarding the ability of contributions to sway policy in privately financed systems. Likewise, Arizona's legislators could not agree on the extent to which campaign contributions influenced their decisions. Some members argued forcefully that contributions did not change their behavior, regardless of their source or size. A Republican with multiple sessions of experience said, "I don't see any quid pro quo...do I remember when a group comes in that was strongly supportive of me? Of course I appreciate that. But it's not going to influence a vote, or even get them access more than anyone else. And I haven't observed anything from others that says I'm different than anyone else."

Other members pointed out that Arizona's contribution limitations were so small ($296 when I conducted interviews in 2007) that vote-buying was a near impossibility. One Republican member of the Arizona House said, "I think it's not right that people think that an individual can give you $296, and I think we're electing very shallow individuals to the legislature if they're going to be influenced by that." A Democratic member cited the importance of his reputation as an independent thinker and his belief that a small contribution could not change that: "When you have a limit of less than $300 that you can get contributed from an individual, nobody's going to buy your vote. Nobody buys anybody's vote. I have people who have contributed to me. Some of them represent interests, some are friends of mine. I vote with them sometimes, and I'll vote against them sometimes. I really like my reputation, that I'm a person who's going to vote my conscience."

Other legislators were not so sure. One member of the Arizona House who had run with public funding paused for a long moment when asked whether campaign contributions influenced the decisions that his traditionally financed colleagues made. While he clearly did not want to suggest that there were votes for sale in the Arizona House, his answer was similar to the opinion of many non-incumbent candidates, who frequently stated that there must be *some* influence of political money, even if subtle and subconscious: "Clean Elections takes the big money out of politics, and it allows those of us who are representing the district just to represent the district. I don't have to sit and think about who gave me money when I look at a bill. 'Am I going to support this, or not?' I do think that happens [for traditionally financed legislators]. I don't think it's conscious, in a lot of ways; in talking with people who run for office the traditional way, they say it doesn't happen, but I think subconsciously it has to, because when you're looking at a bill that's going to affect the person who gave you the most money to run, and it's going to affect them adversely, you know that they're not going to contribute to you the next time."

Another legislator who ran with Clean Elections funding was a bit stronger in communicating a belief that even if the arrangement is not overt, there is a natural inclination to support the people who helped one to get elected. The size of the contribution, in this informant's view, was much less important than the expression of support, which itself created subtle feelings of obligation: "I think that if you are a candidate and you get a $300 check from home builders, and you get elected in the legislature and you have a bill that helps the home builders, you're not quite sure . . . it makes it difficult to be completely unbiased in making that decision. I think what it does is it keeps that candidate more attuned to the voters. If you're going to get those checks, it's just human nature that you're going to want to try to help pay back the person who gave you that check, so I do think that the candidates that take money from special interests will pay a lot more attention to those special interests that gave them money, and I think that's a problem."

While some legislators clearly believed that money holds the potential to affect legislative behavior, even the most pessimistic members felt that the linkage was subtle and would be hard to prove. For most members of the legislature, the issue regarding campaign contributions is not the potential purchase of votes but the disproportionate access that contributors enjoy. One Democrat who had won with public funding reflected on the freedom of not having to use contributions as the basis to decide which people he would see when the session began. He argued that contributors were more likely to get face-to-face interaction with legislators, which he felt is a crucial component of lobbying on an issue. Moreover, he believed that while the interests most likely to desire such interaction would make their support known via bundling tactics that amplified their contributory power, public funding was an effective tool at curbing disproportionate influence: "One person can give you five dollars, the other can give you $16,000 worth of checks. You have three hours' worth of time to spend. You decide to block that off into one fifteen-minute meeting, and one two-hour-and-forty-five-minute meeting. Which person is going to get which meeting? [Contributing] buys access; it buys time to convince the legislator. I just feel that I [having accepted Clean Elections funding] have such freedom that I don't have any of those constraints."

The testimony above underscores the fact that even if vote-buying is not rampant in the legislature, participating candidates can run knowing (and signaling to voters) that they owe nothing to financial supporters. Thus, public funding reduces the appearance of corruption, which is important for maintaining continued public confidence in political institutions. When asked what the state of Arizona is buying with its investment in Clean Elections, candidates who took public funding (both winners and losers) consistently communicated the benefit of reducing not corruption itself but the appearance of corruption in the eyes of the public. One legislator responded, "I think the main thing you're buying, and for me it's unquestionable, is a perception on the part of the public that candidates for elected office are not bought and sold by lobbyists. We could debate the facts of that, but the perception [among the public] is that we are, and [Clean Elections] destroys the perception."

Another publicly funded candidate, this one a first-timer who lost in the general election, said, "You're investing in the incumbent, to make sure that he or she is true and representing the people." This sentiment was echoed by an experienced Democratic member of the Arizona House, who noted that accepting public funding allowed him to focus on objective representation and advancing issues he cared about: "If I were running traditional, lobbyists can give me contributions just like any other stakeholder or person who thinks I'm doing a good job here. To me that's fine. The beauty of publicly financed campaigns is I don't even have to think about that. I don't need to care who gives me the money. I don't care whether they actually live in my district or not. I have issues I care about. [During the qualifying phase] I think I raised less than a thousand dollars. The [traditionally financed] Speaker of the House raised $90,000 at a luncheon. Now which one of us do you think is going to be influenced?"

For fully funded candidates, running "Clean" allows them to know that they are not being influenced and forms the basis to credibly present themselves to voters as such. Because partially funded candidates must still raise money from private donors (including PACs and other organizations as allowed by state law), they retain the risk of appearing to be corrupt. Thus, participating in Clean Elections likely enhances the nonmonetary benefits of the office in Black's model, but the power of partial funding to do this is certainly smaller.

Putting It All Together

Accounting for the elements above, and also assuming that challengers are able to make an accurate calculation of their costs and benefits, that they prefer more money to less, that they are able to qualify for public funding, and that they run a serious campaign (i.e., they actively seek financial resources and votes), we find stark differences in the likely candidate experience in traditionally and publicly funded campaigns. The underlying logic of this claim is the same as that in Black's (1972) model: candidates will weigh the costs of a campaign against the benefits of the office, while factoring in the likelihood that they will win. However, public funding adds more variables to the equation, making candidates' calculus more complicated. Specifically, publicly funded candidates receive an additional benefit from feeling less "beholden" to donors, and many will also believe that the subsidies will improve their likely performance. At the same time, nearly all participating candidates will bear some costs of qualifying for public funds, and some may feel uncomfortable accepting taxpayer funds for ideological reasons. Those who do participate, however, are likely to experience lower net fundraising costs, as they must devote significantly less time to soliciting contributions.

Thus, when potential candidates consider the positives and negatives of a campaign for which public funding is available, they face a more complex set of choices than traditionally funded candidates. Public funding has the potential to simultaneously change all elements of the calculus of running: campaign costs, the anticipated probability of victory, and the perceived benefits of the office. In turn, these changes are likely to alter the conditions in which many candidates will run for office, and how they will behave once they make the transition from citizen to candidate.

This claim provides the beginning of a framework for understanding how public funding affects whether certain candidates will run for office, and how the campaigns of participating candidates might differ from those raising only private money. If a candidate is completely ambivalent about the acceptance of subsidies, then public funding adds no additional costs and benefits to the campaign, and Black's (1972) calculus remains the mechanism by which candidates decide whether a campaign is worth the time and effort. However, if candidates perceive public funding as increasing their probability of victory or decreasing their campaign costs (or both), they will be more likely to choose to run a publicly funded campaign. In some instances, the shifts will be so stark that candidates will enter politics when they would not have done so otherwise.

The results of my 2008 legislative candidate survey are generally supportive of this framework. One of the survey questions asked publicly funded candidates in both partial and full funding systems about their rationale for participating and allowed them to choose all applicable options: increased time flexibility, a greater likelihood of victory,

TABLE 2.1.   Percentage of Publicly Funded Candidates Citing Various Reasons for Participating

	Partially funded states	Fully funded states
	N = 206	N = 106
Greater time flexibility	65.1	73.3
Would not have been competitive otherwise	58.5	40.7
Avoid taking money from interest groups	25.5	65.5
Other	16.0	14.1

the avoidance of taking money from interest groups, or some other reason. Candidates' responses to this question are useful for gaining a sense of their strategic considerations when they began the campaign. The percentages of respondents who cited each answer are contained in Table 2.1.

There are some immediately apparent differences among candidates in the two types of systems. First, a healthy majority of candidates running with Clean Elections funding—65 percent—reported accepting subsidies at least in part because they did not want to rely on contributions from interest groups. In contrast, only about 25 percent of candidates who ran with partial subsidies shared this sentiment. The difference between fully and partially funded candidates likely results from the fact that while the former can confidently envision a campaign devoid of *all* interest group funding, smaller subsidies for the latter mean that they must still solicit contributions from willing donors. In other words, Clean Elections funding allows candidates to credibly claim no dependence on so-called special interest contributors, but partial funding does not afford this luxury.

Second, large proportions of candidates in each type of system cited public funding as vaulting them to a level of competitiveness that they would not have been able to achieve otherwise. Just over 40 percent of fully funded candidates agreed that raising enough money to run a competitive race would have been a problem without subsidies; considerably more partially funded candidates—by about 18 percentage points—agreed with the statement. The high proportion of candidates in both types of systems selecting this response is consistent with the idea that candidates perceive subsidies as enhancing their likely electoral performance, and also that public funding is most helpful to candidates who are least likely to make a strong showing in a traditionally financed environment.

Third, in both full and partial funding systems an overwhelming majority of respondents reported that they saw election subsidies as a means to gain more control over how they used their weekly campaign time. Among partially funded candidates, over 65 percent cited a more flexible schedule as having motivated their decision, while over 70 percent of fully funded candidates did so. These majorities strongly suggest that candidates understand that accepting public subsidies diminishes fundraising obligations. In total, then, Table 2.1 shows that candidates perceive altered costs and benefits associated with the acceptance of public funding in a manner generally consistent with the narrative presented above.

Conclusion

The first step toward a complete understanding of public funding as policy is to grasp its effects on the strategic decisions that candidates make. This claim will seem obvious to some, but it has to date largely eluded study. Academics and analysts alike have focused on broad, macrolevel questions about the relationship between election subsidies and readily observable outcomes. For example, existing studies address the relationship between public funding and variables such as electoral competition, turnout, and the composition of the candidate pool. All of these are worth examining; however, if changes are apparent in these areas, they are likely the result of shifts in the decisions that individual candidates make over the course of an election. Put another way, if political science has established that public funding changes elections, it has to date said little about *why* these changes occur.

The propensity for public funding to dramatically shift strategic incentives is therefore worthy of consideration from both advocates and critics. The former will undoubtedly focus on how subsidies enhance the "positive" elements of the calculus that candidates make when weighing whether to run, namely, the increased probability of victory, lower fundraising costs, and reduced entanglement between donors and candidates. The framework above suggests that many candidates—and non-incumbents in particular— will see public funding as providing a net benefit in all three of these areas. Significantly, candidates perceive public funding as providing these benefits because they are allowed to behave differently than they would have otherwise. These behavioral changes aggregate to an altered electoral environment, be it more competitive, more representative, or more participatory.

It seems shortsighted to conclude that public funding improves competition solely because challengers have more money than they would have otherwise. If public funding frees candidates to perform the tasks that they think are necessary for garnering votes, then a fuller exploration of the mechanism between public funding and vote totals is necessary. Money is certainly important, but the narrative above suggests that a reduction in fundraising costs is also important in terms of the manner in which candidates use their *time*. Shifts in candidates' ability to directly engage and mobilize voters should pay dividends, and must be considered as part of a complete picture of the policy impacts of public funding programs. Thus, a deeper understanding of the candidate mind should prove useful for those hoping to explain why public funding should improve democracy.

For those who might hold more skeptical attitudes about the benefits of public funding, a better grasp of the costs associated with participation in public funding programs will lead to a deeper understanding of how the policies are likely to function in practice. For one, the costs of qualifying have to date been understudied and should be more thoroughly explored. Moreover, if more fiscally conservative candidates bear costs that moderate and/or "liberal" candidates do not feel, then ideology and/or party affiliation is likely to be a crucial cost driver in the participation calculus, effectively determining the likelihood that a given candidate will participate. From a policy perspective, this could lead to disproportionate effects as fiscally conservative candidates feel the need to opt out of a program that would almost certainly benefit them.

3

Campaign Time

Public funding holds great potential to affect the financial fortunes of participating candidates, but it is equally likely to change how they use their time. Whether the act of fundraising is "bad" in a normative sense is debatable, but it stands to reason that since public funding frees them from fundraising obligations, participating candidates are likely to pursue a different set of activities on a week-to-week basis than they would otherwise. Indeed, the framers of Arizona's law recognized that running with traditional contributions "requires that elected officials spend too much of their time raising funds rather than representing the public" (AZ 16-940). Presumably, if candidates receive all the money they need in a single lump sum disbursed early in the election cycle, then they will spend considerably less time fundraising than they would otherwise (Francia and Herrnson 2003).

But a crucial question remains: What do publicly funded candidates do with that time? It could be that candidates reinvest the hours they would have devoted to fundraising, focusing on other campaign activities instead.

This shift would likely result in a more visible campaign as candidates sought out additional opportunities to engage the public. Alternatively, perhaps public funding does not change public engagement patterns, instead drawing candidates who would not have had time to run for office otherwise due to work or family obligations. Or maybe candidates who accept subsidies simply campaign less, spending their fundraising time on family, work, or other interests.

Assuming that candidates intend to earn the highest possible number of votes, it seems safe to expect that if fundraising is removed from the list of necessary campaigning tasks, candidates will redirect the time that would have been spent on fundraising to garnering support from voters instead. Depending on the number of hours that subsidies can regain for a candidate, this shift could lead to significant gains in the number of voters the candidate is able to reach directly via any number of tactics. Considering the potential that increased time flexibility therefore holds for candidates looking to gain additional control over their electoral destiny, it is worthwhile to study how public funding alters campaign strategy and resulting activities.

Public Funding and Candidate Time

Presumably, few prospective candidates look forward to spending a great deal of their immediate future raising money. Fundraising is a necessary task if one is to run a credible campaign (e.g., Cassie and Breaux 1998), but it seems reasonable to assume that given a choice, most candidates would prefer to devote their time to some form of direct communication with voters. There is ample evidence for this among Arizona candidates in the interview sample. For instance, when asked what motivated him to run, one candidate responded, "I wanted to meet the people; I wanted to go to the fairs and the parades and everything else." His desire to meet voters is shared with most other informants, and stems from a common belief that activities such as canvassing and speeches conform to popular conceptions of what a campaign "looks like." In reducing the effort required to raise campaign money, public funding is likely to be viewed by candidates as affording them the ability to perform the tasks they *want* to do as opposed to those they *have* to do.

For many informants, this change resulted in immediate, perceptible returns on the time invested in voter interaction. A first-time candidate running in the general election described these benefits indirectly while expressing surprise in her ability to invest so much time in the campaign: "[I would not have thought] that at my age I could go twenty-four hours a day with three meetings a day, and two parades and a conference. That I had that energy, that was amazing. I was a political junkie before the campaign and it just fed my addiction." Such responses were not uncommon; candidates consistently described a belief that meeting citizens energized their campaign and gave them a sense of efficacy. This feeling was underscored by another informant who described her gradual understanding that interaction with voters was paying off: "As a candidate knocking on a door, or even calling, citizens would say, 'I've never had a candidate even talk to me.' So it was a really positive thing."

Not all candidates seek the same sort of interaction with voters. While some prefer face-to-face activities such as field canvassing, others may choose to phone or mail constituents. These decisions are shaped by the candidate's personality as well as by district constraints; mobilization efforts conform to the realities of media costs and district size in a given election. An Arizona primary candidate described his choices almost defensively, detailing how while he may have preferred to knock on more doors, he felt bound by a feeling of how campaigns were generally conducted in his area and was sensitive to fitting his message with voter expectations: "People get their message out [in a variety of ways], whether it's TV, radio, or mail. In our district, it's mail." Another candidate, whose district covered a large geographical area in rural Arizona, preferred signs and phoning simply due to the difficulties of face-to-face field canvassing: "We relied a great deal on the signs. They really do make a great difference in spite of what people say. What would have made a bigger difference is going door-to-door, but our district is [very large in terms of] square miles, and has a lot of gated communities, so it's really hard to get into some of the places. But we did a lot of calling. We had thousands and thousands of phone calls, and people calling on our behalf. That was a good thing."

Regardless of the chosen method of voter interaction, given a choice between spending an hour communicating their message in some fashion or raising money, none of the informants indicated that they would have chosen the latter. Indeed, many candidates for the Arizona Legislature expressed acute anxiety stemming from the prospect of raising money from private donors. As one primary candidate said, "To me, it just seems awkward to ask people for $500 or $1,000, or to go into businesses asking for money. I just have a problem with that." Another, who ran in the general election with Clean Elections funding, felt that he would not have had much success funding his campaign from traditional sources, and noted that many of his colleagues refused even to raise the allowed seed money in the early phases of the campaign due to an aversion to that activity: "I don't think I would have been very good at fundraising. People hate fundraising; they absolutely despise it. We're allowed to collect $3,000 in seed money on our own, and I collected it all, just over the Internet from my friends. But a lot of people didn't even do that because they just hated asking for that money."

From the perspective of candidates who detest raising money, the problem is that fundraising is a crucial activity in the vast majority of modern American campaigns. The rise of professionalized campaigns increasingly dependent on expensive media operations has contributed to an explosion in campaign spending since the mid-1970s (Malbin et al. 2008), as campaigns increasingly opt for mass-media tactics at the expense of retail politics (Schier 2000, 124). The necessity of fundraising creates an inherent tension for candidates who want to run on the basis of their ideas, as they must choose between two distinct campaigns: one for money and another for votes (Herrnson 2011). This tension is captured in the excerpt below, which is from a first-time candidate who sought the advice of an experienced politician when he first contemplated entering a legislative race: "I talked to him and he said, 'You know, you have two campaigns, and whenever you run for office you have the "political, get out and vote, here are my ideas" campaign, and then the much more important campaign of "where does the money come from, who are you going to get to fundraise for you,"' and I was just horrified. I [thought], 'Well, I don't have any types of those deep community ties to drum up that kind of financial support. My points are good ones, and I think I speak well and articulately about them, and that should get me the votes, coming from an idealistic perspective.' So that was very concerning to me."

The tension expressed in the excerpt above reflects a maximization problem that most American candidates likely perceive: time is a finite resource; few candidates enter politics so that they can spend countless hours raising money, but fundraising is necessary in order to pay for other campaign activities. Raising funds can be a significant challenge that requires tenacity, but for all the effort expended to raise funds, campaign spending itself does not necessarily determine victory (Brown 2013). In terms of expected return on the investment of their *time,* an hour spent raising money therefore imparts an unclear benefit that for most candidates is worse than the utility derived from an hour spent with voters. The act of fundraising certainly conveys positive information about the candidate, but in a well-targeted funding plan, this information is likely to be distributed to individuals and groups who were already predisposed to support the candidate. Moreover, unlike get-out-the-vote efforts, fundraising is not confined to district boundaries, and a candidate might solicit donors who do not have the ability to cast a vote in the election. So even while they feel intense pressure to raise funds, I assume that most candidates will prefer to maximize the amount of time they spend interacting with citizens.

Public election funding holds great potential to resolve this tension. The presence of subsidies offers candidates a choice between a traditional campaign in which they must devote a significant amount of time to fundraising and one in which the state allocates a single, large contribution at the outset, reducing or eliminating the need for raising additional money. Reflecting on his campaign, a Clean Elections candidate acknowledged that fundraising might have presented a burden had he run traditionally because he "would have had to collect money all along the way." Another informant offered a similar take: "If I were funding [the campaign] on my own, or through donations, I would have spent a lot of time fundraising. That's where the difference [in my time] would be."

Consistent with this testimony, Francia and Herrnson (2003) confirmed that fully funded candidates spend less time raising money, which should not be surprising given that candidates in such systems are legally precluded from this activity once they receive the initial grants. However, Francia and Herrnson did not examine how public funding affects candidates' voter mobilization activities, and despite a clear potential for Clean Elections programs in particular to influence candidate behavior, little is known about how public funding changes candidates' ability to directly engage voters. If candidates no longer need to raise money from private sources, it is reasonable to assume that they instead focus more effort on direct voter engagement.

That said, not all funding programs are equally likely to alter candidate behavior. In the partial funding programs of Hawaii, Minnesota, and Wisconsin, subsidies typically amount to less than 25 percent of the average cost of a contested race. In contrast, the fully funded Clean Elections programs in Arizona, Connecticut, and Maine offer subsidies that make up more than 90 percent of average campaign expenses, and candidates are barred from further fundraising once they accept public funding.[1] Thus, the candidate experience in a partially funded system is much the same as in a traditional, privately financed one: challengers, in particular, must still persuade skeptical private donors to contribute, and so they must devote substantial time to fundraising. This implies that the large subsidies in Clean Elections programs are likely to change the behavior of candidates whereas smaller subsidies are not. Since fundraising is not a necessary campaign task for candidates accepting Clean Elections subsidies, they should be more likely than even partially funded candidates to wage a more visible, voter-centric campaign.

There is ample anecdotal evidence that candidates who accepted Clean Elections funding spent more time communicating with voters. In its 2010 report on Clean Elections, the GAO interviewed six Clean Elections candidates from Maine and five from Arizona (GAO 2010, 18, 27); in both cases a majority of interviewees (four and three, respectively) reported that their acceptance of public funding allowed them to devote more time to the "campaign for votes." My analysis of roughly one hundred candidates during the 2006 election in Arizona and Maine (Miller 2011b) was consistent with this conclusion, as was the consensus among the Arizona candidates I interviewed that year. One of the Arizona informants believed that he "wouldn't have gone door-to-door as much as [he] did [had he run with private funding], and it wouldn't have been a grassroots effort. It would have been a media effort" because of the necessity of preserving time for fundraising. Another candidate put it more succinctly, noting that accepting public funding results in "people spending less time having fundraisers and more time going out and meeting the voters." A third candidate expressed the same sentiment more personally: "Once I filed, I just knocked on doors every single night, and every morning. And I wouldn't have been able to do that if I was running traditional."

Clean Elections candidates in Arizona generally felt not only that the time flexibility afforded by full subsidies allowed them to be more visible, but also that participation provided a distinct advantage for them over their traditionally financed competitors. Their narrative was one in which they worked hard to meet voters while their opponents were engaged in less-visible activities for the purpose of raising money. One publicly funded challenger elaborated: "The candidates that I knew this last election that [funded] traditionally were having fundraisers two or three times a week, while [publicly funded candidates] were going out knocking on doors. That, I think, is a big difference in how you spend your time. In an evening after work, I can knock on fifty to seventy doors of people who will actually go to the polls for me, as opposed to that candidate who has to go out and raise and spend two, three hours with lobbyists who often don't even live in their district. Yeah, they're going to get the money, but I'm the one going out and meeting the voters." Moreover, many Clean Elections candidates felt that the time advantage compounded over the course of a campaign as voters came to know them. A first-time candidate running with public funding against a well-known incumbent described how her field-oriented campaign gained traction: "I started in January, nobody had a clue who I was, and by the month before the election I rarely made a phone call or went to a door without them saying, 'Oh yeah, we know who you are.' My [traditionally financed] opponent, people were aware of him because of his incumbency, because of his three terms as a representative. But in terms of being out among the public, I was out more [than he was]."

What Do Candidates Do?

There is no single blueprint for a successful campaign. Depending on their own traits, such as experience or funding, or on characteristics of the district, such as population or geographic size, candidates pursue many different paths to election. In an effort to better understand candidate behavior, the 2008 legislative candidate survey asked respondents to quantify how they used their campaign time during the first week of October, assigning the number of hours devoted to ten separate activities: fundraising, field (canvassing, posting signs, and other so-called retail politics), e-campaigning (e-mail, blogging, and website maintenance), speaking and debate (including preparation for speeches and candidate forums), media activities (staged events, ad production, and interviews), interest group meetings (generally for the purpose of seeking endorsements), mail preparation (including design, envelope stuffing, and mailing by the candidate), phoning (by the candidate), meetings (with staff or supporters for the purpose of setting strategy), and research (conducted by the candidate).

Survey responses shed considerable light on how candidates used their time, indicating that candidates performed a wide range of activities during a typical campaign week. Table 3.1, which pools data from both traditionally and publicly funded candidates, contains the mean number of weekly hours that candidates reported devoting to each task. The table suggests that campaigning is a full-time job, with candidates devoting an average of nearly 45 weekly hours to their campaigns. "Field" activity—canvassing and related activities designed to directly garner votes—leads the way among campaign tasks, taking about 40 percent of this time. Fundraising is also an important campaign activity, occupying more than four hours—roughly 10 percent—of weekly campaign time among all respondents. Candidates in 2008 also devoted more than three hours per week to "electronic campaigning" activities, public speaking, and research, and more than two weekly hours to media, meetings with interest groups, mailing, and phoning. Staff meetings occupy the smallest amount of campaign time, at just under two hours per week.

TABLE 3.1. Mean Weekly Hours Devoted to Campaign Tasks

	Hours	Percent
Field activities	18.3	41.1%
Fundraising	4.1	9.2%
E-campaigning	3.9	8.8%
Speaking/debates	3.6	8.1%
Research	3.2	7.2%
Preparing mailings	2.9	6.5%
Phoning voters	2.4	5.4%
Meeting with interest groups	2.1	4.7%
Media	2.0	4.5%
Strategy/meetings	1.9	4.3%
Total	44.5	100%

If public funding changes the way candidates use their time (relative to traditionally financed ones), then different patterns should be observed between the two groups. Specifically, hours should flow from the "Fundraising" column in Table 3.1 to other activities, with "Field" being the most likely beneficiary. Figure 3.1 therefore depicts the mean percentage of time that candidates devoted to fundraising, "field" activities, and other campaign tasks (collapsing all activities other than field or funding to a single category), arranged by state and candidate funding status. Candidates are not separated into publicly and privately funded groups in Minnesota and Hawaii because only one respondent participated in Hawaii's public funding program and only two respondents opted out in Minnesota. In those states I report overall mean percentages only.

Since full funding should eliminate most fundraising altogether, the most substantial effects should be apparent in the Clean Elections states. The six leftmost bars in Figure 3.1 therefore reflect the time allocations of participating and nonparticipating candidates in those states—Arizona, Connecticut, and Maine—that offer full public subsidies. Within all three Clean Elections states, candidates in the publicly funded group reported devoting a significantly lower percentage of their campaign time to fundraising than those who opted out.[2] Publicly funded candidates in those three states also reported higher mean levels of field activity, although only in Connecticut is the difference statistically significant.[3] That said, the basic picture in the fully funded states is one of candidates spending less time raising funds, allocating the remainder of their campaign time differently than traditionally financed candidates. This is consistent with the notion of a subsidized candidate redirecting fundraising time to the "campaign for votes."

The same cannot be said for partially funded candidates in Wisconsin, which is the only state employing partial public funding for which respondent numbers are sufficiently large to support statistical comparison of participating and nonparticipating candidates. Relative to traditionally funded candidates in Wisconsin, those who took partial subsidies in that state reported slightly lower and higher mean levels of fundraising and field activity, respectively, but in neither case is the difference statistically significant. Moreover, the mean percentage of fundraising time for publicly funded candidates in Wisconsin (and in Minnesota, where all respondents but two accepted subsidies) is comparable to that in many other states

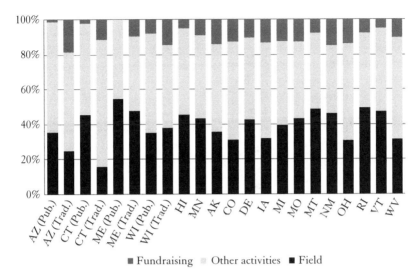

Figure 3.1. Percentage of time spent on campaign activities, by state and funding status. Pub. = public funding; Trad. = traditional funding.

in which no public funding is available. At very least, the patterns evident in Figure 3.1 offer some preliminary evidence that while participation in Clean Elections substantially reduces fundraising time, candidates taking partial funding spend about the same amount of their time raising money as "traditional" candidates who raise all funds from private donors.

Figure 3.2 depicts the data from a slightly different angle, comparing the fundraising behavior of partially and fully funded candidates while restricting the analysis to those who ran in contested elections. The means depicted in Figure 3.2 are calculated from data pooled across states. Two patterns are evident in Figure 3.2. First, within each funding condition (full, partial, or none), incumbent and non-incumbent candidates devote a similar amount of attention to fundraising. Second, Figure 3.2 confirms the intuitive notion that as candidates accept progressively larger subsidies, they spend less time raising money. Specifically, both traditionally funded incumbents and challengers reported spending about 11 percent of their time on fundraising, while mean levels of fundraising for both types of partially funded candidates were slightly less, at 7.9 percent for incumbents and 9.3 percent for non-incumbents. It is worth noting, however, that none of the apparent differences in attention to fundraising between

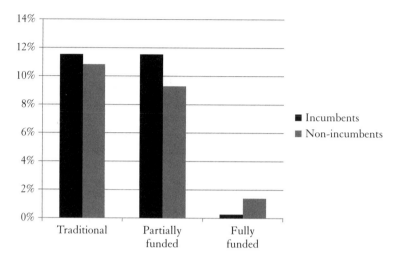

Figure 3.2. Percentage of weekly time devoted to fundraising, by incumbency and funding status, contested elections

traditional and partially funded candidates achieve statistical significance. In other words, candidates who took partial funding spent the same percentage of their time raising money as traditional candidates, statistically speaking.

In contrast, both incumbent and non-incumbent candidates who accepted Clean Elections subsidies reported spending very little of their time on fundraising: less than 1 percent of overall time for the former and about 1.5 percent for the latter. These are statistically significant differences relative to either traditional or partially funded candidates.[4] The apparent conclusion is that while the fundraising commitments of a partially funded campaign are little different from those of a traditional campaign, full subsidies free candidates from the task of fundraising. This is consistent not only with the theoretical expectations and anecdotal evidence described above but also with previous research (GAO 2010; Francia and Herrnson 2003). Not surprisingly, then, when asked their feelings about the time demands of funding their campaigns, 86 percent of fully funded candidates reported that the time they spent raising money "was just about right," compared with about 55 percent of traditionally funded and partially funded candidates.[5]

It is clear that fully funded candidates spend less time raising funds, but the question of what they do with that time remains. If they are interested

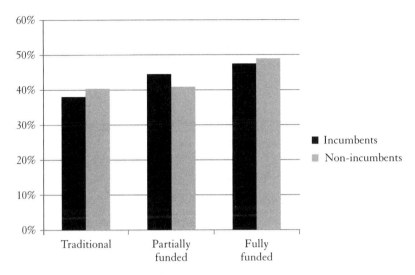

Figure 3.3. Percentage of weekly time devoted to field activities, by incumbency and funding status, contested elections.

in maximizing their vote totals, they should be observed spending more time directly engaging the voting public. Figure 3.3 depicts the percentage of time that candidates in each group devoted to field tasks, the type of activities described by many candidates I interviewed as "grassroots" campaigning dedicated to meeting voters face to face. As with fundraising behavior, there are two apparent trends worth mentioning. Once again, candidates in each funding condition display similar levels of attention to field activities, regardless of their incumbency status. Moreover, Figure 3.3 yields an inverse pattern of field activity to the one observed with regard to fundraising: while partially funded candidates spent about the same percentage of their time on field activity that traditionally funded candidates did, those who accepted full funding reported significantly higher rates of field activity. Non-incumbent Clean Elections candidates reported spending 48.9 percent of their overall campaign time on field activities, which is significantly higher than the levels reported by both their partially funded and traditionally funded counterparts.[6] Clean Elections incumbents spent an average of 47.5 percent of their time on field activity, which is significantly higher than traditional incumbents but not partially funded incumbents.[7]

In tandem, the patterns apparent in Figures 3.1, 3.2, and 3.3 strongly suggest that Clean Elections funding alters the behavior of candidates by effectively eliminating their time commitments to fundraising. Those candidates who accept full subsidies are no longer obligated to pursue private contributions during the course of the general election, and appear to reinvest that time in other activities, namely, direct engagement of voters in the field. Thus, full funding appears to free candidates from a task that they otherwise feel compelled to do by necessity, allowing them to focus on activities that they deem useful for persuading voters and delivering the campaign that they envisioned—one focused not on fundraising calls but on direct outreach.

These are certainly promising findings, but a more thorough analysis of the behavior of publicly and privately funded candidates is necessary to rule out other factors that may obscure the true relationship. One such factor stems from the fact that candidate funding status is not likely to be random. The differential participation among candidates of opposite parties or genders described in GAO (2010) and Werner and Mayer (2007), combined with the correspondent overrepresentation of women and Democrats in the survey sample (see Appendix 1), serves as a reminder that individual and/or district characteristics likely affect candidates' public funding status. If it is true that certain candidate attributes or certain types of districts make participation more likely, then one must be careful in attributing changes to public funding alone.

It is necessary, then, to take a closer look at the relationship between candidates' public funding status and the degree to which they directly engage voters, using statistical techniques both to control for other possible factors causing an apparent change in candidate time and to adjust for the nonrandomness of candidate participation. Specifically, to determine the effect of accepting public funding on campaign time, I fit four separate linear regression models to each dataset (Table 3.2), using sampling weights obtained from matching exercises described in Appendix 3 (see Ho et al. 2007b). All of the models seek the effect of accepting public funding on the public interaction activities of candidates who accepted public funding, but since the campaign activities that make up direct "public interaction" are open to some interpretation, I construct four related outcome variables using additive indices of time measured in raw weekly hours or fractions thereof that candidates devoted to various campaign activities. Following Francia and Herrnson (2003), the dependent variable for each model is the

TABLE 3.2. Candidate Public Interaction Activities: Ordinary Least Squares Regression Coefficients

	Partial funding				Full funding			
	(1)	(2)	(3)	(4)	(1)	(2)	(3)	(4)
Accepted full funding	–	–	–	–	11.673* (2.361)	11.704* (2.074)	12.064* (2.032)	11.625* (2.118)
Accepted partial funding	0.609 (3.082)	1.769 (1.9108)	1.628 (1.433)	0.501 (2.435)	–	–	–	–
Held previous office	10.213* (3.980)	−0.407 (2.271)	3.265 (2.405)	3.507 (2.995)	−2.266 (2.555)	−1.027 (1.448)	−1.756 (2.140)	−2.997 (2.483)
Male	−0.627 (5.940)	−0.440 (1.629)	−1.309 (2.784)	−2.527 (2.998)	−0.299 (2.419)	−2.789 (1.47)	−4.298* (1.68)	−2.817 (3.216)
Dist. population (ten thous.)	−0.803 (1.663)	0.091 (0.704)	−0.772 (0.651)	−0.440 (0.820)	−1.121* (0.123)	−0.259* (0.08)	−0.351* (0.14)	−0.378* (0.107)
Dist. household income (ten thous.)	0.604 (1.693)	−0.080 (0.310)	0.197 (0.721)	0.886 (0.598)	−0.770* (0.277)	−0.266 (0.18)	−0.678* (0.141)	−0.591* (0.159)
Constant	35.942* (15.134)	90.084* (3.681)	78.113* (5.547)	68.528* (6.380)	48.329* (3.868)	92.536* (2.89)	85.158* (2.843)	77.319* (3.042)
N	155	155	155	155	279	279	279	279
R^2	0.06	0.01	0.04	0.04	0.15	0.31	0.19	0.14
Root mean squared error	21.86	9.82	13.55	14.85	19.99	9.09	14.0	16.28
F-statistic	16.70	1.72	17.09	25.38	25.73	41.29	27.26	16.05

Note: Robust standard errors in parentheses, clustered by state. Sampling weights derived from genetic matching.
Dependent variables are the percentage of time (ranging from 0 to 100) devoted to various public interaction indices.
(1) Percentage of time devoted to field activities (canvassing, posting signs, etc.).
(2) Percentage of time devoted to all campaign activities except fundraising.
(3) Percentage of time devoted to all campaign activities except fundraising, research, and staff meetings.
(4) Percentage of time devoted to all campaign activities except fundraising, research, staff meetings, and mail preparation.
*$p < .05$.

percentage of overall weekly campaign time that each candidate devoted to that index of activities.[8]

In other words, the outcome measures incorporate a range of measurements for the percentage of campaign time that candidates devote to interacting with—and persuading—voters. The dependent variable for Model 1 is the percentage of weekly campaign time that each candidate devoted solely to field activity, as described above, and therefore represents the most direct measure of face-to-face interaction between candidates and voters. The outcome measure in Model 2 captures the opposite extreme; it is the percentage of time that candidates spent on all activities *except* fundraising. Note that I exclude fundraising from all "public interaction" indices. While the candidate must interact with the public for fundraising purposes, the fundraising audience is made up of a narrow sector of the electorate with well-known, favorable preferences (Wilcox 2001). In other cases, funds may be solicited from individuals who live outside the candidate's district or state, negating any potential electoral benefit from fundraising activities.

The dependent variables in Models 3 and 4 are intermediate measures of public interaction. In Model 3 the dependent variable is calculated from an additive index of field activity, electronic campaigning, media relations, public speaking, preparation of mailings, phone calls, and interest group meetings, since all these activities can be plausibly construed to be related to direct public interaction with voters. In contrast, staff meetings and research are left out of the index in Model 3 (in addition to fundraising) since they can be viewed as "housekeeping" activities that occur out of the view of voters. The dependent variable in Model 4 subtracts mail preparation from the index used in Model 3, since the time a candidate spends on mail might be interpreted as indirect interaction with voters. If the effect of public funding is substantively similar across the measures, then confidence in the robustness of the findings should be higher.

The independent variable of interest in all models is a dichotomous indicator coded 1 if the candidate accepted public funding and 0 otherwise. I also include several additional control variables to account for variation in public interaction activities between candidates. If the models lend support to the hypothesis that candidates will invest recaptured fundraising time in public interaction activities, then I anticipate that the models of partially funded candidates will return a substantively small and statistically insignificant effect while the models of Clean Elections candidates will display a large, positive, and statistically significant relationship between participation in full funding and public interaction. So, controlling for other possible causes, I expect to find that acceptance of partial funding does not free candidates to spend more of their time with the public whereas participation in full funding does. This expectation is driven by the belief that the fundraising behavior of partially funded candidates differs little from that of their privately funded counterparts, and thus there is no regained time for them to direct toward other activities. In contrast, if Clean Elections eliminates fundraising, then candidates who accept its large subsidies should also devote more time to interaction with voters.

Results from all models are contained in Table 3.2. As noted above, each model employs a separate dependent variable, reflecting a different construction of a public interaction index measuring the percentage of time that candidates devoted to various campaign activities. All models use sample weights derived from the matching exercise described in Appendix 3. I also report robust standard errors clustered by state to account for any nonrandom error variance that may be present due to the multistate composition of the candidate pools. Notably, the results of all models generally agree with those of unmatched data, which are also reported in Appendix 3.

For all four dependent variables in the models of partially funded candidates, the coefficient indicating public funding participation is positively signed, is substantively small, and does not indicate a statistically significant relationship between partial subsidies and the percentage of time devoted to public interaction. It therefore seems safe to conclude that partial public funding does not stimulate direct voter mobilization efforts. This finding is consistent with the expectations described above, and is not surprising considering that the financial realities partially funded candidates face typically require them to raise money from private sources throughout the election.

The picture in fully funded elections is markedly different. The coefficients for the indicator variable for a candidate accepting full public funding are all positively signed, substantively large, and statistically significant. Moreover, the effect size of accepting full funding is similar for all four constructions of the public interaction variable: about 11.5 percentage points. In other words, holding other factors in the models constant, candidates in Arizona, Maine, and Connecticut who accept full public funding devote significantly more of their weekly time to public interaction, and this effect remains stable across various constructions of "public interaction" indices. In contrast to candidates accepting partial funding, who display no change in their public interaction behavior, participation in full funding programs appears to alter the manner in which candidates conduct their campaign.

Clearly, when it comes to having an impact on the things that campaigns do, subsidy size matters. Participation in partial public funding systems has no effect on the way that candidates use their time; the proportions of overall time that partially funded candidates devote to fundraising and field activity are similar to those of traditional candidates, and there is little evidence from the statistical models of any altered behavior resulting from accepting partial funding. However, the acceptance of full funding effectively eliminates fundraising from the list of candidates' weekly activities, which leads to other changes in campaign behavior. Specifically, candidates who accept Clean Elections subsidies redirect the time they would have spent raising money to interaction with the voting public in the form of face-to-face canvassing, phoning, and related activities. With an effect size of 11.5 percentage points, a fully funded candidate entering a legislative race in the first week of June who campaigns at the mean level of total campaign hours (46.8) reported by survey respondents would devote more than 1,000 additional hours to public interaction during the 22-week effort. The shift toward higher levels of interaction with voters therefore has great potential to impart broad effects on mass political behavior, specifically on voters' propensity to cast ballots in state legislative elections in which public funding is present.

Conclusion

The acceptance of full public funding subsidies like those in full public election funding systems (such as Clean Elections) changes how candidates use their time. Full public funding effectively eliminates the necessity of raising money, facilitating a solution to the paradox that traditionally financed candidates face when searching for campaign contributions. Moreover, in freeing them from the necessity of persuading skeptical donors to contribute to a long-shot cause, full funding allows candidates to focus solely on the campaign for votes, which results in many more direct interactions with voters. This finding marks a crucial first step toward a fuller understanding of public funding as policy.

Given conventional wisdom about the role of money in American politics—namely, that more money equates to more votes—it is perhaps easy to assume that providing greater funding to challengers will allow them to purchase more mailings or advertising, which will in turn persuade a higher number of people to support them instead of the incumbent. There is certainly some truth to this logic, but it is not the whole story. Fully funded candidates reported that the *time* flexibility the subsidies afforded was a driving reason for their participation, and their testimony suggests that they leveraged that flexibility for a campaign that was more focused on personally soliciting votes. If fully funded challengers are making headway against incumbents, their increased ability to personally interact with voters—which often comes with little or no financial cost—is certainly a component of their success. Increased time flexibility must therefore be considered a likely component of the causal linkage between public funding and observable changes in any number of areas, such as enhancing electoral competition or driving up voter participation.

There are also implications beyond elections for more voter-centric campaigns. Certainly, heightened interaction between candidates and voters would result in increased information levels among the latter, but the benefits of such interactions flow in both directions. Candidates with "extra" hours to directly engage voters are likely to develop both deeper connections with the electorate and an understanding of issues important to the district. If good representation flows from candidates—and subsequently, legislators—who are well tuned to public opinion, then the possibility for enhanced interaction between subsidized candidates and the public has great potential to improve government responsiveness. Such a question is beyond the scope of this book but is certainly worth exploring in future research.

4

Voting Behavior

Particularly during presidential election years, state legislative candidates face a challenge in capturing the attention of voters, who are more likely to focus on high-profile races. But given that full public funding heightens interaction between the public and candidates, it seems reasonable to expect that the subsidizing of campaigns will also have implications for mass voting behavior. If voters are more likely to receive a high-quality contact from a state legislative campaign, they should gain crucial knowledge about that election. Whether by disseminating information about a candidate's policy positions or biography, or by raising the perceived salience of the job of state representative, increased contact between candidates and citizens should lead the latter to conclude that voting is important. We should therefore expect to find heightened levels of mass voting in elections contested by at least one publicly financed candidate.

Enhanced voter participation is important for several reasons. In very close contests an increase in the number of voters (especially if they prefer one candidate over another) could conceivably change the outcome of the election. However, public funding is most likely to affect voting propensity by raising confidence in voters' minds that they have sufficient information to choose the candidate who best represents their interests. More people will therefore vote "correctly" (Lau and Redlawsk 1997), raising the probability of election for the candidate whose positions best reflect those of the district. This in turn will indirectly enhance the quality of representation in the legislature, regardless of whether it alters the competitiveness of elections. It is difficult to argue that this is a negative outcome, but at the very least the potential connection between public funding and voting behavior is worth studying.

Yet the demonstration of a link between public funding and rising turnout has eluded political science. This failure, though, is the result of an inattention to the goals of low-visibility campaigns. Presumably, few people base their decision about whether to turn out on the goings-on of a state house election. Indeed, quite a few of them go to the polls, vote for federal and statewide offices, and leave. The true strategic goal for candidates in state legislative and other down-ballot contests is therefore to persuade voters to cast a preference on the entire ballot, not just the high-visibility races. Thus, turnout is the wrong place to look for an effect of public election funding on mass voting behavior. Instead, we should examine patterns in other measures, namely, whether public funding leads to the casting of more complete ballots.

Getting Them There or Keeping Them There?

Campaign field operations attempt to mobilize voters with a combination of mass media and direct solicitation. Despite recognizing a need to be visible via advertising and mail, most of the candidates I interviewed felt that campaign methods should be personalized whenever possible and that campaign efforts were best devoted to well-targeted, meaningful interactions with voters. The candidate interviews conducted in 2007 underscore the fact that the importance of personal campaigning is not lost even on seasoned politicians. As one incumbent noted, "Legislative elections, at least in Arizona, are generally decided by who can knock on the most doors. When we knocked off the incumbent in my first race, so many people said, 'I voted for you because you came to my door.'" Another Arizona legislator described how shortly after hiring a consultant in his first campaign, he asked what the most effective strategy would be, "and [the consultant] said, 'If you want to win, you've got to knock on doors.' So [that] encouraged me to meet a lot of voters, and I did. And I still do." Even first-time candidates quickly realized the effectiveness of face-to-face interaction for fostering support. Reflecting on a losing campaign, one said, "I did much better in the precincts where I knocked on every door than in the ones where I didn't. As a challenger, you can live by getting out to knock on every door."

Other informants described the effects of face-to-face interaction in terms of building party bonds and broader efficacy, as expressed by another challenger who traveled to a rural county for a monthly party meeting: "I went to a meeting. They could only gather about ten people to come to the meeting, but they said, 'This is the first time we've ever clapped eyes on a candidate up here in twenty years.' So you know, that's good for them." Most candidates believed that those feelings of efficacy extended to the broader electorate via door-to-door canvassing, when voters were given the chance to have a two-way conversation with candidates. One first-time candidate, who won an improbable victory, summed up this sentiment: "I was on the phone, and I was walking door-to-door. It was hard work. I had no idea how hard it was going to be. But you have to do grassroots, on the phone, door-to-door, you have to go visit the people and say, 'I would appreciate your vote; this is what I believe in.' And when they have that personal touch, they're more likely to vote, because they feel like they can make a difference." Candidates are careful with their resources; most do not knock on random doors, opting instead for a well-targeted field strategy. One effective method of targeting is gaining an understanding of influential people within communities (Rosenstone and Hansen 1993), and a sitting legislator described his campaign strategy of knowing not only all the neighborhoods in the district but also who was at the center of the networks in them: "The people love it [when you knock on their door]. 'Oh, you're the candidate! Sit down, this is great!' Because you don't see candidates anymore, you know, you'll see them on the television, especially congressional candidates; I know they mean well, but it's just impossible. For these legislative districts, you should know all the neighborhoods, and you should be comfortable meeting with all the heads of the neighborhood associations, and I think it helps to see the candidates running around with people they know instead of going to fancy dinners with people they don't."

Another candidate, this one a neophyte who lost a close Democratic primary race, relied on more modern methods of targeting via the party's Voter Activation Network (VAN), which identifies the partisan affiliation and voting propensity of registered voters: "I was already irritated with how much I had to do in the way of going to events, and debates...and that stuff really pulled me away from prime-time walking, because I felt that I did the most good, even if it was just going through a neighborhood going door-to-door and seeing twenty or thirty people in an afternoon or evening, because I was talking to people I had already targeted with the VAN as likely primary voters. I'm not going and trying to convince them to vote; I'm going and trying to convince them to vote for me because I pretty much know they're going to vote."

Such efforts hold great promise to mobilize voters in support of a campaign: a growing number of mobilization experiments have found that compared with mass-mobilization techniques, well-targeted, intimate messages are particularly effective mobilization tools. For instance, phone calls designed to get out the vote have been shown to have little effect when they are delivered from large professional phone banks in both a nonpartisan (Gerber and Green 2000, 2001; McNulty 2005) and partisan (Panagopoulos 2009) context. The ineffectiveness of professional phone banks is likely due to the "low quality" of the solicitations, which are often hurried and impersonal (Nickerson 2007). In contrast, a positive effect on turnout has been demonstrated when phone solicitations come from volunteers able to more effectively engage voters (Nickerson et al. 2006; Nickerson 2005, 2006). Face-to-face canvassing techniques appear to be the most efficacious voter mobilization tools, particularly when delivered on time to targeted populations (e.g., Gerber and Green 2000; Niven 2001, 2002).

If the presence of a Clean Elections candidate in a state legislative election raises the likelihood that a voter will communicate with a campaign in some fashion, and if candidates focus their field efforts on well-targeted, high-quality interaction, then it seems reasonable to expect that the presence of a Clean Elections candidate will increase mass participation. Such an increase would appear to be consistent with the primary objectives of public funding laws as well as some scholarly evaluations of partial public funding programs. In its 2010 report on the impact of Clean Elections in Arizona and Maine, the GAO noted that "increasing voter participation, as indicated by...voter turnout, was a goal of public financing programs in Maine and Arizona" (GAO 2010, 81). Moreover, at least one analysis has determined that the presence of public funding in gubernatorial elections boosted turnout (Gross and Goidel 2003).

Yet studies of campaign finance laws generally (Primo and Milyo 2006) and Clean Elections specifically (Miller and Panagopoulos 2011) have yielded little reason to conclude that such policies improve mean levels of efficacy among the electorate. Primo and Milyo's (2006) study, which accounted for inherent differences among states, contrasted with Gross and Goidel (2003) in finding no association between gubernatorial public funding and turnout. Such findings are generally consistent with the prevailing viewpoint of candidates in the interview sample, few of whom felt that the passage of Clean Elections on its own had stirred democratic passions. One Democratic legislator said that in 2006, even after three elections with public funding, a substantial percentage of people still did not know that the program existed: "Six years later, you have to explain it to fewer people, but there are still a lot of people out there who don't know about it."

Given the apparent anonymity of the program among voters and no evidence of increased mass political efficacy, it is not particularly surprising that Milyo et al.'s (2011) analysis, which examined the impact of both gubernatorial and legislative public funding programs on turnout, found no evidence of higher turnout in publicly funded states. Indeed, their study finds a *negative* relationship between available public funding in legislative elections and voter turnout, and also determines that there is little difference between the effect of partial and full funding. Yet Milyo et al. do not make in-state comparisons of turnout in races where public funding was actually used with those in which all candidates opted out. Since it is worth wondering whether public funding should be expected to affect elections in which it is not utilized, the question of whether legislative public funding affects turnout requires further scrutiny.

More important, turnout is not the best measure of voter participation in elections to non-statewide offices. Contrary to the GAO's report, there is in fact little statutory evidence that increasing voter turnout was a primary goal of public funding supporters in Arizona or Maine, as evidenced by the fact that the word "turnout" does not appear in the text of the laws themselves. In Arizona, where the statute (AZ 16–940) contains a lengthy "findings and declarations" section, the policy actually declares that public funding "will encourage citizen *participation* in the political process" (emphasis mine). However, few people are likely to base their decision of whether to vote *at all* on the goings-on of a state legislative election. This is especially true in a presidential election year, in which the high salience of the presidential race is likely to further obscure the events in more localized state house elections.

If voters either know more about a low-information contest or have been persuaded that it is important, they might be more likely to cast a vote in that election when they might have otherwise abstained. In other words, the strategic objective for state legislative candidates is to break through the din of more high-profile races to communicate the details and importance of their contest, since doing so should compel more citizens to cast ballots in the legislative election after voting for higher-profile offices. Heightened interaction between candidates and voters in a state house race may not compel a citizen to visit a polling place, but it should diminish voter "roll-off," which occurs when voters *who have already turned out* stop marking their ballots when they get to the lower offices.

Roll-off is a difficult phenomenon to reconcile with the classic rational-choice voting models (e.g., Downs 1957; Riker and Ordeshook 1968), which predict that citizens will vote when the cost of doing so approaches zero, as it does when a voter is already in the booth. However, when voters know little or nothing about the candidates in a given race, the odds that they will make an "incorrect" decision increase (Lau and Redlawsk 1997). Most partisan voters in low-information elections can use party labels as reliable cues, even if they know little else about the candidates, but Feddersen and Pesendorfer (1996) demonstrate that when weak partisan voters face a great deal of uncertainty, they have an incentive to abstain from voting and delegate the choice to more informed citizens.

Thus, in low-visibility elections (such as those for a state legislature) information is a crucial commodity. Much of the existing political science literature has approached roll-off as a problem to be solved by raising mass awareness of the candidates and issues in a given contest. Many of these studies have been conducted to better understand a well-documented racial gap, in which African American voters are significantly more likely to roll off (Feig 2007; Knack and Kropf 2003; Vanderleeuw and Engstrom 1987). Previous research has also found that African Americans appear to be more likely to vote in a given contest when black candidates run against white candidates (Vanderleeuw and Utter 1993; Engstrom and Caridas 1991), particularly when black candidates make focused mobilization efforts (Vanderleeuw and Liu 2002).

These findings underscore the importance of information and salience in reducing roll-off in low-visibility elections. Wattenberg et al. (2000) found that voters approach ballots in much the same way as a test, abstaining when they lack sufficient knowledge to make a clear decision. Indeed, many candidates see themselves as serving the valuable function of information dissemination, reasoning that if they can provide voters with sufficient facts to make informed decisions, there is a greater likelihood that they will vote. As one Arizona legislator noted, "So many people today are unaware of who their elected officials are, unaware of the issues, and everyone laments that we need greater participation, and to educate the voters. I think that candidates are some of the best to do that, and to get that information out there."

Information in professional, media-heavy campaigns is easier to obtain than in less visible ones, yet the attention that the high-profile campaigns receive makes it even more difficult for less visible candidates to provide voters with many of the useful heuristics they use to make a decision, such as incumbency, occupational background, or endorsements (e.g., Lau and Redlawsk 2001; McDermott 2005). Particularly in low-visibility elections such as those for most state assemblies, the higher levels of interaction between fully funded candidates and the public hold great promise to increase the probability that voters will express a preference in a given contest if they have already turned out to vote.

The logic here is not complex: when candidates interact with voters, the latter learn about the candidate's background, issue positions, and other key pieces of information. Moreover, candidates might describe to voters the function served by the office they are seeking and why voting in that race is important. Thus, levels of information and salience almost certainly rise when candidates are engaging in more interaction, such as field canvassing, mailing, and phoning. If fully funded candidates are more likely to perform these activities (see Chapter 3), and if increased information and salience lead to diminished roll-off, then lower roll-off should be observed when at least one candidate accepts public funding in a given district. I make this claim based on the fact that it should take only one candidate to raise general levels of awareness about a given race. Exposure to a candidate might compel a voter to support that person, or the voter might decide that the alternative is better. Either way, increased exposure aids in preference formation and should therefore reduce average voter roll-off in state legislative elections. So if the heightened public interaction activities of fully funded candidates increase information and/or salience levels among voters, then roll-off should be lower in districts where a publicly funded candidate runs.

Does Public Funding Reduce Roll-Off?

In the search for effects of public funding on mass voting behavior, I analyze voter roll-off trends in the fully funded state legislative races of Arizona, Connecticut, and Maine, both before and after the implementation of public funding, since interaction between candidates and voters in those (fully funded) states is higher when the former accept Clean Elections subsidies (see Chapter 3). To carry this out, I compiled precinct-level vote totals in all three Clean Elections states for both president and the applicable state legislative office, in all precincts where voters cast ballots for only one house or senate district, and used this information to calculate roll-off for each legislative district, calculated as the percentage of people who cast a ballot for president but not for the applicable legislative office.

For the purposes of isolating the true effect of public funding on voter roll-off, I exploit an opportunity created by the rules that govern candidate participation in public funding programs. Given that participation in public funding is optional, not all districts are contested by a publicly funded candidate in a given year. Since whether a voter will interact with a fully funded legislative candidate is determined solely by the district in which that voter lives, I borrow from the language of experiments, dividing districts into "treatment" and "control" groups. I assign districts to the treatment group if at least one candidate accepted public funding during the election when it became available and to the control group if all candidates raised money solely from private sources in that year. If public funding decreases roll-off, then roll-off should be significantly lower in the "treated" districts. For more information about group assignment and methods in this area, see Appendix 3.

Before we look at trends in roll-off over time, it seems worthwhile to compare roll-off in districts where a publicly funded candidate ran in the first election when Clean Elections was effective with those in which all candidates ran with private contributions, since lower roll-off in the districts where at least one candidate accepted subsidies would provide some early support for the link between public funding and voter participation. To that end, Figure 4.1 depicts mean levels of district roll-off in both state house and state senate elections in Arizona, Connecticut, and Maine in the first election after the implementation of Clean Elections. The means are portrayed by a district's "treatment" condition; treated districts are those in which at least one candidate ran with Clean Elections subsidies.

The relative pattern is the same for all six elections: mean levels of district-level roll-off are lower in those that saw a fully funded campaign. The largest differences are evident in Arizona and Connecticut house elections, in which roll-off in treated districts was lower by about twelve and fourteen percentage points, respectively; these differences are statistically

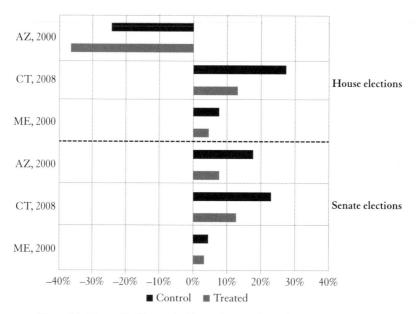

Figure 4.1. Mean roll-off in state legislative elections, first cycle with clean elections

significant in both cases.[1] Significant differences are observed in the 2000 Maine House elections, in which treated districts saw roll-off levels about four points lower than control districts (3.5 to 7.5 percent, respectively).[2] While the mean level is lower in treated districts, roll-off rates in Maine Senate races were separated by about one percentage point, and levels in the two groups were statistically indistinguishable from each other. However, the ten-point differences apparent between treated and control groups in the Arizona and Connecticut senate races are both statistically significant.[3] In short, the roll-off rates depicted in Figure 4.1 show a consistent pattern for all six examined elections: roll-off is lower when at least one candidate accepted full subsidies, and these differences are statistically significant in four of the six cases.

Yet Figure 4.1 still allows some room for skepticism, mainly due to the fact that it cannot rule out reverse causation. It is possible that publicly funded candidates emerge in districts that are predisposed to low voter roll-off due to education levels or other pertinent demographics, or that less observable characteristics such as a well-organized local party contribute simultaneously to both candidate recruitment and voter mobilization. One way of dealing with this issue is to calculate the "difference in differences," that is, the difference in the slope of the trend line for each group from analyzed trends in roll-off *within* legislative districts between Election 0 (when no public funding was available) and Election 1 (the first election during which candidates could accept subsidies).

This approach has two major benefits. First, the examination of differences within districts excludes district factors that are time-invariant (or relatively so), such as racial composition or political preferences, as potential confounding variables. Second, the logic of the difference-in-differences design supports a causal framework, since I assume that the roll-off trend in the control group (districts with no publicly funded candidates) approximates the mean of what would have occurred in the absence of public funding. This assumption establishes a counterfactual baseline for comparison of roll-off trends between the treatment and control groups. It could be that roll-off rose overall between Election 0 and Election 1, but if it rose by significantly less in the treated group, the difference-in-differences framework would allow one to conclude that the presence of a publicly funded candidate diminished roll-off. The same would be true if roll-off declined overall between the two time periods but shrank at a larger rate in the treatment group. So the difference-in-differences framework is an improvement over simple comparison of means.

To that end, mean same-district roll-off differences from state house and senate elections in the three states are depicted in Figure 4.2, with districts again portrayed by treatment condition. Thus, Figure 4.2 shows the difference between roll-off in 2000 and 1996 in Arizona and Maine, and between 2008 and 2004 in Connecticut. In five of the six legislative houses mean roll-off increased for districts in the control condition between Election 0 and Election 1; the lone exception is in elections to the Arizona Senate, where roll-off levels were essentially the same in 2000 as in 1996. Yet roll-off in treated senate districts of all three states *decreased* over the same period. The difference between these trends (the difference-in-differences) is certainly supportive of the theoretical arguments advanced above, but it is important to note that the pattern observed in the senate elections supports no firm conclusions. As noted previously, statistically based conclusions in the senate elections are difficult due to the small size of the groups, and none of the differences in the senate elections is statistically significant.[4]

Examination of same-district roll-off difference-in-differences in house races yields more confidence. Same-district roll-off in Connecticut House elections shows a similar pattern to that apparent in the senate

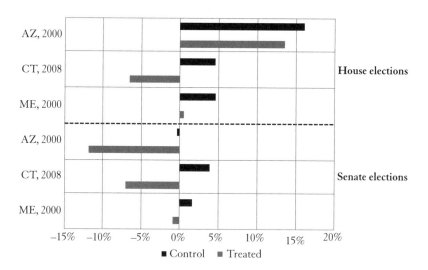

Figure 4.2. Mean difference in same-district roll-off

contests: roll-off increased by about 4.5 percentage points in the control districts and decreased by about 6.5 points in the treated districts between 2004 and 2008. Moreover, the difference in mean roll-off change between the two groups is statistically significant.[5] Mean roll-off rose for both the treatment and control groups in both Arizona and Maine house elections between 1996 and 2000, but in both states it rose much more in control districts. In Maine, roll-off increased by 4.5 points for districts in the control condition, compared with a very small increase in the treated districts of about one-half of one percentage point; this is a significant difference.[6] In Arizona, same-district roll-off rose 13.5 points in treated districts but 16 points in control districts. While the difference in Arizona is not statistically significant, it is consistent with a clear pattern apparent in elections to *all other offices:* mean roll-off trends higher in districts where no candidate ran with public funding after its implementation.

The patterns in both Figure 4.1 and Figure 4.2 are consistent with the notion that roll-off will be lower in elections contested by at least one fully funded candidate. However, the observed patterns do not wholly confirm that hypothesis. Small sample sizes confound statistical tests in most instances, and even conclusions based on the relationships that do achieve statistical significance cannot definitively rule out confounding variables such as contestedness as the true cause of changes in roll-off. I therefore now turn to the results of four regression models designed to isolate the effect of a fully funded candidate on roll-off in Connecticut and Maine elections, where group sizes support statistical inference (for more information, see Appendix 3). Compared with basic comparisons, the main advantage of these multivariate statistical models is that theoretically relevant covariates can be held constant, isolating the effect of the presence of a Clean Elections candidate on roll-off differences. Table 4.1 therefore contains coefficients and robust standard errors (clustered by district) from the regression models used to calculate the difference-in-differences estimators for lower house elections in Connecticut and Maine, which reflect roll-off changes in those states from Election 0 to Election 1, holding relevant covariates constant.

Several trends in Table 4.1 bear mentioning. First, money raised in a district is significantly and negatively related to roll-off in three of the four models, indicating that roll-off declined when candidates in a given district collectively raised more money in Election 1 than in Election 0. This result is consistent with expectations; more money in the election leads to more

TABLE 4.1. Ordinary Least Squares Regression Coefficients, Calculation of Difference-in-Differences Estimators of Voter Roll-Off in State House Races, Connecticut and Maine

	Connecticut		Maine	
	(1)	(2)	(1)	(2)
At least one publicly funded candidate running	−4.277* (0.852)	−2.076* (0.556)	−1.794* (0.500)	−1.530* (0.465)
Diff. in money raised by candidates in district (thousands)	−0.019 (0.018)	−0.024* (0.012)	−0.104* (0.024)	−0.110* (0.024)
Diff. in major-party contestedness	−21.362* (0.978)	–	−12.387* (1.404)	–
Diff. in presence of incumbent	0.671 (0.885)	0.761 (0.718)	−0.544 (0.284)	−0.628* (0.268)
Diff. in number of minor-party candidates	−0.139 (0.493)	0.343 (0.523)	−0.905 (0.719)	−0.394 (0.583)
% of African Americans in district	0.151* (0.055)	0.098* (0.046)	0.797* (0.393)	0.719 (0.403)
Constant	0.769 (0.637)	−0.113 (0.451)	0.978* (0.338)	0.881* (0.331)
N	129	82	97	91
R^2	0.877	0.333	0.693	0.306
Root mean squared error	4.32	2.44	2.31	2.16
F-statistic	114.77	6.36	27.59	9.37

Note: Robust standard errors in parentheses, clustered by legislative district.
Dependent variable for Connecticut is the difference between 2008 roll-off and 2004 roll-off. For Maine, the difference is between 2000 and 1996. The control group for Connecticut is partially constructed from Rhode Island House districts (explained in Appendix 3). Specification (1) fits a model to data from all districts in which elections were contested by two major- party candidates in the first election after public funding implementation. Specification (2) fits the model to all districts in which both elections were contested by two major-party candidates.
*$p < .05$.

advertising, staff, and mailings, all of which help to raise awareness of candidates among the electorate. Second, incumbency does not appear to be a significant determinant of roll-off. In three of the four models there is no statistically significant relationship between differences in incumbent candidates running and roll-off trends.

Third, the percentage of African American residents in a district appears to be positively associated with roll-off trends, suggesting that in districts with a larger black population, roll-off rates were higher in Election 1 than in Election 0. Fourth, the models suggest a slightly negative relationship between the presence of third-party candidates and roll-off. This is consistent with expectations, since the presence of a minor-party candidate might create the opportunity for some citizens to more accu-rately express their preferences, leading them to vote when they might oth-erwise have abstained. However, the models indicate that the relationship between minor-party candidates and roll-off is not statistically significant. The most likely explanation for this is that voters whose interests are re-flected by third parties will support those candidates when they run but will otherwise "settle" for a candidate of one of the major parties.

Finally, Specification 1 (see Table 4.1) includes an additional variable reflecting changes in the contestedness of the election by major-party can-didates in each state. As expected, the models demonstrate that major-party contestedness is a powerful attenuator of roll-off; when an election was contested in Election 1 (but not Election 0), roll-off in that district was significantly lower. The relationship between contestedness and roll-off is statistically significant and consistent with expectations; partisan voters are likely to abstain from voting in elections when their preferred party does not advance a candidate.

With regard to the question of interest, all four models indicate that the presence of a publicly funded candidate in a given district diminishes mean roll-off. In both Connecticut and Maine the treatment dummy vari-ables for all four models prove to be negative, statistically significant pre-dictors of turnout, holding the other variables constant. For the models of data from Connecticut, Specification 1 returns a negative effect of about 4 points while Specification 2 returns a negative effect of about half that size.[7] The reduction in Maine is 1.79 percentage points in Specification 1 and 1.53 percentage points in Specification 2; both of these coefficients are statistically significant.[8]

The effects in both states are fairly large, considering the mean roll-off levels apparent among the control groups depicted in Figure 4.1, which shows that control districts in Connecticut overall displayed roll-off levels of 27.3 percent in the 2008 election. If only contested races are considered, the roll-off level in Connecticut was 9.9 percent in that year. In Maine, roll-off rates in 2000 were 7.55 percent overall and 3.1 percent in contested races. Again, the models of contested elections show that roll-off is reduced by about 2 points and 1.5 points in Connecticut and Maine, respectively, when a publicly funded candidate is present. In short, controlling for rele-vant additional factors, roll-off decreases by about 20 percent in both states when a publicly funded candidate runs.

Conclusion

Candidates in down-ballot elections may see their core goal as "mobilizing" voters—persuading them to leave their homes or workplaces, travel to the polls, and cast a ballot—but the reality is that state legislative campaigns are likely not the driving factor in voters' decisions of whether to turn out (especially in presidential election years). That said, they do possess the capacity to influence whether voters view the state legislative contest as an important one, and can also disseminate information to aid voters in confidently expressing a preference in what might otherwise be a low-visibility affair. It remains an open question whether information or salience is the primary mechanism linking public funding and voter roll-off.

One answer might be that, as Wattenberg et al. (2000) suggest, increased interaction between candidates and voters simply lowers voters' information costs, providing them with a political education sufficient to allow a clear choice. Another possible explanation is that when voters meet candidates, the personal connection leads to higher levels of mass political efficacy, which has been shown to be particularly important in reducing roll-off among African Americans (Vanderleeuw and Utter 1993; Vanderleeuw and Liu 2002).

Likely, the truth is somewhere in between. However, for candidates interested in reducing roll-off—thereby increasing the number of votes cast in their race—the mechanism is secondary in importance to the result. Heightened interaction is a crucial element in any narrative linking public funding to voting behavior, regardless of whether voters are responding to more information, an altered opinion about the importance of the contest, or both. Simply put, the acceptance of public funding allows the candidate to focus on voters, who for whatever reason respond.

These findings are important for those who see public funding as a protector of election integrity. Full public funding like Clean Elections appears to increase the number of people voting in the relatively low information setting of a state legislative campaign. The desirability of more voting is a matter of some dispute if voters are unmotivated or uniformed (Brennan 2012). It remains unknown whether voters in Clean Elections states actually possess higher knowledge levels as a result of increased interaction with publicly funded candidates, but given the greater propensity for interaction described in the previous chapter, it seems safe to assume that they do. Thus, public funding may propel citizens to cast more informed preferences, raising the probability of an election result that reflects the true will of the district. This has obvious implications for representation as well.

Finally, it is worth noting that these findings are useful for forming future research questions about campaign effects in state legislative elections generally, regardless of whether subsidies are present. Political science may be missing a crucial theoretical component of the narrative when it comes to understanding both the objectives of low-information campaigns and the results in those elections. My assertion that many campaigns are interested less in persuading people to go to the polls than in encouraging them to simply continue voting once they have turned out may be controversial in some circles, but it bears further consideration. Broader studies of roll-off in legislative elections will likely lead to a deeper understanding of how money and campaign activities can affect voting behavior.

5

CANDIDATE QUALITY

When it comes to assessing public funding's efficacy as policy, no outcome has received more attention from political scientists than its potential to enhance electoral competition. This focus is understandable, given the relatively uncompetitive nature of American politics. It is a well-documented truth that when incumbents seek reelection to Congress (Jacobson 2009) or state legislatures (Carsey et al. 2008), they can reasonably expect to win more than 90 percent of the time. Moreover, as Carsey et al. (2008) demonstrate, only about one-third of state legislative elections are won with less than 60 percent of the vote, and congressional elections are similarly uncompetitive (Herrnson 2011). The bottom line is that a career as an American legislator comes with a great deal of job security.

These trends do not appear to be lost on politically savvy prospective candidates, who recognize that most incumbents are practically unassailable. Indeed, many such "high-quality" challengers—those with the means and experience to run a strong, well-funded campaign—appear to be quite opportunistic, usually emerging when local conditions appear to weaken the incumbent (Krasno and Green 1988) or when there is no incumbent at all (Cox and Katz 1996). When the strongest potential challengers cede the field to less seasoned candidates, the potential for competition is further eroded. Political neophytes are less likely to possess the connections and experience necessary to fund a strong challenge, and the donors they do solicit are likely to judge them a poorer investment than a more experienced candidate. Thus, these "low-quality" challengers find themselves the victims of a crippling paradox, as they must raise money to be viewed as strong challengers, but the "strong challenger" tag comes only when one has money in the bank. Thus, most of the time, incumbents are able to bury challengers in campaign cash.

Public election funding is delivered to candidates who meet minimum qualifying thresholds, regardless of how much money they would have raised in a traditional, donor-driven system. Subsidies therefore allow even the most inexperienced challengers to solve the paradox described above, facilitating a well-financed campaign regardless of the candidate's inherent "quality." Publicly funded challengers are likely to control more money than they would have otherwise and will spend it to enhance their name recognition and to spread their message. In short, they should be expected to run stronger, more visible campaigns than traditionally financed challengers.

While that story is certainly true, little research has been done about the interplay of public funding, competition, and candidate "quality" in state legislative elections. The availability of campaign subsidies could encourage the entry of experienced candidates looking to challenge incumbents. Such challengers might gauge public funding as a vehicle to improve their funding position for a race that they may well have undertaken eventually, regardless of whether subsidies were available. Alternatively, public funding could empower political neophytes, encouraging them to wage a campaign that they may never otherwise have considered. Full funding in particular holds the potential to draw candidates into even the most unwinnable races, giving them the tools to run a serious campaign. If that is true, then Clean Elections programs could serve as springboards that vault candidates into the "high-quality" category regardless of their previous political experience, connections, or name recognition.

Untangling this question is therefore a crucial step in understanding how public funding affects challengers' ability to run well.

Reducing Campaign Costs in "Losing Races"

In aiding challengers who may otherwise find fundraising a difficult chore, public funding has long been seen as a tool with the potential to stimulate electoral competition. Political science has generally found that subsidy size is an important determinant of the ability of public funding to achieve this end, with larger subsidies apparently having a much greater effect. Examining evidence from Wisconsin, for example, Mayer and Wood (1995) report no evidence that partial public funding encouraged challenger emergence in districts with entrenched incumbents or that it narrowed election margins. In an early study of partial public funding in Minnesota, Jones and Borris (1985) also found no apparent connection between public funding and electoral outcomes in close races. One reason for this, the authors suggested, was that candidates who believed their races would be close opted out of partial public funding to avoid its spending ceilings, which were quite low during the period under study. Donnay and Ramsden (1995) found that once appropriate controls are included, there appears to be a relationship between competition and public funding in Minnesota's incumbent-contested elections. However, Donnay and Ramsden note that the effect sizes are substantively small and their impact is unclear in circumstances in which both the incumbent and challenger take public money.

The picture is clearer in Clean Elections states. Before the implementation of full funding programs in Arizona and Maine for the 2000 election, a simulation study suggested that more generous subsidies would lead to narrower victory margins (Goidel and Gross 1996). Since then, scholarly analysis has largely confirmed this prediction in fully funded environments. For instance, the GAO found statistically significant changes in the winner's victory margin in both Arizona and Maine during years for which public funding was available (GAO 2010, 35). Examining data through 2004, Mayer et al. (2006) found "compelling evidence" of heightened competition in both Arizona and Maine after 1998, with fewer incumbents receiving more than 60 percent of the vote. Werner and Mayer (2007) extended this analysis to include the 2006 elections, with similar findings. Malhotra (2008) employed two dependent variables and multiple specifications of a regression model to measure the effect of Clean Elections in state senate elections in both Arizona and Maine, and found that incumbents saw diminished margins when they were met by a publicly funded challenger.

Despite growing evidence of heightened competition in fully funded environments, all the Arizona candidates I interviewed in 2007 recognized the strategic and institutional advantages that sitting legislators enjoy. In particular, they cited factors such as fundraising connections, name recognition, and the experience gained from previous elections. Asked to comment on the difference between running as incumbents and running as challengers, one challenger lamented the uphill battle of running against an incumbent, who is always better known among the electorate: "The incumbent will still have an advantage just from being out there in the community. Not much you can do about that." Another noted the relative ease with which incumbents can raise money from lobbyists and interest groups via established connections, an advantage that can lead to wide funding gaps between incumbents and challengers. "If [the funding system] was just traditional like back in 1998 or whatever, my opponent would probably have raised $25,000 just because she's got lobbyists and other networks already in place. I could have probably raised maybe three or four thousand." A final challenger was more blunt: "My opponent's a terrible legislator, but he knows how to run for office."

While they generally agreed that the deck was often stacked in the incumbent's favor, *every* Clean Elections candidate I interviewed believed that the public funding program had positively affected the competitive climate in Arizona. One challenger preferred to focus on the things he could control rather than those that could not be changed: "Name recognition and incumbency, that's just part of electoral politics. Although Clean Elections gives the challenger a better opportunity than they ever had before, all things considered." Even a Republican legislator who opposed Clean Elections as policy conceded that it was making elections closer, saying, "[Clean Elections] certainly levels [the playing field] more than it would have been without it—I think wrongly, but it does level it more."

Yet few political elites in Arizona view Clean Elections as a panacea for stagnant competition in that state. Rather, most informants saw the policy as a mechanism by which inexperienced candidates in unfavorable districts could enter races and run credible campaigns even if they were almost certainly going to lose. Some legislators, particularly those in leadership roles, came to see Clean Elections as a tool to foster competition in districts that might not have otherwise been contested at all. One Democratic member responsible for recruiting candidates in the early 2000s described how the party gradually came to realize that Clean Elections could serve as a valuable recruiting inducement. Asked about whether the party employed any strategic thinking on this front, he said: "In my first term, we were very conscious of the need to recruit more candidates. There were many districts where we were not even opposing incumbents. In certain areas, it did go through our thinking, our strategy,... 'as long as we can get this person qualified for Clean Elections, they will have the money to run a campaign.'" It is important to note that the goal of this informant was simply recruiting *more* candidates, regardless of their political experience or the circumstances of the district. The parties have an interest in fielding a complete slate of races, and thus public funding allowed party leaders to recruit candidates who might not have otherwise run because, given the makeup of their district, losing was a near certainty. Nearly all candidates who accepted public funding in these circumstances acknowledged that they began the campaign with the understanding that their effort would probably not be successful, even with the infusion of public subsidies. For instance, a Republican candidate who ran in a senate district containing a solid majority of Democratic voters reflected on the power of public funding to alter the competitive dynamics of a race. "Competition," to him, meant providing voters with a meaningful choice, even if everyone involved—including the candidate—understood that the outcome of the election was predetermined. "If [incumbents] are running traditional and the people support them, more power to them. I didn't win my campaign, but at least people had the opportunity to say, 'I choose this person or I choose that one.' To me, that's the quintessential part of democracy."

"Choice" was a recurring theme among Clean Elections candidates, many of whom saw their role as not to win but to carry the party banner and take a meaningful conversation to the voters. One candidate who realized he was likely going to lose his bid for the state senate contrasted the efficacy of the campaign he had with Clean Elections to the one he would have had otherwise. He also alluded to providing voters with a choice: "I suppose I could have done it without Clean Elections. I could have gotten on the ballot. Nobody's going to give you any money to run in a race that you really can't possibly win [in a traditional system]. So it really allows people to run, especially in districts that are not considered very winnable....But with Clean Elections, you know, hey, if I'm willing to roll up the sleeves, knock on the doors, do the time to get the five dollars, to me democracy is all about having the choice when you go to vote in November."

Most publicly funded candidates echoed this general sentiment, viewing a "competitive" race merely as one in which voters were given a choice and candidates ran on equal footing. These candidates deemphasized their odds of victory and focused instead on the necessity of presenting options to voters that may not have otherwise existed. Public funding may trump the "market forces" of politics that make for an uphill battle for challengers, but Clean Elections candidates mainly see subsidies as encouraging a conversation in places where the market dictates that no such conversation should occur. The words of one publicly financed challenger underscore this belief: "I ran a fantastic campaign. I did door-to-door, canvassing about eight hundred households. I did all the fairs and all the parades. I did TV ads, radio ads, print media ads, and when all was said and done I got 35 percent of the vote." One Clean Elections candidate was more succinct: "There's something to be said for Clean people to run these losing races."

Many of the Clean Elections challengers I interviewed stated that they understood they would run a viable, *losing* campaign, and blamed other factors, such as incumbency advantage and district demographics, for creating unwinnable races. The senate candidate quoted above, who ran in a district that strongly favored the opposite party's incumbent, described feelings of frustration with the political dynamics of his race. However, he felt that had he run with private contributions, "it would have been even more frustrating. It's kind of great getting that money to run. I guess you could say that it's kind of a waste giving somebody who can't possibly win money to run, but that's their fault for the way they've gerrymandered the districts in this state." One traditionally financed incumbent was more concise: "Clean Elections really gets used a lot in races that are so lopsided that it really doesn't matter."

An examination of election statistics yields some support to the notion of candidates running against long odds. Figure 5.1 depicts the percentage of Arizona and Maine house incumbents who were challenged by at least one major-party candidate in the general election, pooling data from all available years before and after public funding became available (except for redistricting years), and separating incumbents in "competitive" districts (where the last race was won with less than a 10-point margin) from those in "safe" districts (where the incumbent won the previous election with more than 55 percent of the vote). Data from years following redistricting are excluded from the data used to calculate means in Figure 5.1, since the political conditions are often not readily clear in such circumstances.

Figure 5.1 suggests that in both states, Clean Elections appears to have a stronger effect on rates of challenge in the less competitive districts. To be fair, there is little room for improvement in Maine, where 96 percent of incumbents in competitive districts were challenged before Clean Elections took effect. However, that rate *declines* slightly, to 94.6 percent, in elections when public funding is available. In Arizona fewer incumbents—82 percent—were met by at least one challenger in competitive districts before the implementation of Clean Elections, but that rate rose to 94.4 percent during Clean Elections years.

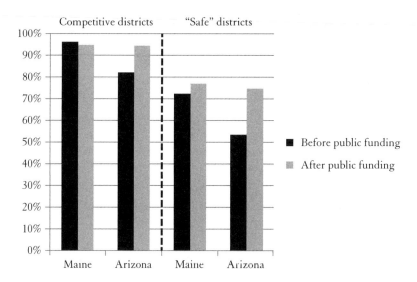

Figure 5.1. Percentage of incumbents challenged before and after public funding, by district competitiveness. Arizona figures reflect incumbents challenged by *at least* one major-party candidate.

The magnitude of the difference in challenges between traditional and Clean Elections years is much higher in the "safe" districts. In both states the percentage of challenged incumbents in those districts is considerably lower both before and after Clean Elections took effect. However, in Arizona the mean percentage of challenged incumbents rose from 53.5 percent before public funding to 74.5 percent afterward, a difference that is not only statistically significant but also more than twice the size of the difference in competitive Arizona districts.[1] In Maine the mean challenge rates rose to 77 percent in the Clean Elections era, compared with 72.5 percent before, but the difference is not statistically significant.[2] Nonetheless, Maine adheres to the pattern demonstrated in Arizona: while incumbents *overall* appear to be more likely to face a challenger in years when Clean Elections funding is available, this change is driven by challengers being more likely to emerge in districts where they stand little reasonable chance of winning.

This pattern suggests that full funding reduces the costs of campaigning to such a level that would-be candidates perceive *any* campaign—however quixotic—as a worthwhile endeavor. Such a framework is generally consistent with the notion that public funding should provide the greatest entry incentive to candidates who would otherwise have had the most difficulty raising funds. However, it is at odds with the expected behavior of a "strategic candidate" who enters when the probability of victory is high. So-called high-quality candidates—who possess skills and experience that facilitate strong campaigns—appear to be the most strategic entrants of all (Jacobson and Kernell 1981; Krasno and Green 1988). Since public funding dramatically alters candidates' perceived costs and benefits, the characteristics of participating candidates are therefore worth examining, particularly with regard to "quality." It could be that strategic, experienced candidates emerge when subsidies are available due to the much lower costs of running, regardless of their judgment about the likelihood that they will win. Or perhaps the lower costs are irrelevant to strategic candidates, whose main goal is to maximize the chances of victory. In such a scenario, public funding might encourage entry mainly by neophytes who do not have to worry about giving up an existing political office to run for a higher one. Assuming (as political science has) that high-quality, strategic candidates run better campaigns, these alternate possibilities lead to very different conclusions about how public funding might affect elections.

Public Funding and "Quality" Candidates

It is worthwhile to explore the factors that encourage candidates to participate in public funding programs, since public funding may tip the balance for strategic challengers who would otherwise avoid entering politics because they perceive either the cost of campaigning as too high or the probability of winning as too low. This calculus is consistent with the legislative intent of the Arizona Clean Elections Act (AZ 16-940) itself, which declares that among other problems, the privately funded campaign finance system that preceded Clean Elections "[drove] up the cost of running for state office, discouraging otherwise qualified candidates who lack personal wealth or access to special-interest funding."

It seems reasonable to assume that candidates with neither political experience nor the corresponding access to an established network of campaign contributors will see the largest reduction in campaign costs if they accept public funding. Such candidates would exert a considerably larger effort than an established politician to raise a fixed sum from private donors and would therefore perceive public subsidies as a larger aid. Alternatively, candidates who *do* possess tools necessary for building a strong campaign, but who sit out due to a belief that they will not win, may perceive the performance bonus of participation as a sufficient incentive to run.

Thus, it is unclear whether public funding should be expected to increase the "quality" of the candidate pool. Political science has traditionally recognized the importance of candidate quality in predicting the electoral success of non-incumbents in both congressional (Jacobson 1989) and state legislative elections (Van Dunk 1997). However, researchers have acknowledged the difficulty of coming up with a universal framework for what a high-quality candidate looks like in traditionally financed elections. Presumably, a higher-quality candidate will raise more campaign cash and will have an easier time attracting and mobilizing supporters (see Bond et al. 1985). Yet while there is a range of attributes that would aid candidates in garnering contributions and supporters, such as fame in the district, party connections, or failed bids for office in the past (Krasno and Green 1988), many determinants of "quality" are hard to observe. To overcome the practical problems associated with determining the impact of every attribute of candidates, political scientists frequently rely on a shortcut to define a high-quality candidate: previous elected experience (Jacobson 1989; Van Dunk 1997).

Candidates who have already won an office (presumably a lower one) have experienced the rigors of a campaign; the daily grind will be less surprising, and such a candidate will likely be able to rely on experience to gain efficiency. Moreover, the process of campaigning for a lower office is useful for a candidate's subsequent pursuits, since donor and voter lists can be mined in future campaigns. Thus, a candidate's previous political experience is a useful shortcut for observers looking to distinguish between those candidates who are likely to raise enough money to wage a serious campaign and those who will probably fail to attract much support.

Because public funding dramatically changes the costs and benefits involved in running a campaign, previous research has searched for a noticeable difference in quality among the pools of candidates (or potential candidates) running for office when such funding is available. For instance, La Raja's (2008) survey of potential candidates in Connecticut found some evidence that full funding provides an incentive for the entry of high-quality candidates. Dowling (2011) found that public funding led to a substantial increase in the number of experienced candidates running in open-seat gubernatorial elections, but only for those of the incumbent party. Moreover, Dowling found no effects for incumbent-contested elections. In tandem, these findings suggest that public funding generally (Dowling 2011) and Clean Elections specifically (La Raja 2008) *could* lead to a higher likelihood of experienced candidates running in some circumstances.

The 2008 legislative candidate survey is a useful tool for further exploring the relationship between public funding and candidate quality. As noted, inexperienced candidates with little political experience and/or established networks of contributors face the highest hurdles to funding a campaign: in political science parlance, they are "low quality." Public election funding, and especially full funding systems such as Clean Elections, should serve as a larger incentive for inexperienced candidates to run, since many would not have been able to raise the subsidy amount from private donors. The survey responses of non-incumbent publicly funded candidates bear this out: while 44 percent of experienced participating candidates reported that they would not have run had full public funding not been available, 66 percent of inexperienced candidates would have stayed out of the race. The opposite is true of partially funded candidates, among whom a larger proportion of experienced candidates (43 percent) than inexperienced candidates (28 percent) said they would not have run without some public funding.

A similar pattern emerges when the percentage of "quality" candidates in each funding condition is examined, at least for fully funded candidates. Figure 5.2 depicts the percentage of lower-house candidates who reported previous experience as an elected official in the candidate survey, by public funding status. Since the "quality" question generally centers on the attributes of non-incumbent candidates, I present mean levels of experience only for candidates who were not running for reelection. Experience levels are depicted separately for candidates in privately funded states who had no option of taking public funding, those in the two types of public funding states (partial and full) who opted out, and those who accepted partial and full subsidies.

Among candidates running in states that offered no public funding, about one-third (34 percent) had experience as elected politicians before the 2008 election. This proportion is essentially equal to the mean experience level of candidates who opted out of partial funding programs (primarily in Wisconsin and Hawaii) and slightly greater than the 31.5 percent of

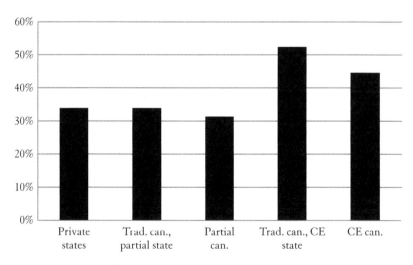

Figure 5.2. Percentage of non-incumbent candidates possessing previous elected experience, by public funding status. Trad. = traditional; Can. = candidate; CE = Clean Elections.

partially funded candidates (primarily in Minnesota) who had experience in elected office. Mean levels of political experience are higher in the states offering full public funding: about 45 percent of candidates who accepted Clean Elections funding reported previous elected experience in the Clean Elections states. However, this figure is about six percentage points lower than the proportion of experienced *traditional* candidates in those states. Especially considering that none of the differences therein are statistically significant, Figure 5.2 offers little evidence that public funding increases mean levels of candidate experience in the general election pool: relative to candidates who opt out of the two types of public funding, those who participate appear no more likely to have held previous elected experience.

Logistic regression models, whose coefficients and standard errors are contained in Table 5.1, allow for the determinants of public funding acceptance to be more fully described. I report separate models for partial and full funding states, and each model includes state fixed effects. Model specification is described in Appendix 3. The dependent variable in each model is a dichotomous indicator coded 1 if the candidate accepted public funding and 0 otherwise. Positive coefficients demonstrate a positive relationship between an independent variable and the odds of a candidate accepting public funding.

The coefficients for the indicators of whether a candidate was a Democrat are positive and statistically significant in both models, indicating that partisan affiliation is an important determinant of whether a candidate opts into public funding. Democrats appear to be significantly more likely than Republicans to take Clean Elections subsidies, other variables in the model being held constant (I explore this finding more fully in the next chapter). That similarity aside, the models yield few additional clues about when a candidate is more or less likely to run with public funding. In neither type of system does work status, incumbency, gender, or partisan balance of the district demonstrate a statistical relationship with participation, suggesting that they are not important explanatory variables of why a candidate opts into partial or full public funding. The coefficient for whether a candidate was unopposed is negatively signed in both types of states but is statistically significant only in the model of Clean Elections states. This finding makes intuitive sense when one considers that unlike Clean Elections subsidies, for which candidates must expend a nontrivial effort to qualify, partial funding usually comes with few qualification requirements. Indeed,

TABLE 5.1. Determinants of Accepting Full and Partial Public Funding: Logistic Regression Coefficients and Standard Errors

	Partial states	Full states
Unopposed	−0.780	−2.518*
	(1.271)	(0.625)
Incumbent	−0.695	−0.294
	(0.891)	(0.532)
Experience	−0.430	−0.316
	(0.701)	(0.534)
Male	1.043	−0.454
	(0.802)	(0.464)
Democrat	1.730*	1.986*
	(0.819)	(0.502)
Employed Full-time	−0.267	−0.575
	(0.782)	(0.515)
Employed Part-time	0.429	−0.653
	(0.802)	(0.586)
% of Vote for candidate's party, 2006	−0.003	0.004
	(0.013)	(0.010)
Constant	3.130*	2.499*
	(1.299)	(0.856)
Observations	190	250
Initial Log Likelihood	−130.42	−113.18
Final Log Likelihood	−40.94	−87.92
Chi-Squared	178.96	50.52
McFadden's R^2	0.69	0.22

Note: Standard errors in parentheses. Dependent variable is dichotomous indicator of whether a candidate accepted public funding. State fixed effects.
*$p < .05$.

winning the nomination is often sufficient for obtaining partial funding. Unopposed candidates, who know they will win, are not likely to invest much effort to secure Clean Elections funds, but will take any partial funding that comes with no additional effort.

As for the experience question, the coefficient for previous experience is negatively signed in both partial and full funding states, which is to be expected given the pattern apparent in Figure 5.2. However, the failure of either coefficient to achieve statistical significance suggests that, holding the other factors constant, previous political experience exerts no independent effect on a candidate's decision of whether to run with public funding. The failure of the model to find a relationship between candidate experience and public funding acceptance suggests that public funding has little effect on the "quality" of the candidate pool one way or the other, at least if quality is defined by a candidate's previous electoral experience. Yet that may be a suboptimal definition.

While the survey data presented above lend little support to the notion that public funding changes the pool of "quality" candidates as traditionally defined in political science, candidate testimony reveals a wide gulf between how political neophytes and more seasoned legislators viewed the impact of Clean Elections on attracting more and/or better candidates to the electoral arena. Most Arizona candidates and legislators resisted the political science definitions of candidate quality (i.e., dichotomous measures of candidate experience), opting instead for an "I know it when I see it" approach. As such, descriptions of "quality" were wide-ranging among the candidates I interviewed. Some incumbents, and Republicans in particular, were less than optimistic about the effects of Clean Elections on the quality of legislative candidates. One Republican incumbent said as much: "People will run if they have a base of support. If you've had a city council position, that's how you start [in a traditional system]. I feel like [Clean Elections] is artificial. It creates candidates that otherwise wouldn't be there. 'Oh well, free money, I might as well run.' Some people might see that as healthy, but I really don't. I think that the traditional system works just fine. If someone is doing a bad job, even with the power of incumbency and all that stuff, I think in most cases there will be an opponent, or there will be a group that will run somebody against them. But on the flip side, Clean Elections artificially gets people into the races, and creates an opponent because of this money."

This informant alludes to a marketplace that rewards political experience and candidates who have paid their dues. Subsidizing neophytes allows them to skip several rungs of the political ladder. Clean Elections is therefore an "artificial" force in the eyes of some because it allows candidates to move up the political ranks too quickly, before they have taken the time to build connections in the community, understand local issues, or establish a base of political support. Another Republican incumbent reiterated this sentiment, saying, "You better have some roots in this community to go out and raise some money if you want to challenge me. Clean Elections just lets them move up five steps. Five dollars from two hundred people...does that mean you have roots in the community?"

The implication of this statement is that establishing roots in the community allows candidates a chance to learn about the community's political tastes, who its leaders are, and how to represent it. Thus, a candidate who lacks a solid existing district network will be of low quality in the sense that she will not have a clear understanding of the key political players and issues. A third Republican candidate spoke to this directly: "I think [Clean Elections] attracts a lot of people that really aren't ready for prime time, and you know, some get elected. They haven't been involved in politics, other than saying, 'This sounds like a neat idea.' I'd prefer people who know the process. Some people are very good in a traditional sense, good business people, community activists, maybe they didn't run for city council, they're really good people. But by and large, I think most people do follow a ladder in the political process, and I think there's a reason for that. I think that's why we tend to be skeptical if someone runs for governor right out of the gate, never having been to elected office before."

Even some Democrats joined in. As one said, "I think [Clean Elections] allows somebody that's not in the system to get in the system and run. That can be a good thing, but not always. Maybe the person that's not in the system shouldn't be running." A number of informants felt that one major result of not being "ready for prime time" was that, in their view, candidates in both parties getting elected with Clean Elections funding were more apt to focus on narrow or even single-issue legislative agendas, and were therefore less likely to take up the overall objectives of the parties in government. A Republican member echoed this criticism more forcefully: "The only thing [Clean Elections] has truly accomplished is giving people with no ability to do the job the ability to get money to run for the office, and in some cases they actually get elected. And they're one-issue people; they don't understand what governing is about. The issue might be pro-life, but they don't have the overall broad experience to really understand even what you're trying to accomplish."

Most informants critical of Clean Elections also believed that the candidates with narrower objectives tend to be more radical as well, which is consistent with early evidence that legislators who enter the chamber with the aid of Clean Elections are more ideologically extreme (Masket and Miller 2013). The underlying assumption is that Clean Elections funds all who qualify, diminishing parties' ability to direct campaign resources to candidates who will toe the line. While they would have failed to attract sufficiently broad financial backing in a traditional system, such candidates, in the words of one Democratic legislator, "who happen to be of the right stuff with some narrow segment of the electorate, and particularly on social issues, are going to get elected. They couldn't get the funding before, but if they have the funding [with Clean Elections], they're going to get elected."

In sum, Clean Elections skeptics—at least in Arizona—felt that certain forces in traditionally funded politics provide some crucial benefits and that political experience is a useful heuristic for identifying candidate quality. For one, politicians who take the time to follow a career course through local government will build a base of support in the community while learning the political ropes. Along the way, they gain political savvy and learn the importance of being part of a partisan team. Critics of public funding felt that while some good candidates were undoubtedly aided by public funding, subsidies had also opened the door for candidates who did not possess the hard-to-define traits that come with being a high-quality politician. One legislator put it this way: "There are some really good, wise, sharp people here. Some of them are here because of Clean Elections. There are some real idiots here. Some of them are here because of Clean Elections."

Clean Elections candidates were aware of these criticisms. As one Democratic neophyte said, "There were plenty of people who told me that I had no business running for that high of a position when I had never been in political life before." However, despite a consciousness of their own inexperience, all such candidates displayed a markedly similar unapologetic attitude, standing their critics' arguments on their heads in favoring a citizen legislature. One informant who lost a close Democratic primary election was adamant in questioning whether experience was the best measure of "quality" in terms of candidate recruitment. He argued that if the effect of Clean Elections was to encourage more citizens to run, then it was actually moving Arizona politics closer to the intended arrangement of a citizen legislature. "[A citizen legislature] was the whole goal [of the Arizona Constitution], and unfortunately in Arizona with the existing body right now, I think existing legislators on both sides would say that incumbency and previous offices are not very good measures of quality."

First-time candidates who ran with Clean Elections funding returned to a common phrase: "people like me." The pervasive view among neophytes was that they either would never have run without the availability of Clean Elections funding or would not have had much funding success. But unlike Clean Elections' critics, those who ran with public subsidies saw this as a good thing. Asked to describe the most important effect of public funding in Arizona elections, a losing Democratic candidate said, "It allows people like me, not that I was the best candidate, but it allows people like me to run for an office without knowing a lot, without having a lot of contacts." Another expressed exasperation at the critics who judged her, as a first-time candidate, to be unqualified: "As a citizen, the more people we have in this thing, and the more people who we want to get out there, and give a voice, and give a platform, that's what it's supposed to be all about, for crying out loud, so what's wrong with that? I don't think anything's wrong with that. Quite to the contrary, I think it's quite good, and might in and of itself be worth the investment [in Clean Elections]."

When asked what would happen to the federal government if it replicated Clean Elections for congressional campaigns, another Democrat, this one a successful candidate who won her first-ever campaign, said: "If we get total public funding [in the rest of the country], it's going to be different. We're going to have people like me. You know, ordinary citizens running for office more so than these people who have this grand scheme of running for greater offices, for bigger offices, for the stepping-stone. It doesn't mean that they don't start at the local level and then go to the national level, but from what I have seen in our caucus here, it's the people like me that never would have thought about running for office [who run]. So that's adding a different dynamic; it's adding, I'm hoping, a positive thing to the electoral process, because we don't have an agenda. We don't have a political career. We're the citizen-politician that I think our founding fathers planned on. That's how I feel."

Nearly all Clean Elections candidates stressed their credentials as citizens first. One member of the senate described the campaign of one of her traditionally financed colleagues: "My first term here there was a pediatrician from Yuma. He went into debt something like $16,000 for a job that paid $24,000. I would have had to mortgage my house." Another Democrat "decided to go Clean Elections because I'm not a wealthy person and I don't have corporate or PAC support." Perhaps the most succinct statement was, "Does Clean Elections make a difference? I think so! Because I wouldn't be here otherwise."

One first-time candidate recalled how her party used Clean Elections as a recruiting tool to overcome the objections of candidates reluctant to raise money. When she was approached by party elites asking her to run, she said, "'Well, I can't raise money.' And they said, 'Well, you don't have to, because there's Clean Elections.' So I didn't really know that much about it, and then I learned, once I got going, what it meant. It meant everything. It meant that I could run." This testimony underscores the importance of Clean Elections in shifting the necessary qualifications away from fundraising toward other areas of the campaign. One experienced legislator commented on how the elimination of fundraising affected the entry calculus for candidates and served as a strong incentive for citizens to run: "See, in the past, that 'Are you good at fundraising' qualification was first. I'm not good at fundraising, you know what I mean? I'm especially not good at fundraising for myself. I think it's a shame, you know people say, 'Why don't we have better people running for office?' And it's because people say, 'I'm not going to touch that fundraising.' So you have a relatively small percentage of people who are interested in this stuff anyway, and then you take all of the ones who aren't any good at fundraising and we say, 'I don't want you to play.' I think we eliminate so many people who would be good public policy stewards or, you know, statesmen, and we make it a contest, a popularity contest of who can raise the most money to get the message out. I don't think that whether you can raise money to get your message out has anything to do with whether you would be a good statesman or steward of things."

It seems safe to conclude that proponents of Clean Elections in Arizona were not very enthusiastic about defining quality in terms of previous experience. A Democratic member of the Arizona House leadership, asked about the "quality" of candidates in his caucus, said, "We've got eleven new freshmen in my caucus this time, and with rare exceptions, they're bright, energetic, and hardworking. That's quality." Those characteristics alone are not sufficient to get someone elected in most of America's legislative districts, but Arizona's candidates consistently acknowledged that accepting public funding is a fairly reliable mechanism to transform an inexperienced candidate into a high-quality contender with the tools to do the job.

Manufacturing Quality?

Elites—especially incumbents—who are critical of Clean Elections tend to define a "quality" candidate as one who possesses the talent and knowledge to run a good campaign and/or an effective legislative office, or in the words of one of the informants above, one who is "ready for prime time." This is a subjective measure of quality that contrasts sharply with much of the political science literature, which has necessarily sought a clearer definition. Thus, it seems prudent to explore quality in terms of whether candidates are more or less likely to feel in command of sufficient resources when public funding is available.

One shortcoming of the dichotomous "experience" measure of quality is that it says very little about how candidates orient to their own campaigns. Under the "I-know-it-when-I-see-it" framework of candidate quality that many political elites appear to use, higher-quality candidates should be better able to muster the resources necessary to wage a strong campaign and should be less surprised by the rigors of daily politics, regardless of their previous political experience. With that in mind, I now turn to questions about, first, whether accepting public funding markedly improved candidates' financial position and, second, how publicly funded candidates *felt* about their campaigns relative to those who opted out. To that end, Figure 5.3 depicts the extent to which non-incumbent survey respondents agreed with two statements, collapsing "Strongly Disagree" and "Disagree" into one category and "Strongly Agree" and "Agree" into another. The first one read, "When I began this campaign, I underestimated how difficult it would be to raise money." The second one was, "I have sufficient time, money, and staff to mobilize voters who will support me." Candidate responses are broken down by whether a candidate ran with private funding only, partial public funding, or full public funding.

Two patterns emerge in Figure 5.3. First, the feelings of partially funded candidates are comparable to those of traditionally financed candidates on these issues. About 45 percent of candidates in both groups agreed that they had underestimated the difficulties associated with fundraising while about 30 percent disagreed. Roughly 30 percent of candidates in each group also felt that they had sufficient resources to mobilize their voters. Notably, a higher percentage of partially funded candidates disagreed with that statement, suggesting that compared with traditionally financed candidates, fewer partially funded candidates felt that they had sufficient campaign resources. On the whole, however, partially funded candidates appear to feel about the same, not only toward their ability to fundraise but also toward their overall resource position, as those who raise money from private sources alone.

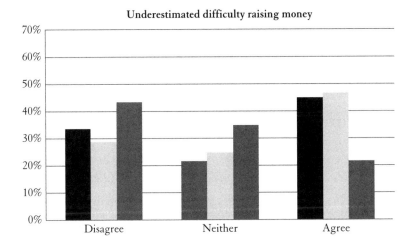

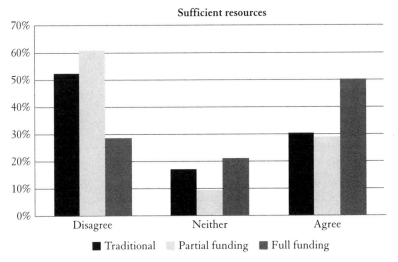

Figure 5.3. Non-incumbents' responses to survey questions: underestimated difficulty fundraising and sufficient resources

In contrast, candidates who accepted Clean Elections subsidies appear less likely to feel that they had underestimated the difficulties of fundraising and more likely to believe that they commanded enough resources to win. Relative to traditional candidates, the percentage of candidates taking full funding and who agreed with the "difficulty raising money" statement was much less: about 25 percentage points. A similar gap— about 20 points—is evident in the percentage of fully funded candidates who agreed that they had sufficient resources to mobilize voters; both of these differences are statistically significant.[3] Thus, Figure 5.3 suggests that non-incumbent Clean Elections candidates appear to possess more control over their campaigns, demonstrating less anxiety about their campaign resources and less surprise about the rigors of daily fundraising activities.

Yet Figure 5.3 does not account for possibility that other factors are driving the differences in candidate opinion. I therefore model candidate responses to the two questions with three ordered probit regression models each (Table 5.2). Specification 1 models all survey data and contains separate indicators for Clean Elections and partially funded candidates. Specification 2 models data from the matched dataset of fully funded candidates, and Specification 3 utilizes the matched dataset of partially funded candidates (these datasets and models are fully described in Appendix 3). The models examine the relationship between candidates' funding status and their responses to the questions, holding other traits of the candidate and the district constant to eliminate those variables as confounding factors. Coefficients and standard errors can be found in Table 5.2. The referent category for all models is "Strongly Disagree." Thus, positive coefficients in Table 5.2 indicate that respondents are more likely to agree with each statement as the independent variables grow larger, if the other variables are held constant.

I first examine the models of responses to the statement, "When I began this campaign, I underestimated how difficult it would be to raise money." The control variables indicate that, unsurprisingly, incumbents are significantly less likely than challengers to be surprised by the rigors of fundraising. The same is true of open-seat candidates in the model pooling all survey data and the one using the matched dataset of fully funded candidates (but not the matched partial funding dataset). The model of matched partial candidates indicates that men appear to be more likely to feel that they had underestimated fundraising difficulty, but that effect is not present in the other two models. None of the models suggests that either previous experience or the partisan balance of the district (defined here as the percentage of the vote that the candidate's party received in 2006) are significant predictors of responses to the fundraising difficulty question.

The coefficient for participation in a partial public funding program appears in Specifications 1 and 3. Those coefficients are positively signed in both models, but neither achieves statistical significance: compared with those who fund their campaigns entirely through private contributions,

TABLE 5.2. Ordered Probit Regression Coefficients and Robust Standard Errors

	Underestimated fundraising			Had sufficient resources		
	1	2	3	1	2	3
Accepted full funding	−0.007 (0.233)	0.086 (0.349)	–	0.567* (0.224)	1.141* (0.347)	–
Accepted partial funding	0.358 (0.299)	–	0.051 (0.299)	−0.477 (0.304)	–	−0.606* (0.302)
Incumbent	−0.759* (0.112)	−0.930* (0.225)	−0.905* (0.275)	0.894* (0.112)	0.750* (0.215)	1.351* (0.293)
Open seat	−0.202* (0.100)	−0.432* (0.189)	0.084 (0.298)	0.439* (0.100)	0.335 (0.184)	0.545 (0.304)
Male	0.118 (0.079)	−0.065 (0.146)	0.411* (0.199)	0.046 (0.078)	0.206 (0.141)	0.229 (0.205)
Previous elected experience	0.014 (0.087)	−0.047 (0.174)	0.106 (0.212)	0.144 (0.087)	0.416* (0.171)	0.276 (0.219)
Lagged party vote %	0.000 (0.002)	0.001 (0.004)	−0.002 (0.005)	0.004* (0.002)	0.002 (0.004)	−0.001 (0.005)
Cut 1	−1.587* (0.223)	−1.425* (0.417)	−2.121* (0.466)	−0.866* (0.225)	0.122 (0.407)	−0.668 (0.464)
Cut 2	−0.562* (0.219)	−0.477 (0.413)	−0.931* (0.439)	0.326 (0.223)	1.231* (0.408)	0.980* (0.449)
Cut 3	0.106 (0.218)	0.427 (0.413)	−0.392 (0.434)	0.807* (0.224)	1.765* (0.412)	1.484* (0.456)
Cut 4	1.013* (0.221)	1.324* (0.420)	0.908* (0.449)	2.067* (0.230)	3.174* (0.435)	2.848* (0.495)
Observations	840	239	153	864	257	152
Initial log likelihood	−1292.45	−358.45	−226.27	−1281.85	−376.61	−215.29
Final log likelihood	−1233.79	−333.44	−207.44	−1179.54	−339.22	−187.53
Chi-squared	117.34	50.02	37.65	204.64	74.78	55.53

Note: Analysis restricted to contested candidates. Models include state fixed effects.
*$p < .05$.

partially financed candidates exhibit about the same attitude toward their fundraising ability. A similar picture emerges for fully funded candidates. The coefficient for the variable indicating participation in Clean Elections can be found in Specifications 1 and 2. While the signs of those coefficients do not agree, neither one is a statistically significant predictor of candidates' estimation that they had underestimated how difficult it would be raise money. So, if we control for other factors, neither candidates who took partial subsidies nor those who ran with Clean Elections funding differed from traditionally financed candidates in the extent to which they underestimated fundraising obligations.

I now turn to the models of the extent to which candidates agreed with the statement, "I have sufficient time, money, and staff to mobilize voters who will support me." Again, incumbency is a powerful predictor: all three models indicate that incumbents are significantly more likely than challengers to feel that their resources are sufficient. In the model of pooled data, open-seat candidates were also more likely than challengers to agree with the statement. Experienced candidates in the model of matched fully funded candidates, and candidates in more favorable partisan conditions, were also more likely to agree in the fully matched and pooled data, respectively. No other control variables achieved statistical significance.

In Specification 1 the coefficient for the variable indicating participation in partial public funding is negative but not statistically significant. The coefficient for the same variable in Specification 3 (using matched data) is also signed negatively, but in that case it achieves statistical significance. Thus, the conclusions about how partially funded candidates viewed their campaign resources range from (at best) that they are no different than traditionally financed ones, to (at worst) that partially funded candidates are significantly *less* likely to feel as if they controlled sufficient resources. In contrast, the coefficient for accepting Clean Elections subsidies is positive and significant in both specifications in which it is present, indicating that Clean Elections plays a significant role in determining candidates' belief that they possess sufficient resources to be competitive, independent of the other variables included in the models.

In short, relative to candidates raising money in traditional systems, fully funded candidates are more likely to agree that they had enough resources at their disposal. There is no evidence that partially funded candidates were more positive about their resource position. Indeed, the models cannot rule out the possibility that they actually held more negative feelings than their traditionally financed counterparts. There are no apparent effects of public funding (of either type) on candidates' beliefs that they had underestimated the difficulty of fundraising. Regardless, the attitudinal shift apparent among fully funded candidates on the resource question is suggestive that Clean Elections *manufactures* high-quality candidates by providing them with the resources that would normally accrue mainly to experienced candidates in traditionally financed systems. In other words, defining candidate quality by previous elected experience might be less useful in fully funded systems than in other campaign finance schemes.

An examination of campaign finance records underscores the potential of Clean Elections funding to reduce the importance of candidate experience in determining funding levels. Figure 5.4 depicts the mean sums raised (in 2008 dollars) by contested challengers and open-seat candidates from 2000 to 2008 in Arizona and Maine and for the 2008 election in Connecticut. Mean fundraising is shown by public funding status. Three trends are apparent. First, comparing the funding levels of traditionally financed candidates running in elections for an open seat with those who challenged an incumbent reveals that the former raised much more money on average, which is consistent with the increased attention and heightened competition in open-seat races. Second, making the same comparison between publicly funded challengers and open-seat candidates in all three states reveals that fully funded non-incumbents raised about the same amount regardless of whether there was an incumbent in the race. This is perhaps not terribly surprising given that the presence of an incumbent does not affect the subsidy amount. Third, comparing publicly funded candidates with those who opted out demonstrates that both publicly funded open-seat candidates and challengers generally controlled larger sums than their traditionally financed counterparts. In Arizona and Connecticut the average gap between publicly and privately funded candidates is vast, while it is considerably narrower in Maine elections, which are much less expensive. Thus, in the comparatively expensive legislative races in Arizona and Connecticut, Clean Elections appears to bolster challenger finances, levying resources that would probably not exist otherwise.

Yet Figure 5.4 does not account for differences in candidate experience. Perhaps less experienced candidates opt out of public funding, exacerbating the differences in funding capability between "high-quality" and "low-quality" candidates. Figure 5.5 therefore depicts the percentage of funding in a paired race that non-incumbent respondents to the legislative candidate survey controlled (for example, if the challenger spent $4,000 and the incumbent spent $6,000, then the challenger would control 40 percent of the funding in the paired race). With one exception, the pattern in Figure 5.5 is consistent: non-incumbent candidates lacking experience as previous elected officials appear to control a smaller percentage of the funding in a given race than those who have successfully run for office previously.[4]

In states where no public funding is available, experienced candidates controlled more of the money in a paired race, by about seven percentage

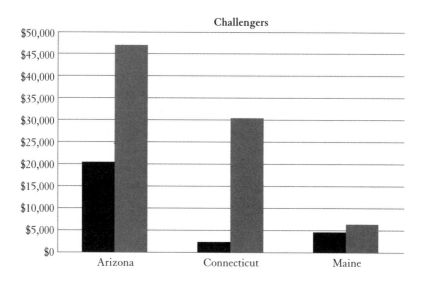

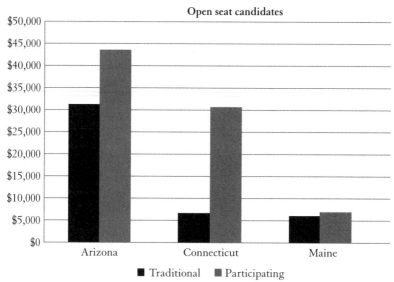

Figure 5.4. Lower-house candidate fundraising by public funding status, clean elections states. Pooled Data. Arizona and Maine: 2000–2008 elections. Connecticut: 2008 election. Figures in 2008 dollars. Data Source: National Institute for Money in State Politics.

points. Experienced candidates who participated and opted out of partial funding had about four and six percentage points more money, respectively, and those who opted out of full funding outperformed their inexperienced counterparts by about 30 points. In contrast, experienced non-incumbents

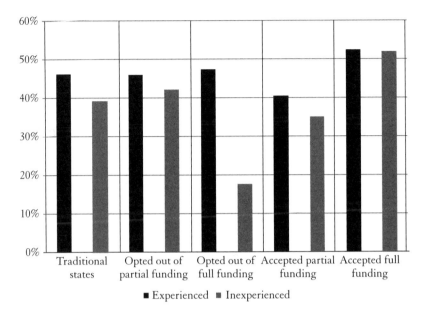

Figure 5.5. Percentage of funding in paired race controlled by non-incumbent survey respondents, by experience and public funding status

participating in full public funding controlled almost exactly the same percentage of funding in an election as their inexperienced counterparts: about 52 percent. Notably, candidates who accepted full funding—regardless of their political experience—*out-raised* incumbents, on average. This is true of no other candidate group illustrated in Figure 5.5, and strongly suggests that full funding diminishes the importance of elected experience in determining candidate "quality."

Conclusion

The critics of public funding I interviewed in 2007 saw it as eroding the importance of the traditional political career arc, which begins at the local level and advances to progressively higher offices. These candidates saw the corresponding process of network-building and partisan experience as necessary traits of a high-quality candidate. According to them, subsidies allowed candidates to fund a campaign without establishing these relationships, propelling them to the state legislature before they were ready. Meanwhile, Arizona candidates who accepted public funding viewed the program as having provided them with tools that they would have otherwise lacked, precisely because they did not have access to a ready network of donors. These candidates viewed hard work and a commitment to voters as the core components of "quality," and felt that they would not have run a strong campaign without the help granted by the subsidies.

There is evidently some disagreement among informants in Arizona as to whether public funding improves the average quality of the candidates running for office. If subsidies merely encourage neophytes to run before they are "ready for prime time," then perhaps this funding serves to effectuate the campaigns of low-quality candidates. Indeed, the analysis in this chapter yields little evidence that candidates who accept public funding are more likely to possess political experience than traditionally financed candidates in their states. By the conventional definitions of candidate quality in political science, which lean heavily on a candidate's level of previous political experience, one might conclude that public election funding does little to improve the quality of the candidate pool.

However, there is substantial evidence that public funding reduces altogether the utility of the "experience" measure of candidate quality. Regardless of whether they possess political experience, fully funded candidates raise more money and exhibit a more positive attitude toward their ability to wage an effective campaign than traditional candidates. In short, they look to an outside observer much like a high-quality candidate in a traditional election. The full subsidies of Clean Elections systems appear to help candidates to run the campaign they originally envisioned. Previous experience may provide a useful shortcut for funding prowess in traditional funding systems, but public funding is agnostic to such attributes: anyone who qualifies may participate. Thus, while public election funding may not *attract* high-quality candidates, it appears to *manufacture* them, at least as they are defined by the Clean Elections–funded informants in Arizona.

This is an important finding, for at least two reasons. First, from a political science perspective, previous definitions of candidate quality are evidently not useful when a candidate accepts full funding. Previous political experience is a good proxy for quality in traditional financing systems because experienced candidates are likely to have the experience and tools to do the job. Experience is, in short, the best backward-looking measure of a concept that is famously difficult to observe directly, because quality is something that "we know when we see it." However, if a well-funded, hardworking candidate is the thing we are looking for in our search for quality, then a candidate's public funding status is likely a more important determinant of quality than experience, since anyone can get funding if they meet the qualification threshold.

Second, public funding may create a different kind of legislator. Public funding appears to encourage challenging campaigns by "normal" citizens in even the most quixotic conditions. Indeed, Clean Elections candidates consistently returned to the "people like me" theme when describing the effects of subsidies on the democratic system. In their own words, subsidies facilitated the emergence of a different "type" of candidate, less opportunistic and career-focused and more akin to the citizen-legislator. If true, then any number of changes might be observed in legislative behavior, including shorter tenures and diminished aggregate power of organized interests. Further research might therefore explore how public funding affects legislative bodies after the election.

6

Ideology and Partisan Participation

Although subsidies impart a clear benefit to the fundraising-challenged, other candidates might view a publicly funded campaign as having a higher net cost than a traditionally financed one. For instance, those who can easily self-fund may find the qualification costs to be relatively oner-ous. More likely, however, those candidates who perceive participation to be costly will do so because of a personal, ideologically based objection to the program. Given the rather overt expenditure of direct subsidies, it should not be terribly controversial to assume that candidates who think of themselves as "fiscally conservative"—and are therefore likely to possess an ideological desire to reduce government spending—will oppose public funding as an unwarranted utilization of government funds. Such candi-dates would eschew subsidies because accepting them would be inconsis-tent with their values.

This implies that in Clean Elections states, where subsidies are quite large relative to both spending limits and the cost of a typical campaign, there is likely a higher proportion of candidates whose main motivation for opting out of public funding is its incongruence with their political values. Even if they recognize that public funding would improve their financial resource position (and would likely enhance their odds of victory), candidates with very conservative fiscal ideologies will perceive the emotional or political costs of accepting government subsidies as too much to bear. Moreover, assuming that party affiliation is a useful proxy for candidate ideology, the higher costs of participation for conservative candidates imply that Republican candidates will be less likely than Democratic candidates to accept large public subsidies such as those in Clean Elections systems.

If it is a strong determinant of participation, then ideology is important in more than a descriptive sense. Advocates of public funding often describe it as a means to make elections more equitable. Generally, this rhetoric takes the form of "evening the playing field," implying that the election will be determined less by incumbency or money, and more by the quality of ideas. These are noble goals, and they mark a distinct departure from the conditions in most American elections. However, if an entire class of candidates is likely to perceive participation in public funding as more costly, then it is important to reflect on whether the benefits that the subsidies impart accrue evenly or whether some candidates are inherently advantaged. Put another way, it is worth considering whether the playing field is more even for Democrats in full funding systems.

The Ideology Opt-Out

The candidate survey asked candidates who chose to opt out of public funding why they did so. The survey question allowed candidates to choose all applicable options from a menu, including a belief that the spending limit would prove too limiting against their competition, a strategic desire to keep other candidates away via the raising of a large war chest, and opposition to public funding on ideological grounds. Table 6.1 contains the proportion of candidates in both fully and partially funded states who selected each option. Since subsidy sizes or eligibility are generally determined by contestedness, I restrict the responses in Table 6.1 to those of candidates who faced major-party opposition. Of the survey respondents, 60 candidates ran in contested elections in the partially funded states of Hawaii,

Minnesota, and Wisconsin but opted out of public funding; all but 2 of these were from Hawaii and Wisconsin. In the Clean Elections states of Arizona, Connecticut, and Maine, 25 survey respondents opted out of public funding in contested races.

The most-cited rationale for opting out of partial funding is a concern that spending limits are unrealistic: more than 60 percent of traditional candidates marked that reason as factoring in their decision in the partially funded states. Given the fact that most of the traditional candidates in the sample ran in Wisconsin and Hawaii, where spending limits in 2008 did not reflect the cost of a typical competitive race, this result is not surprising. Roughly one-quarter of nonparticipating candidates in partially funded systems reported opting out on ideological grounds. Substantially fewer candidates—about 12 percent—felt that the spending limit would inhibit their ability to build a large war chest in order to scare away the competition.

A different pattern emerges among candidates who opted out of full funding programs. Ideological objection is the leading determinant of nonparticipation for candidates in Clean Elections states by a large margin, with over 84 percent of respondents reporting opposition to full funding programs on those grounds. In contrast, only about 16 percent of traditional candidates felt that in order to win they needed to spend more than Clean Elections would allow. The low percentage of respondents choosing this option relative to those in partial funding states likely reflects the fact that Clean Elections subsidies in all three states are well in line with typical legislative campaign spending levels. Finally, about 12 percent of candidates in Clean Elections states cited the necessity of building a formidable war chest as a component of their decision.

The leading factors in the opt-out decisions for candidates in each type of system suggest two preliminary conclusions worth deeper exploration. First, a majority of candidates in partial funding systems perceive the spending limitations to be inadequate in comparison with the spending typical of viable campaigns in their state. These results are primarily driven by candidates from Wisconsin and Hawaii, where spending limits were quite low relative to mean campaign spending in 2008. Second, while relatively few candidates in Arizona, Connecticut, and Maine take issue with Clean Elections' subsidy sizes or spending limits, a sizable majority objects to the programs on ideological grounds. These results imply a

TABLE 6.1. Percentage of Traditionally Funded Candidates in Contested Races Citing Various Reasons for Opting Out

	Partially funded states	Fully funded states
	N = 60	N = 25
Had to raise more than spending limit	63.3	16.0
Desire to raise large war chest to dissuade challengers	10.0	12.0
Ideological opposition to public funding	26.7	84.4
Other	13.3	20.0

different calculus in the partial funding states relative to those with Clean Elections systems. In the former, candidates opt out because they do not see participation as sufficiently increasing their chances of winning. In the latter, the ideological costs that come with much larger subsidies are too much for some candidates to bear.

Describing Ideological Objections

Interviews with candidates in Arizona shed additional light on the calculations that various candidates made as they weighed whether to run with Clean Elections subsidies. Many conservative candidates expressed an acute opposition to Clean Elections that had existed since the policy was placed on the ballot in 1998. One Republican legislator, reflecting on his voting decision on the initiative measure, described it as a "very simple" decision: "I opposed the concept of taxpayer money being used for campaigns."

This statement is a succinct summation of the objections that many conservatives expressed. It is worth noting that while no Democratic candidates mentioned a philosophical discomfort with Clean Elections, support among Republicans displayed a considerable range. Some Republicans advocated its immediate repeal, but others unflinchingly endorsed public funding in Arizona. For instance, one first-time candidate who took on a Democratic senate incumbent in a heavily Democratic district utilized Clean Elections funding without hesitation. He saw the program as having the blessing of a majority of citizens who voted on it, which legitimized the policy and made it "safe" to use: "As far as philosophically being opposed to it, I can kind of see where [other Republicans] are coming from, but you know, over 50 percent of people voted for Clean Elections. Just going through what I went through, having that opportunity, I would wholeheartedly support Clean Elections. I mean, I just think it's a fantastic program."

It is possible that this sort of testimony stems from the fact that the candidate was running in a Democratic-leaning district where the issue is simply unimportant to voters. The costs of accepting public funding, at least in terms of a voter backlash, likely seem less acute in such districts. Other candidates reported similar nonreactions in districts that did not contain large majorities of Republican voters. For instance, a self-described "moderate Republican" member of the legislature who ran with traditional funding reported few conversations about Clean Elections with voters. "The typical voter I don't think is too tuned in to how you're running one way or the other. I explain it a little when fundraising, but typically when you're with a group or a forum, that seldom comes up."

However, the dynamics appear to be different in districts where conservative voters dominate. Another Republican member of the Arizona Legislature, this one a "conservative Republican in a conservative district," recounted his successful efforts to overcome the program's high-minded name in persuading voters to see it his way: "It's gotten this terrible misnomer, I think; 'Clean Elections' is unfair to anyone trying to attack it. People in my campaign said, 'Don't refer to it as Clean Elections, refer to it as taxpayer-funded campaigns.' For that very reason, most people think if you're not for Clean Elections, then you must be for dirty elections. I think [voters are] aware of Clean Elections, but that they haven't thought through the ramifications of it. Usually when I tell them the details and I'm opposed to it, they tend to agree with me…they say it sounds like a Communist system or whatever." The negative reaction from many Republicans, as the allusion to Communism suggests, appears to originate from the belief of many of those respondents that politics, like business, reflects winners and losers as determined by a market mechanism. The underlying logic of this position is that if candidates are able to raise large sums in a privately funded system, it is merely a reflection that voters and interest groups endorse their position.

This, in turn, creates a feeling of responsibility as candidates become stewards of the trust that donors place in them. Ideological opposition to Clean Elections is therefore formed around what is seen as an unnecessary intervention in a market. One Republican informant described what he viewed as an incongruence between Clean Elections and his own ideological perspective, saying, "It removes the economic market forces in a campaign. And I believe strongly in market forces, whether it's in the economy, in education, or in politics." Another Republican legislator who ran with traditional funding used almost the same language in describing how, in his view, the market of political contributions rewards good candidates while Clean Elections removes the accountability that traditional candidates feel toward their donors: "I have accountability. I go and raise money from people, I get $296 [the contribution limit] from you . . . I have some accountability to those people, much more than someone who receives public funds, because these people that have given to me, they're going to expect that I not be a clown. So I would say that [Clean Elections] removes market forces that makes people do things with sincerity."

This kind of argument for "market forces" was lost on many Democratic candidates. Like their Republican counterparts, Democrats discussed accountability as a factor in their decision, but they were more likely to express a preference for avoiding entanglements with private donors in order to be accountable to the broader electorate. One Democratic candidate, who won her first-ever campaign for the Arizona House, ran with a copartisan "teammate" (Arizona's house districts are represented by two members each) who also accepted public funding. She noted that in contrast to traditional candidates, "We were responsible to the state of Arizona, the Citizens' Clean Elections Commission, and the Secretary of State. They funded us, so the only people we owe is the government itself. That was a lot better than being indebted to a corporation." When asked to summarize how Republicans viewed appropriate campaign finance regulations, another Democratic legislator expressed a frustration with the broader logic of their accountability argument. "[Republicans] say it's more appropriate to get your support from corporations, but I can't figure out the logic behind that. Why? Well, because 'that's the way politics should be.' That's their answer."

The debate over the market mechanism extends beyond the relationship between donors and candidates, to a question of whether Arizona citizens should be compelled to pay into the Clean Elections coffers when they are assessed civil fines (see Chapter 1). Democratic candidates were much more likely to draw a distinction between "taxes" and "fines," and were therefore more comfortable with a system that is subsidized indirectly by citizens' bad conduct as opposed to a uniform tax. However, some Democrats expressed frustration about trying to communicate this position to voters who objected to the mandatory subsidization of candidates whom they would not have supported otherwise. One Democratic candidate who lost a general election for the state house suggested an advertising campaign to raise voter awareness on the sources of Clean Elections funding: "I think that the Clean Elections Commission needs to have a public relations firm working on its behalf, not for those who are going to run for office but for the citizens who say that they don't like Clean Elections. I say [to them], 'You're not really using public funds, it's not coming from your tax base, so I'm not sure why you're so concerned about it. This was extra money that was set aside from fines, so you may not even be participating in this. You may not have given a dollar to my campaign, so I don't know why you're so upset.'"

Republican informants were much more likely to see the distinction between "taxes" and "fines" as practically meaningless, and viewed Clean Elections as compelling citizens to perform an action that they would not have done otherwise. Some of them employed this logic during the campaign by making Clean Elections a campaign issue. One Republican challenger, running in a crowded primary field, chose to attack two candidates in his district for accepting public funding. In the process, he considered whether the difference between a tax and a fee was sufficiently important to clarify it for voters. Ultimately, he determined that it was not: "I personally took out the piece of mail against the two other candidates criticizing them for running with taxpayer funds. I think it was very effective. It was sent to Republican households, and for most Republicans, I think it strikes a chord for them. I remember when we were putting the piece together I wondered if it was accurate to say 'taxpayer dollars' because there's more that goes into it than that... but we just said that 'taxpayer dollars' is a true statement, so it was the sort of message that people could quickly grasp."

These calculations exemplify the process by which Republican candidates scrutinized Clean Election funding as it relates to market forces in politics. Ultimately, many concluded that a dollar moving from a citizen to the government, and then to the campaign coffers of a candidate unknown to the citizen who provided the money, is part of a system of "taxpayer-financed elections." Many conservative Republicans came to reject the imposition of an actor between the contributor and the candidate. For instance, one Republican member expressed frustration with a system that compelled people to pay for a program that they might not have otherwise chosen to support. Thus, it is the removal of choice that creates the objection that this respondent (and many other Republicans) had to the program: "[Democrats] say it's voluntary, but it's not voluntary. There is a surcharge on fines that you have to pay, and I believe in my heart that money is being extorted from our citizens.... I think it's wrong to force people [to pay]. I just think it's inappropriately funded, and yet I will say [Clean Elections] would go away if people were just donating money to it, because you wouldn't get enough people to donate money."

These responses depict a wide disparity between candidates of the two parties on the question of what makes up fairness in the election "marketplace." While Democrats spoke more in terms of fairness and equality for *all* voters and candidates, Republicans were more likely to consider fairness for those whose money actually funded elections. In other words, the underlying partisan difference of opinion regarding Clean Elections is apparently driven by ideological considerations. A Democratic member of the state house alluded to this ideological divide in equating Clean Elections to the redistributive programs that Republicans traditionally favor limiting. When asked who opposes Clean Elections, he responded: "Republicans are against it. I say that broadly. Well, some Republicans. Anything that ends up in an expenditure, a very large and costly state program, it's clear from the record that instead of funding anything at all, any entitlement, any program, education, healthcare, they much prefer to give tax credits to people that have plenty of money. So the people that don't like any type of state meddling in any type of system, they don't like [Clean Elections] at all." Another Democratic candidate was more blunt: "Here's their ideological opinion: 'We shouldn't be spending the taxpayer's money.' Baloney! That's no ideology. I think their ideological purpose is a bunch of crap."

A considerable number of Democratic respondents refused to acknowledge the legitimacy of Republicans' ideological objection at all, seeing it as a convenient political excuse to mask ulterior motives. One Democratic senate candidate felt that Republicans are more likely to use Clean Elections funding to reach the legislature but then defend their seats with traditionally funded campaigns: "Some [Republican] legislators run with Clean Elections, but once they get connected to the lobbyists, now they're opposed to it. They use it to get in." A Republican member who had run campaigns using both traditional contributions and Clean Elections subsidies acknowledged that there may be truth to this accusation, at least in his own case: "When I was elected to the senate, most of us [Republicans] who were elected ran Clean. So are we hypocrites, or are we taking advantage of the system? We're grabbing the lowest fruit on the tree."

However, it is worth noting that unlike his Democratic colleagues, the Republican informant just quoted did not see his behavior as indicative that ideology was an ersatz excuse for opting out of public funding. Rather, he viewed the trend as reflecting a very real tension that conservative candidates face: accepting public funding might be undesirable, but it is also difficult to raise private money as an unknown challenger. Thus, for many conservatives, taking public funding is a necessary evil. In the informant's words, "I ran Clean Elections my first time because it was an easier route, not having any built-in foundation for fundraising. It seemed to make [strategic] sense." Another (Democratic) legislator expounded: "For the seasoned politician, running Clean is probably a very effective way to do it without going after constituents over and over again. Their names are out, they're incumbents, they're more likely win, more likely to get coverage. For the new candidates, I think Clean Elections provides the foundation to become a politician." Yet another legislator, this one a Republican opposed to Clean Elections, criticized the willingness of some Republicans to trade ideological opposition for strategic advantage: "It's gone from a realm of this high-moral-ground philosophy, to strategy, and I don't feel very good about that. But that's the key. It's a strategic move." Reflecting on his strong aversion to public funding, the same informant described the tension he felt during his first election: "My district is almost two-to-one Republican. So [when I got in the race] of course I started talking to people. I had a lot of people telling me, 'If you don't run Clean Elections, you can't win. The deck is stacked against you...you've got to run Clean Elections. We all hate it as Republicans, but you've got to do it. There's no shame in it, there's lots of Republicans doing it now.' And I continued to say that I don't want to run as a participating candidate...I really believe in doing your own fundraising as a traditional candidate."

The informant just quoted opted in the end to run with private contributions, but for many other Republican candidates, the ability of public funding to enhance their financial position—and ultimately, their odds of winning—outweighs their ideological objections. In the words of a

Republican member of the Arizona Legislature, the end result for quite a few Republican candidates (and for non-incumbents in particular) is that "a lot of them just hold their noses and participate."

Partisan Effects

The apparent ideology-driven difference in candidates' orientation toward Clean Elections is not particularly surprising. Indeed, La Raja (2008) found that Clean Elections in Connecticut serves as a greater incentive for liberal citizens to enter politics than it does for conservatives. While a candidate's personal political ideology is in many cases not directly observable, the interviews described above serve as a reminder that partisan affiliation can provide a reasonable proxy for ideology, facilitating relative comparisons. Assuming that Republicans are more conservative than Democrats on average, then Republican candidates should face higher average costs of running a publicly funded campaign than Democratic candidates because of stronger reservations stemming from personal ideology. Republican candidates should therefore view public funding with greater skepticism and demonstrate lower participation rates than Democratic candidates.

Figure 6.1 depicts the percentage of survey respondents in the partial and full funding states who agreed with the statement, "I believe that public funding improves democracy in my state."[1] As is evident in the figure, Democrats are much more likely in both system types than Republicans to view public funding favorably. In the partially funded states the partisan difference on this question was about forty points, with nearly 80 percent of Democratic respondents viewing public funding favorably. The partisan gap is even larger in the Clean Elections states, in which 37 percent of Republicans saw public funding as improving democracy compared with more than 83 percent of Democrats. The partisan differences are statistically significant in both types of funding environment.

Given this finding, it seems reasonable to expect corresponding differences in the rates of partisan participation. This is particularly true in the fully funded states, where subsidies are considerably larger and where candidates must bear meaningful costs of qualification. Indeed, previous research has shown such a difference in both Arizona and Maine (Werner and Mayer 2007; GAO 2010).

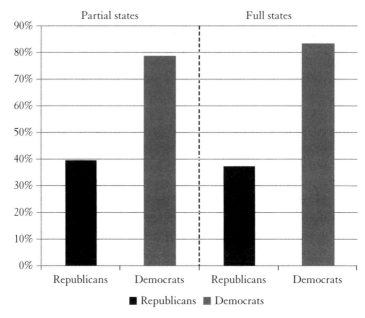

Figure 6.1. Percentage of candidates who agreed that public funding improves democracy

Figure 6.2 shows the percentage of Republican and Democratic general election state house candidates who accepted public funding in Arizona, Connecticut, and Maine from 2000 to 2008, and allows the analysis of partisan participation trends to be extended through 2008 with new data from Connecticut. In both Arizona and Maine, where comparison over time is possible, a similar trend is apparent: while participation levels for both parties are generally higher in 2008 than 2000, in every election a higher proportion of Democrats than Republicans chose to run with public funding. This is true even in 2004, when Republican participation peaked in both states before leveling off in Maine and falling somewhat in Arizona. In the 2008 Connecticut election the difference between Democratic and Republican participation was approximately six percentage points. An unfamiliarity with the programs is one possible explanation for lower overall participation rates early in their histories, but the enduring partisan gap is consistent with the theoretical cost differential that makes participation more difficult for some Republican candidates.

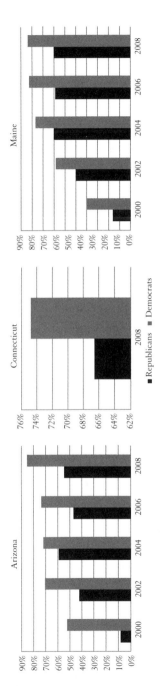

Figure 6.2. Percentage of state house candidates accepting public funding, by party. Source: Data from the National Institute on Money in State Politics. http://www.followthemoney.org.

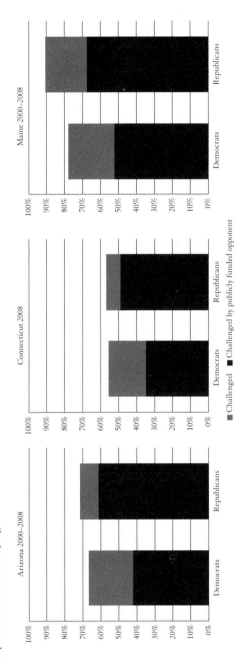

Figure 6.3. Incumbents challenged, and challenged by publicly funded candidates, clean elections states

What implications might differential partisan participation have for elections? Previous scholarship has commented on the relationship between ideology or party and Clean Elections participation, but there has been no systematic analysis of whether partisan affiliation affects how Clean Elections bears on the dynamics of incumbent-challenged elections. In the context of an incumbent-challenged election, Republican incumbents should be more likely than Democratic ones to face a publicly funded major-party challenger.

I examine incumbent-contested elections using election data from all three fully funded states, since (as noted previously) participation rates in the fully funded states yield groups of traditional and publicly funded candidates sufficiently large for statistical analysis. Moreover, the survey responses depicted in Table 6.1 suggest that ideological opposition is a more important factor in the fully funded states. Figure 6.3 therefore depicts the percentage of incumbents in each state who were challenged by major-party opponents, as well as by publicly funded opponents, during years for which public funding was available. In Connecticut, Republican and Democratic incumbents were challenged at about the same rate in 2008; just under 60 percent of incumbents of both parties faced major-party competition. However, while slightly more than 30 percent of Democrats faced a publicly funded opponent, nearly half of Republicans did. A similar trend is apparent in Arizona, where incumbents of both parties were challenged by at least one candidate of the opposite party about 70 percent of the time, but the percentage of Democrats and Republicans facing at least one publicly funded challenger was about 42 percent and 62 percent, respectively.

The same pattern is observed in Maine, where since 2000 Republicans have been much more likely than Democrats—by about 15 percentage points—to face a major-party challenge. However, it is worth noting that in contrast to Arizona and Connecticut, Republican incumbents were also challenged overall at higher rates in Maine. Still, the gap in overall challenges cannot wholly explain the apparent difference in the likelihood of facing a publicly funded challenger, and it seems safe to conclude that the summary statistics in Figure 6.3 support the theoretical framework advanced above.

Yet Figure 6.3 does not allow for conclusive inference. To that end, the results of separate logistic regression models predicting the likelihood of

TABLE 6.2. Arizona, Connecticut, and Maine Incumbents Challenged by Publicly Funded Opponents: Logistic Regression Coefficients and Robust Standard Errors

	Arizona	Connecticut	Maine
Dummy: Incumbent Is Republican	1.61*	1.43*	0.932*
	(0.007)	(0.519)	(0.243)
Dummy: Incumbent's First Defense of Seat	0.646	–0.134	–0.12
	(0.518)	(0.606)	(0.243)
Margin over Top Major-Party Opponent in Last Election	–0.007	–.021*	–0.003
	(0.007)	(0.007)	(0.004)
Dummy: Same-Party Incumbent Running	0.508	–	–
	(0.629)		
Constant	–1.642	0.446	–1.657*
	(0.875)	(0.417)	(0.348)
Observations	83	130	413
McFadden's R^2	0.18	0.11	0.20
Log Likelihood	–65.10	–77.88	–227.24

Note: Robust standard errors in parentheses, clustered by legislative district. Election cycle fixed effects.
Reelection-seeking incumbents are the unit of analysis; redistricting years are omitted.
The dependent variable in Connecticut and Maine is a dichotomous indicator of whether the incumbent was challenged by an opponent who accepted public funding. In Arizona it is a dichotomous indicator of whether the incumbent was challenged by at least one opponent who accepted public funding.
*$p < .05$.

an incumbent facing a publicly funded challenger in Arizona, Connecticut, and Maine (holding obvious potential confounding variables constant) are contained in Table 6.2. The models—which are described in greater detail in Appendix 3—include fixed effects for election cycle and utilize standard errors clustered by legislative district. Reelection-seeking incumbents in non-redistricted years serve as the unit of analysis for all models, and the dependent variable in each is a dichotomous indicator coded 1 if the incumbent faced a publicly funded major-party challenger and 0 otherwise. The independent variable of interest is an indicator coded 1 if the incumbent was a Republican; positive, significant values of this coefficient indicate that Republicans are more likely to face a publicly funded challenger, holding the other factors constant.

The model control variables—for the incumbent's previous margin of victory, whether she was making her first attempt at reelection, and in the case of Arizona, whether she was running with a copartisan incumbent—do not prove to be significant predictors of facing a publicly funded challenge in most cases. The dummy variable for a candidate's first defense of her seat is not a significant predictor of a publicly funded challenge in any state, suggesting that freshmen are not more likely to face a publicly funded challenger. While the coefficient for lagged victory margin is negatively signed in all models, it achieves statistical significance only in Connecticut, where stronger incumbents appear to be less likely to face a publicly funded challenge. The additional control variable in the Arizona model, indicating whether the incumbent ran as part of a two-member team of copartisan incumbents, also fails to achieve statistical significance at conventional levels, signifying that publicly funded challengers are equally likely to run against one or two incumbents in a given two-member district. However, in all three states the coefficient for the Republican dummy variable is both positive and highly significant, indicating that Republican incumbents are more likely than their Democratic counterparts to face a publicly funded challenge. In Arizona, Republican incumbents are significantly more likely to face *at least* one challenger who accepted Clean Elections subsidies. This all adds up to the possibility of a different reality for Republican incumbents. At least one longtime Arizona incumbent believed this was the case: "Things are different now. Some very conservative Republicans [are feeling] a little bit of pressure after coming through a very close election when they should not have even had a race."

Conclusion

Fiscally conservative candidates face two potential challenges with regard to running a publicly funded campaign. First, they must overcome their own personal aversion to the program. Second, they must answer to an electoral base of conservative voters. Most fiscally conservative candidates saw "market forces" at work in traditionally financed politics, with donations flowing to candidates with attributes that made them attractive to donors. Public funding, they argued, disrupted these forces, potentially allowing for candidates to run who would not otherwise have attracted much support. In contrast, liberal candidates tended to see public funding as encouraging fairness in the electoral process and reducing the potential for nefarious entanglements between donors and legislators. Simply stated, in having to "hold their nose" if they want to accept subsidies, many conservative candidates face considerations with regard to public funding that their more liberal counterparts do not. It is therefore not surprising that Democrats are more likely to participate.

One practical result is that, when they seek reelection, Republican incumbents in Arizona, Connecticut, and Maine are significantly more likely to face a publicly funded challenger than their Democratic counterparts. Since Clean Elections appears to be achieving the goal of enhancing electoral competition in the elections where it is used (Mayer et al. 2006; Werner and Mayer 2007; Malhotra 2008), its net effect might be to provide a competitive advantage to Democratic challengers, reducing the average systemwide margins of Republicans (relative to Democrats) to a greater degree. This chapter might therefore give pause to advocates who see Clean Elections as an evenhanded reform, as it seems worthwhile to consider whether the *practical* effects of full funding may be uneven.

That said, this chapter offers no empirical support for the notion of systemic Republican disadvantage. Indeed, since all candidates are free to opt into or out of public funding as they see fit, and since this chapter offers some anecdotal evidence that quite a few conservatives still utilize public funding as a way to get elected (despite ideological objection), it is difficult to make a normative argument that public funding is inherently unfair to more conservative candidates. However, assuming that partisan affiliation serves as a useful proxy for ideology, conservative candidates appear to face higher nonmonetary costs of participation than their more liberal counterparts. While this conclusion is not particularly surprising, the candidate testimony offered in this chapter provides substantial insight into how personal ideology affects orientation to public funding, and how uneven costs may bear on candidate participation, subsequent campaign strategy, and election results.

Clean Elections at the Supreme Court

On March 28, 2011, the United States Supreme Court heard oral arguments in *McComish v. Bennett,* a First Amendment challenge to the matching funds provisions of Arizona's Clean Elections law. The case was consolidated with *Arizona Free Enterprise Club's Freedom Club PAC v. Bennett* (since they were argued together, I refer to both cases with the *McComish* citation). In the weeks leading up the argument, supporters of public funding maintained that it was making elections fairer and more democratic, and that matching funds were an integral component of the program's success. Meanwhile, its opponents claimed that the incentives that matching funds create were effectively destroying the speech rights of nonparticipating candidates.

Given the Court's recent decisions on campaign finance cases, on the morning of the argument it seemed all but certain that the justices would move to strike down matching funds. It was also possible that they would go further. Indeed, as the Court convened, any number of outcomes were possible, and it is not much of a stretch to say that the future of public election funding in the United States was at risk. Accordingly, interested parties on both sides contemplated the potential ramifications for public funding programs like Clean Elections. Would the Court, against expectations, uphold matching funds and preserve Clean Elections as originally constructed? Would it sever the matching funds and leave the subsidies intact? Or would it take this opportunity to eliminate public funding as a regulatory tool altogether? The answers to these questions would not only determine the fate of existing programs but also set the trajectory for future public funding reform efforts.

Gaming Arizona?

The question in *McComish* turned on the constitutionality of Arizona's matching funds provisions. Like those in Connecticut and Maine, the Clean Elections law in Arizona allowed for the provision of matching funds allocations to participating candidates when they were outraised or outspent; the extra subsidies mandated financial parity even when some candidates chose not to participate in the program.[1] In Arizona primary elections, matching funds were triggered when money was spent. In general elections, participating candidates were matched either when their opponent reported *raising* money or when an independent expenditure was made against them. In either instance, expenditures beyond the publicly financed candidate's subsidy amount were matched dollar-for-dollar to an aggregate limit of three times the original allocation.

The importance of matching funds to participating candidates, as well as their uniqueness compared with the dynamics of a partially funded system, is perhaps best understood through a hypothetical comparison of publicly funded candidates in partially and fully funded states with spending limits of $25,000 running against an opponent who raises and spends $75,000 (see Table 7.1). In a system of partial funding, in which a candidate receives a subsidy equivalent to 45 percent of the spending limit, a publicly funded candidate would still be facing a spending deficit of nearly $64,000. In Arizona's Clean Elections system, however, the opponent's expenditures would trigger matching funds allocations, preserving funding equality. Since participating candidates can be outspent in only the most exceptional cases, matching funds provide a strong incentive for candidates to accept subsidies.

TABLE 7.1. Public Funding Scenarios

	Opponent spending	Spending limit	Subsidy amount	Matching funds	Funding gap
Clean elections	$75,000	$25,000	$25,000	$50,000	$0
Partial funding	$75,000	$25,000	$11,250	–	$63,750

From the perspective of the nonparticipating (traditional) candidates I interviewed in 2007, once the original subsidy threshold was breached, a dollar spent was in effect a dollar contributed to the other side. Traditional candidates therefore paid careful attention to expenditure levels so as not to benefit a publicly funded opponent. One traditional candidate described a campaign that, in order to mitigate this effect, was "very calculating in how much we sent out to keep spending as low as possible." Another traditionally funded incumbent reached the same conclusion, saying, "If I raised $100,000 and he capped out at $69,000, that would give me a $30,000 advantage. I don't know that I could raise that much, so I think we would probably be equal. I would spend a lot of time and money raising that money...just [to] give it to him." Still another incumbent clearly articulated the degree to which matching funds call for careful attention to spending: "I don't want to raise money and give my opponent money. If I can keep the spending down, me as an incumbent, I have a tremendous advantage.... If I am a traditional candidate, and I raise $50,000, he's going to get that money, and he's going to use it to get more voters out. So I'm getting advice from both camps now. I'm getting advice that says, 'You need to raise $100,000, because you need to get your message out, you need to get your voters out,' and I hear the other people saying, 'You need to go clean, because you don't need to be raising money for him, and in a low-spending race, it's you as an incumbent that has the advantage.'"

The desire for cost efficiency is present in all campaigns, but the effects of matching funds shift the spending calculus well beyond simple husbandry. While all traditional candidates interviewed expressed concern about the effect of matching funds on their opponents, some described conscious decisions to withhold expenditures for items that might have increased their performance at the polls: "Every dollar I spend over the threshold starts feeding the alligator trying to eat me. So I have to be very careful with how I spend money, which meant that I sent out a lot less mail and held a lot less events than I would have but for my hands feeling like they were tied under this system. That really irritated me, because I'd say, 'I'd love to rent a big tent, and we'll have an old-fashioned ice cream sundae thing in the park' or whatever, but I didn't want to do it unless everything was absolutely essential so that we didn't trigger more money to our opponent. Quite honestly, I would have sent probably twice as much mail." Stories like this one were echoed by every candidate I interviewed who had ever run traditionally against a Clean Elections opponent. One challenger who ran with public money observed that "those who want to go for the hundred-thousand-dollar campaign, they're not so sure they want to do it because they don't want to give me matching funds. I'm sure that they don't want a level playing field." Another challenger noticed that her traditionally financed opponent had stopped spending in order to avoid triggering matching funds: "He spent just the amount in the general election to avoid having to give me matching money."

While traditional candidates pondered the advantage of not spending, those who accepted public subsidies cared little if their opponents spent large sums because they were protected by matching funds. When asked whether he would take issue with his opponent spending $75,000 against him, a first-time challenger in a long-shot race said, "That would be O.K., because I like the matching funds clause. If my opponent wants to go raise traditional funds so I can get more money to spend for my campaign, I think I'm fine with it." However, there was a great deal of anxiety among participating candidates regarding the timing of opponent expenditures. One newly elected legislator, fresh from a tough fight in the general election, echoed the sentiments of the others but added an important clause: "I think in some ways [my opponent] does think about [the effects of matching funds], and he limited his fundraising. I only got $2,500 in matching funds because of that. And he had a primary, and his one opponent was Clean Elections, and the other two were traditional, and the other two raised money like they were running a traditional campaign, not realizing that it impacted the Clean Elections candidate in huge ways. That Clean Elections candidate got huge amounts of money. *But they wait until the last minute and spend it,* to avoid that" (emphasis added).

The belief in the existence of strategic expenditure timing was ubiquitous. According to *every informant I interviewed,* traditionally funded candidates tried to maximize the competitive effect of the money that they did spend by releasing funds at the last moment, giving the Clean Elections candidate little time to react. Traditional candidates conceded that while the timing of expenditures was not an initial component of their strategy, by the end it was crucial in maintaining control of the political message. So although late spending "[was not] like a Manhattan Plan or anything, [it] was part of our thinking...let's spend as little as possible early on, so that we could control the debate." By releasing a mailing on the Friday before the election, traditional candidates were aware that even if their opponent was matched on the same day, it was prohibitively difficult to spend money over the final weekend in any meaningful fashion.

One experienced candidate described how traditional candidates maximized their strategic advantage: "You want to have a strategy and a plan of using those funds so that the matching funds are least beneficial to your opponent. In most cases you would think that that's at the last second, so they can't counter it. I think there's benefit to that. I think that's wise." An incumbent who funded her campaign traditionally said, "We...think about [spending at the last minute], frankly. At least I do. Sometimes we may have planned what we're going to do, but we don't initiate anything, because the minute we sign a contract or the minute we initiate anything, we have to report." Other candidates detailed how one can "really...work the system" by "spend[ing] money at the last minute if you're a traditional candidate.... The clean candidate gets that money, that match, the day before the election." An incumbent with multiple cycles of election experience described this phenomenon: "In terms of opponents incurring expenditures right before the elections, you know, the Friday before, that's happened both times that I've run. And so you pick up a check from the Clean Elections department, you know, that Friday night, for the matching money—good luck trying to spend $5,000. So that has definitely played into most campaigns now, you know, people know that if you are going to go over the expenditure limit, you do it that weekend before." Yet another legislator noted that campaign strategies have fundamentally changed as candidates play this game with ubiquity: "If a traditional candidate waits towards the end, and has some expenses that go over the limits, then the Clean Elections candidate gets matching funds, but if you do that farther down the road and the clean candidate doesn't know about it, then she's not going to have much time to plan how to spend that money, so there's some strategic advantages that a traditional candidate has. It would not be an exaggeration to say that Clean Elections is shifting strategic considerations."

Traditional candidates who purposely spent late had little sympathy for their publicly funded opponents, viewing a failure to adequately prepare for the expenditures on the final weekend as a lapse in proper planning. One legislator who had run as a traditional candidate described the importance of a prefabricated plan for publicly funded candidates to deal with late spending, saying, "I think I'm a good enough campaigner and strategist to figure that out." Some Clean Elections candidates who faced this situation effectively anticipated late expenditures and took steps to respond. One incumbent who had been the victim of last-minute attacks by traditionally funded candidates in the past behaved differently the next time, saying, "I got smarter the second time around...thinking that our opponent would probably spend, and [I] had a strategy ready to go on how we could spend that money quickly if we got matched." Another experienced candidate said that when independent groups spent money against her in the closing weeks, she was ready to respond by hiring a group of people to walk on her behalf: "In my last race, every other day there was a hit piece. Every other day I would get matching funds. What do you do when you get $4,000 right before the election? If you're smart, you have a strategy, and you think, 'O.K. if I get $4,000 two weeks out, I'm doing this.' If I get it right before the election, I'm doing something else. I'd already preplanned that I would hire union people who were out of work to work on Election Day for me, because it was something that represented my values, and was a financially prudent thing to do."

The expectation of strategically timed spending was not limited to those with political experience. One first-time candidate in a crowded primary field had heard the stories of last-minute spending in other races but had failed to assemble a formal response plan. However, the possibility of spending during the final weekend was present in the back of his mind, and he was able to mount an effective counterattack in the last moments of an ultimately unsuccessful campaign. In his case, it was an independent group, and not the opposition, that released funds with only days remaining before the election: "I was attacked by a group...they put out a hit piece. I was able to use that immediately to get myself qualified for another $3,000 worth of money to send out my own extra last-minute piece, which was a really good one actually...I barely had time to respond. I had run out of money, because that's what happens. I really wanted to do another piece, but I just couldn't budget for it. So I had a couple of ideas sitting on the back burner, and then it just happened." Despite the preparedness of some of their peers, many publicly funded candidates were not so savvy and were caught unaware. Another first-time challenger described feelings of helplessness accompanying the realization that large amounts of money had been spent against him at the last minute, leaving him with matching funds but no time to spend them: "The last day, or the day before the election, they do all this stuff, and you don't really have time to plan real well. I could do better if I did it a second time. As a matter of fact, I gave some money back, because I got five or six thousand dollars the last day. The traditional people, they do that so well. Some people said, 'You should do something,' and I said, 'I can't use it effectively, and I'll give it back.'"

Another neophyte faced a similar situation, and was disappointed with a system that was supposed to guarantee an even playing field. Outspent at the last minute, she was unable to respond and faced the reality that despite her expectation of financial parity, she had been outflanked in the election's closing hours: "I believe [my opponent] spent a great deal of money in the time after the last reporting of expenses and income, so that they wouldn't have to balance how much money I had with how much she had. You can't plan; you can't buy the media if you don't know what they're going to do. It would happen in a regular campaign anyway, but to be on the same playing field, we're not, because Clean Elections candidates are guaranteed this amount of money and the others are not, but if they get to this amount or higher, we'll raise the bar. And they can eventually outspend you. That's not fair." The allusion to "fairness" is an important one, because fairness is a theme running through the narratives of both traditional and publicly funded candidates. To the former, Clean Elections unfairly constrained their speech rights, encumbering their ability to campaign. In contrast, participating candidates felt that it was unfair for traditional candidates to game the system by strategically timing their fundraising and/or spending; in their view, doing so violates the spirit of the law.

Answering the question of whether matching funds lead traditionally financed candidates to speak *less,* or whether they simply choose to speak *later,* is an important first step in determining whether Clean Elections is consistent with the speech protections in the First Amendment of the U.S. Constitution. Before the arguments in *McComish,* however, there was little empirical evidence for a link between Clean Elections and less political speech. Indeed, matching funds distribution patterns are generally consistent with informant descriptions of intentional gaming by traditional candidates.[2] As Table 7.2 indicates, in no election between 2002 and 2006 did the proportion of matching funds expenditures released in the last week of a cycle fall below one-third. Some of this activity is attributable to the natural flow of campaign spending, but if the traditionally financed candidates who trigger matching funds allocations are as conscious of the effects of their spending as they seem to be, a substantial portion of late spending is delayed to maximize its strategic effect. Further, matching funds allocations within one day of the election generally make up a substantial percentage of overall last-minute expenditures. During the 2006 general election, in which the informants quoted above participated, over 40 percent of expenditures occurring in the last week were released just hours before the polls opened. The majority of these matching funds allocations are no doubt the result of strategic expenditure as traditional candidates and outside entities seek to gain favor with the electorate while leaving the publicly funded candidate little or no opportunity to respond.

TABLE 7.2. Timing of Matching Funds Allocations, 2002–2006 Arizona State Legislative Elections

	Primary election			General election		
	Matching funds allocations	**Allocations within one week of election**	**Allocations within one day of election**	**Matching funds allocations**	**Allocations within one week of election**	**Allocations within one day of election**
2006	95	48 (–50.50%)	10 (–20.80%)	124	44 (–35.50%)	18 (–40.10%)
2004	120	54 (–45%)	11 (–20.40%)	124	56 (–45.20%)	6 (–10.70%)
2002	119	50 (–42%)	38 (–76%)	107	69 (–64.50%)	22 (–31.90%)

Note: Percentages in "One Week" columns reflect the percentage of all allocations occurring in the final week. Percentages in "One Day" columns reflect the percentage of final-week allocations occurring on the last day.

In tandem with Dowling et al. (2012), who could find no support for the idea that matching funds suppress *overall* spending levels among traditional candidates, the pattern in Table 7.2 suggests that if it affects speech at all, Clean Elections seems to encourage traditional candidates to spend money later in the election, but not to spend less. At the very least, it seems safe to conclude that the matching funds provisions originally included in Clean Elections laws altered the political communication strategies of participating and traditional candidates alike. Ultimately, however, it became a matter for the Supreme Court to decide whether the matching funds provisions violated the First Amendment.

The Road to the Supreme Court

In 2008 Arizona state senator John McComish and a group of five other traditionally financed Arizona candidates brought a federal lawsuit challenging the constitutionality of Arizona's matching funds provision on the basis that it created disincentives to raise money and campaign for office. Their suit was joined by two independent groups, the Arizona Free Enterprise Club and the Arizona Taxpayer's Action Committee. Both of these groups had affiliated political action committees (PACs) that donated money to candidates; the groups therefore had legal standing to join the suit on the basis that like the traditional candidates, they had disincentives to make expenditures against publicly funded candidates (such as a television ad) that would trigger a matching funds contribution to the candidate they advocated against. The case, which was first known as *McComish v. Brewer* (Jan Brewer was the attorney general of Arizona in 2008), was initially argued at the Arizona District Court in August 2008, when the plaintiffs moved to enjoin the state from disbursing matching funds for the remainder of the 2008 election.

In *Buckley v. Valeo* (424 U.S. 1 1976) the Supreme Court had ruled that spending money in a political campaign is tantamount to speech and is therefore protected by the First Amendment. In *Buckley* the Court found that restrictions may be placed on political speech only when the government could show a compelling interest for doing so, such as reducing either actual corruption or the appearance thereof. Thus, while the size of contributions to candidates could be limited (in an effort to prevent individuals from appearing to purchase favors), limitations on candidates' expenditures of their own personal funds were held as unreasonable restrictions on their speech.

In the *McComish* case both the candidates and the independent groups argued that while there was no limitation on their spending in the text of the law, the incentives spawned by Clean Elections meant that the practical effect of the matching funds provisions was to make any reasonable non-participating candidate spend less money. As such, the petitioners argued that the matching funds rule violated their First Amendment rights by chilling their speech in the manner described above, and also that it violated the equal protection clause of the Fourteenth Amendment because traditional candidates were subjected to reporting requirements to which publicly funded candidates were not. The petitioners therefore asked the district court to halt the distribution of matching funds during the 2008 election. Arizona, in turn, argued that all candidates were free to participate in the program, there was no limitation in the wording of the law on the spending of candidates who did not willfully accept one, and any indirect restrictions on political speech were justified by the reduced appearance of corruption in a publicly funded system, a position that is consistent with the *Buckley* precedent.

Judging a law on its effects rather than its statutory wording presents some difficulties, and the district court recognized that there were cases from various states in which courts had ruled on both sides of the issue. In tandem, the court found that these conditions had "muddied the matching funds landscape."[3] When deciding whether to enjoin matching funds, the district court found salvation in the 2008 U.S. Supreme Court's decision in *Davis v. FEC* (128 S. Ct. 2759 (2008)), which had been released only two months before. At issue in that case was the so-called Millionaire's Amendment in the 2002 Bipartisan Campaign Reform Act (BCRA). The BCRA adjusted campaign finance rules in federal elections, doubling to $2,000 the maximum amount that citizens had been allowed to donate to a candidate before passage of the act. However, the BCRA also required candidates to declare how much of their own money they intended to spend during the election; one spending more than $350,000 of personal wealth "triggered" different contribution limits for her opponent, which were raised to $6,000 to allow her to compete with the "millionaire" self-funder.

John Davis, a businessman who ran for a U.S. House seat in upstate New York, challenged the Millionaire's Amendment in federal court.

Davis argued that the BCRA violated his First Amendment rights to use his own money for political speech, because he recognized that there existed an incentive to constrain his spending to less than $350,000. In short, Davis's claim was grounded on the strategic considerations that the BCRA created. Although there was no statutory spending limit in the BCRA, Davis asserted that the Millionaire's Amendment would lead a rational candidate to self-impose one.

In a 5–4 decision, the Supreme Court agreed with Davis and struck down the triggers in the Millionaire's Amendment as a violation of the First Amendment. Significantly, the Court ignored the fact that as several reform-minded groups noted in an amicus brief, "there is no proof in the record that [the Millionaire's Amendment] has chilled any candidate expenditures or speech—much less the 'substantial' quantity of speech required to sustain a facial challenge."[4] Writing for the majority, Justice Samuel Alito held that "the unprecedented step of imposing different contribution and coordinated party expenditure limits on candidates vying for the same seat is antithetical to the First Amendment" (128 S. Ct. 2759). In other words, the Court found that the law was *facially* unfair, and so its *actual* effects were meaningless.

Davis's argument was clearly similar to that of the traditional candidates and independent groups who brought suit in the *McComish* case. Rather than trigger higher contribution limits to the opponents of candidates who spent their own money above a certain threshold, the Clean Elections law triggered direct contributions from the state's fund to the opponents of traditional candidates who spent money above a certain threshold. The petitioners therefore argued that the *Davis* precedent should be applied, and that the district court should find that the practical effect of the triggering provisions was to chill their speech.

Arizona defended the constitutionality of matching funds, arguing that there was an important difference between it and the Millionaire's Amendment: all funding under the BCRA originated from contributors or the candidates, whereas funding in Clean Elections came from the state with no contribution limitations. Since spending above the Clean Elections subsidy amount did not lead to a scenario in which the two candidates were subject to different rules, and since traditional candidates were always free to accept public funding, Arizona asserted that Clean Elections "imposes no asymmetrical burden on a traditional candidate's ability to contribute or expend his or her own money," and was thus a wholly different scenario than the issue in *Davis*.

The district court failed to find Arizona's argument sufficiently compelling. Judge Roslyn Silver wrote that "though the Arizona Act's mechanism for funding differs, the effect, which forces a candidate to choose to 'abide by a limit on personal expenditures' or else endure a burden placed on that right, is substantially the same [as in *Davis*]." In short, Silver ruled that matching funds violated the traditional candidates' First Amendment rights. Yet the district court refused to issue an injunction barring matching funds in the 2008 campaign, citing the lateness with which the plaintiffs had filed their challenge (August 21). Judge Silver felt that halting matching funds so close to Election Day would interfere with Arizona's interest in running smooth elections, as well as with the good-faith intentions of candidates who had constructed campaign strategies with the expectation of receiving matching funds. So although the substance of the traditional candidates' argument seemed sound, their timing was poor.

In 2009 the plaintiffs tried again, this time leaving plenty of time for the ruling in advance of the 2010 election. Once again Judge Silver issued the decision. In a summary judgment issued in January 2010 the judge described some doubt about the speech burdens conferred by matching funds triggers. For instance, she noted that because the plaintiffs' speech led to matching funds contributions that would presumably be spent by their opponents, the net result would be more speech instead of less; thus in her words, "the 'burden' created by the Act is that Plaintiffs' speech will lead directly to more speech."[5] Moreover, the triggers existed within a system of public election financing, which the Supreme Court had already held to be constitutional. Thus, Judge Silver was quite clear in her belief that it was the incremental nature of the delivery of public subsidies, and not the delivery itself, that was at issue: "Plaintiffs are left to argue their First Amendment rights are violated not by the fact of public financing, or the level of that financing, but by the fact that Arizona provides incremental grants linked to their activities. If a single lump sum award would not burden Plaintiffs' free speech rights in any cognizable way, finding a burden solely because of the incremental nature of the awards seems difficult to establish."

Nonetheless, the judge believed that she was obligated to find the matching funds provisions burdensome because of the similarity between the plaintiffs' strategic considerations and those described in *Davis*. Specifically, the judge noted that the "plaintiffs face a choice very similar to that faced in *Davis:* either 'abide by a limit on personal expenditures' or face potentially serious negative consequences." While in *Davis* those consequences came in the form of higher contribution limits for opponents, for the *McComish* plaintiffs they were delivered—literally—as extra cash. Thus, Judge Silver reaffirmed her earlier stance that under the precedent in *Davis* she had to rule that the matching funds provisions violated the First Amendment. This time she issued an injunction halting the distribution of matching funds in Arizona during the 2010 election.

Arizona appealed the district court's opinion, and the Ninth Circuit Court of Appeals heard the case in April 2010. The parties to Arizona's side of the case had changed by then because Ken Bennett had replaced Jan Brewer as Arizona secretary of state in 2009. Accordingly, he also supplanted her as the defendant in the official capacities of that office, and the case became known as *McComish v. Bennett*.

The appellate court ruled that while *Davis* provided a reasonable framework in which to discuss the burdens imposed by matching funds, the "regulatory framework the Supreme Court examined in *Davis* is different from the one" in *McComish*.[6] Specifically, the Court held that there was no public funding at issue in *Davis,* and the real problem from a First Amendment perspective was the fact that spending large sums of one's own money essentially created different, asymmetrical regulatory environments. The Supreme Court had ruled in favor of Davis because it believed he was being penalized for being wealthy. In contrast, the Court of Appeals reasoned that because participation in public funding was optional, and because the trigger does not distinguish between personal and contributed campaign funds, the Clean Elections law does not make "identity-based distinctions."

Moreover, the Court of Appeals held that there was actually little evidence to support the traditional candidates' claims that their speech had been chilled. It noted some empirical evidence for this, citing campaign finance data indicating that spending in Arizona politics was higher in the Clean Elections era, and noting that no candidates could cite specific instances in which they had restricted spending. Thus, the court reasoned that a substantial burden on speech did not exist. The majority wrote that "*Davis* does not require this Court to recognize mere metaphysical threats to political speech as severe burdens. We will only conclude that the Act burdens speech to the extent that Plaintiffs have proven that the specter of matching funds has actually chilled or deterred them from accepting campaign contributions or making expenditures." Because it held that the "matching funds provision…imposes only a minimal burden on [plaintiffs'] First Amendment Rights," and that the state's interest in preventing the appearance of corruption via quid pro quo exchanges of contributions for favors outweighed the plaintiffs' speech claims, the Ninth Circuit Court of Appeals overturned the district court's decision and reinstated matching funds.

This time it was the plaintiffs' turn to appeal. Days after the Ninth Circuit Court issued its opinion on May 21, the traditional candidates filed an emergency application to the U.S. Supreme Court, asking it to temporarily enjoin matching funds in the 2010 election pending their appellate action. The Supreme Court did so on June 8, and on November 29 it granted *certiorari* and agreed to hear the case in early 2011. In the months leading up to the argument more than two dozen amicus curiae briefs were submitted to the Supreme Court by outside groups and individuals. A number of briefs came from ideologically oriented interest groups that wrote to share their view either that matching funds chilled speech or that the benefits from Clean Elections outweighed any burdens imposed on the speech of traditional candidates. Several political science and constitutional scholars offered empirical evidence and their expert interpretation; all these briefs supported Arizona's contentions that its system was constitutional and/or that the program did not result in less speech (see Panagopoulos et al. 2011; Corrado et al. 2011; Kendall et al. 2011). The state of Maine argued for the constitutionality of matching funds in its own Clean Elections program (Bliss et al. 2011). Other states, including Iowa, Connecticut, Maryland, New Mexico, and Vermont, wrote to "share [their] view that public financing of state elections should remain available as a tool to restore public confidence" (Miller et al. 2011). The U.S. government made a similar claim (Katyal et al. 2011).

Arizona Free Enterprise Club's Freedom Club PAC v. Bennett and *McComish v. Bennett* were consolidated and argued at the U.S. Supreme Court on March 28, 2011. The U.S. Department of Justice joined the case on Arizona's side, given its vested interest in defending the constitutionality of public funding programs. At the argument the petitioners reiterated their belief that the practical effect of matching funds was to chill speech and that such an effect was unconstitutional under the *Davis* precedent.

William Maurer, counsel for the petitioners (the traditionally financed candidates and interest groups), wasted no time in getting to the point. The first sentences he said were, "This case is about whether the government may insert itself into elections and manipulate campaign spending to favor its preferred candidates. Arizona does this in a manner that is even more burdensome to free speech than the law at issue in *Davis v. FEC.*"[7]

Maurer went on to argue the petitioners' position that while they did not dispute that public election funding was consistent with the Constitution, the Court's decision in *Davis* had made triggering provisions unconstitutional. When Justice Ginsburg asked him whether the petitioners would object to the state simply giving all candidates the maximum subsidy (three times the original one) that matching funds would allow, Maurer responded: "This case is not about whether the State of Arizona may provide campaign financing using public funds, nor is it about whether the ability of Arizona to ensure that those who receive the public funds can run effective campaigns. What this case is about is whether the government can turn my act of speaking into the vehicle by which my political opponents benefit with direct government subsidies."

Indeed, Maurer argued that the benefit accruing to the opponents of traditional candidates in Arizona's Clean Elections system was greater than it was for opponents of self-funders in *Davis,* since in the latter case those opponents "still had to go out and actually raise the funds that the Millionaire's Amendment permitted him to raise." Maurer reasoned that since "elections are a zero-sum game" in which there can be only one winner, a benefit to one candidate necessarily constituted a harm to the other. Thus, the petitioners' argument rested squarely on the *Davis* precedent: in raising and spending money above the spending limit, traditionally funded candidates were keenly aware that their actions would harm them by resulting in a contribution to their publicly funded opponent. Accordingly, there were clear incentives for them to withhold their political speech. Or, as Maurer said, "Our concern is that their speech is turning into the mechanism by which their political goals are undercut. So each time they speak, the more work that they do, the more their opponents benefit."

Arizona's counsel, Bradley Phillips, argued, "Public funding of elections results in more speech and more electoral competition and directly furthers the government's compelling interest in combating real and apparent corruption in politics." Arizona defended matching funds by citing the available empirical evidence that no candidate or group had withheld spending due to a fear of triggering matching funds, and also that aggregate spending had risen since Clean Elections was implemented. Phillips argued that in encouraging participation in public funding, matching funds "combats corruption by providing for more candidates running, more political speech, and more electoral competition, all of which have happened in Arizona."

William Jay, assistant to the solicitor general of the United States, echoed this position, saying that "the only consequence of running an independent expenditure...is that another party will get to run a responsive ad, and the sum of speech will be increased." Moreover, Phillips argued that political spending was not a zero-sum affair; presumably, it was reasonable to expect that each candidate would think that her own message was superior. Thus, even political spending that triggered a direct contribution to one's opponent should render a net benefit. "[The] petitioners assume that essentially this is a zero-sum game and that because if I spend $10,000 the other guy is going to get $10,000 to respond, that somehow that's a wash. Well, it's not a wash, first, because I think my speech is more persuasive so I'm going to do it anyway, because I'd rather get it out there; and secondly, because I may be spending my $10,000 on getting out my voters, and I need to do that regardless. And that's why you don't see in the statistics any evidence that this actually suppresses speech."

In short, the position of Arizona and the United States was that any burden on traditional candidates could not be too onerous since there was no empirical evidence of suppressed spending by traditional candidates or groups. Moreover, the respondents asserted that in encouraging participation in Clean Elections, matching funds aided the government in fulfilling its objective of reducing the appearance of political corruption.

The opinion was released in June. Writing for a 5–4 majority, Chief Justice John Roberts held that Arizona's arguments about preventing corruption were unpersuasive since "reliance on personal funds reduces the threat of corruption."[8] Roberts also rejected the argument that matching funds increased aggregate amounts of speech in the political system, noting that such an enhancement was asymmetrical, as "any increase in speech resulting from the Arizona law is of one kind and one kind only—that of publicly financed candidates." Finally, in reply to the state's claim that there was no evidence that candidates suppressed their speech in response to matching funds triggers, Roberts wrote that "it is never easy to prove a negative—here, that candidates and groups did not speak or limited their speech because of the Arizona law." In other words, the majority felt that the issue should turn not on empirical evidence but on what it perceived to be a clear precedent in *Davis v. FEC*. As such, it did "not need empirical evidence to determine that the law at issue is burdensome."

Rather, Roberts wrote, the matching funds provisions of Arizona's Clean Elections law indeed created a real incentive structure that impeded the speech of the traditional candidates, as the Millionaire's Amendment had for self-funders. The premise of public funding survived, since determining its "wisdom," according to Roberts, was "not our business. But determining whether laws governing campaign finance violate the First Amendment is very much our business." Roberts held that it was the delivery method, "in direct response to the political speech of privately financed candidates and independent expenditure groups," and not the size of the subsidies involved that failed to pass constitutional muster. Simply stated, the majority ruled that the matching funds provisions were so similar in practice to the Millionaire's Amendment in creating a chilling effect that the law could not stand, regardless of external evidence. However, in her dissenting opinion, Justice Kagan disagreed: "Arizona...offers to support any person running for state office. Petitioners here refused that assistance. So they are making a novel argument: that Arizona violated their First Amendment rights by disbursing funds to other speakers even though they could have received (but chose to spurn) the same financial assistance. Some people might call that *chutzpah*."

Conclusion

Public funding survived the *McComish* case, but the message was clear: incremental matching funds were over. Beginning with the 2012 election, candidates could still accept full funding via Clean Elections grants—but with no dollar-for-dollar matching funds provisions, there is a greater likelihood that they will be outspent. It is unclear how much of an impact the loss of matching funds will have on how candidates view Clean Elections, and whether the absence of financial parity will curb participation. One possible result is that candidates will perceive a weaker incentive to run with public subsidies; this is particularly true for those who believe either that their opponent will control a relatively large sum or that their race may attract spending by outside groups. If enough candidates think this is likely, it is possible that, in the words of one legislator I re-interviewed in 2011, "the lawsuit, by gutting the engine of the program, has effectively killed Clean Elections." Notably, participation trended downward in Arizona after the suspension of matching funds: half of all candidates participated in 2010, down from about two-thirds in 2008 (Arizona Citizens' Clean Elections Commission 2011).

However, there is little reason to believe that *McComish* will be a death knell for Clean Elections in the long term. Arizona campaign finance records indicate that of 767 Clean Elections candidates for the state house and senate between 2002 and 2008, only 87 received matching funds grants (and 30 of those candidates received less than $10,000).[9] Moreover, Dowling et al. (2012) report no evidence that nonparticipating candidates stopped spending money at the threshold when matching funds were available. It is possible that traditional candidates will unleash a torrent of pent-up money now that Clean Elections candidates cannot get matching funds, but if extra grants were triggered in only 11 percent of races to begin with, it seems premature to conclude that full funding programs cannot function as single-subsidy systems.

Indeed, in the days following the *McComish* decision, Connecticut secretary of state Denise Merrill was publicly optimistic about the future of Clean Elections in her state, saying that "while the supplemental grants are important in a world of high-spending self-funded candidates and independent expenditures, Connecticut proved last year [2010] that our system can and does work in the face of these challenges" (Connecticut Secretary of State 2011). Merrill was alluding to the fact that although Connecticut had suspended its matching funds triggers for the 2010 election in response to the federal court activity, 70 percent of legislative candidates still participated that year, down only three points from the program's debut in 2008 (Connecticut State Elections Enforcement Commission 2011). Connecticut's participation trend compared well with that in Maine, which did not eliminate matching funds for the 2010 election and in which 77 percent of legislative candidates took Clean Elections funding in 2010, down slightly from 81 percent in 2008 (Maine Ethics Commission 2011).

To paraphrase Mark Twain, rumors of the death of Clean Elections may have been greatly exaggerated. Yet it is apparent that public funding efforts in the post-*McComish* era will necessarily look different.

Conclusion

Reform in the Future

The Supreme Court's decisions have narrowed the available policy options when it comes to campaign finance, but it is important to note that the Court has consistently upheld the constitutionality of optional public funding programs established in *Buckley,* despite ample opportunity to strike them down. The Court has held that it is the government's prerogative to allow candidates to opt into public funding programs because such subsidies help to reduce public perception of corruption. In no case since *Buckley* has the Court questioned whether this is a justifiable goal. Indeed, since Arizona and Maine implemented their Clean Elections programs in 2000, a number of other states, including Connecticut, New Mexico, and North Carolina, have followed suit for elections to at least some offices. Thus, there is no indication that public funding generally will cease to be part of the campaign finance reform toolkit in the near future.

That said, there are at least four realities that public funding advocates must confront. First, the fiscal difficulties that many states and municipalities faced in the "Great Recession" meant that some public funding programs were placed on the fiscal chopping block. For instance, even though it had expanded public funding to judicial elections for the 2010 election, Wisconsin eliminated all public funding programs (including the one described in this book) in 2011 when Governor Scott Walker's budget significantly weakened the program, which was subsequently defunded altogether by the Wisconsin Legislature. And in Portland, Oregon, by a narrow margin, voters ended the city's five-year-old public funding program offering full subsidies to candidates for city offices in 2010. As rationale to terminate it, opponents cited its cost of nearly $2 million during its existence as well as at least two instances in which candidates abused the program. The experiences of Portland and Wisconsin demonstrate that in a period of scarce government resources, voters must perceive public funding as a value-added policy if it is going to survive at all, much less function well.

Second, the direct partial programs of the 1980s and 1990s, such as those functioning in Hawaii, Minnesota, and Wisconsin (until 2010), are not likely to expand elsewhere. Evaluation of the efficacy of partial programs in terms of goals such as curbing spending growth or enhancing competition has been mixed at best (i.e., Kraus 2006, 2011; Schultz 2002; Malbin and Gais 1998, 136; Mayer and Wood 1995; Jones and Borris 1985). Furthermore, the analyses described throughout this book consistently demonstrate that partial programs appear to do little to alter the campaign activities, outlook, or traits of candidates relative to traditionally financed ones, and therefore we should not expect commensurate changes among the general electorate. While partial funding programs may reduce somewhat the influence of business, labor, or issue advocacy organizations, these relationships have not been fully studied. Considering what is known, there is little reason for states or municipalities that might be inclined to implement public funding to seek partial programs. Perhaps predictably, then, partial funding has become less prevalent among public funding schemes.

Third, while the Court has not banned the provision of direct subsidies to candidates, its decisions in *Davis* and *McComish* have created some additional rules for the game. The main guideline for future programs is that campaign finance regulations must apply evenly to all candidates and cannot contain "trigger" provisions under which the activities of one candidate affect the financial position of another. Although candidates in full funding states are still eligible to receive large grants capable of funding a viable campaign, the matching funds elements of Clean Elections laws—at least as originally designed—are no more. The major difference for participating candidates is that they are no longer ensured of competing at financial parity with their opponents. It remains to be seen how the end of matching funds will affect the findings reported earlier in this book, if at all.

Fourth, recent federal court decisions beyond *McComish* have dramatically altered the regulatory landscape. The U.S. Supreme Court's 2010 decision in *Citizens United v. FEC* (558 U.S. 130 S. Ct. 876) held that corporate and union entities can spend freely to communicate a political message in elections, and the District of Columbia Circuit Court's decision in the same year in *SpeechNow.org v. FEC* (599 F.3d 686 (2010)) eliminated hard-money limits on contributions to so-called super PACs that spend only on advertising and make no direct contributions to candidates or party units. As such, super PACs can (as of 2010) accept unlimited donations so long as their funds are used only for direct communication (and not contribution to or coordination with campaigns). Various other corporate structures require no donor disclosure at all. While it remains to be seen how these developments will affect the campaign finance environment in the long term, aggregate spending by nonparty entities nearly doubled from 2008 to 2010, when corporate and super PAC activity were first allowed (Campaign Finance Institute 2010). An environment in which actors outside political campaigns control a significant proportion of money spent will no doubt pose challenges for regulatory systems like public funding that attempt to control spending by imposing limitations on candidates.

Nonetheless, as noted above, there is little reason to believe that public funding in some form will cease to exist any time soon. As of 2012, there are at least two other major public funding policy options being evaluated at both the state and federal level.

The New York System

New York City's public funding program, stemming from its Campaign Finance Act (CFA), encourages candidates to seek the financial support of New York City residents via small contributions. Significantly, the program does not offer large one-time payments akin to those in either the partial or full funding programs discussed throughout this book. Rather, the system requires candidates to secure small contributions from individuals residing in the city, and these contributions are then matched from the public fund. The program was passed in 1988 and was implemented in time for the 1989 municipal elections (for a detailed history, see Kraus 2011). In 2013 the program provided a six-to-one match on the first $175 of an eligible contribution. In other words, if a municipal candidate received a donation of $175 from a fellow New Yorker, the program provided a public subsidy of $1,050 (six times the original amount), making the original small contribution worth $1,225. New Yorkers are free to contribute more than $175 (2013 aggregate individual contributions limits ranged from $2,750 for city council candidates to $4,950 for mayor), but the city's fund matches only the first $175 that a given individual donates to a particular candidate.

Candidates qualify for matching funds by raising a predetermined sum from small donors. For instance, a candidate for city council in 2013 had to raise $5,000 from a minimum of 75 small donors. For mayoral candidates, the qualifying threshold was $250,000 from at least 1,000 donors, though as with matching contributions, only the first $175 received from any single donor counts toward the qualifying amount. In exchange for the subsidies, candidates make several concessions. First, they limit spending. In 2013, spending will range from $168,000 for a city council election to $6,426,000 for mayor; the subsidies provide a maximum of 55 percent of this amount. These limits are per election: candidates spend to these limits in the primary and then again in the general election. Second, they agree to rigorous reporting requirements, including the filing of daily financial reports in the last two weeks of the election. Third, candidates agree to participate in at least one debate during the course of the campaign. Thus, in addition to engaging small contributors, the program focuses on reducing spending via spending limits and facilitates at least slightly more available political information via the debate requirement.

The New York system is a viable reform tool in the post-*McComish* era since its matching funds are triggered by the activities of participating candidates—regardless of the activities of those who opt out. Indeed, it has provided inspiration for New York governor Andrew Cuomo and other policymakers looking to overhaul campaign finance regulations at the state level. In his 2012 State of the State Address, Cuomo told the New York

Assembly, "We must achieve fundamental campaign finance reform by implementing a system of public funding of elections. New York City's public financing system provides a good model for statewide reform. The system has helped to increase the number of overall contributors—and especially the number of small donors—in city elections. To make sure we are protecting taxpayers, we will enact strict limits on total public funding per election, and we will phase the system in gradually."[1]

As of 2013, there appear to be few signs that the New York State Assembly entertains serious notions of expanding the CFA to state elections, but preliminary evidence indicates that the program has made some progress toward encouraging broader citizen participation. For instance, Malbin et al. (2012) reported that the six-to-one matching program has resulted in a greater role for small donors, both in number and in the percentage of overall campaign funding they contribute. Malbin et al. also found that the small donor match has resulted in a donor pool more representative of the city at large, with more money coming from geographic areas that are less white, less educated, and less wealthy. Moreover, Kraus (2006, 2011) found that the CFA has slowed spending growth in citywide races and broadened the fundraising base of participating candidates. Yet Kraus also found *increased* spending in city council elections during the CFA era, and reports little reason for optimism regarding the program's ability to increase electoral competition, with fewer "competitive" city races in 2003 than 1985 and more uncontested elections in the CFA era. Thus, existing evidence for the efficacy of the CFA is mixed.

The Fair Elections Now Act

The Fair Elections Now Act (FENA) currently pending in the U.S. Congress would create a system of public funding for congressional elections. The FENA was first introduced in 2009 and has been sponsored in every session since. In 2011 the bill was sponsored in the Senate by Dick Durbin (D-IL) and in the House by John Larson (D-CT), Walter Jones Jr. (R-NC), and Chellie Pingree (D-ME). It is worth noting that all three of the House sponsors come from Clean Elections states (North Carolina employs a Clean Elections system for its judicial elections). As in the New York City system, one intended effect of the FENA is clearly to persuade candidates to seek small donations from individual contributors. However, the FENA as proposed at this writing also displays several similarities to Clean Elections programs, and it is therefore best classified as a hybrid of sorts between the large initial grants of full funding systems and the small donor matching funds in New York.

Like candidates in Clean Elections states, those in the proposed FENA system would qualify for public money by raising a predetermined number of small contributions from citizens of their state. In House races these contributions may not exceed $100 and candidates must surpass the $50,000 mark from a minimum of 1,500 in-state contributors to be eligible for public funding. The formula for Senate qualification is more complicated. Senate candidates must attract 2,000 contributors plus 500 more for each of their state's congressional districts. Thus, a Senate candidate in North Dakota (with one congressional district) would need 2,500 contributors to qualify whereas one in California (with 53 districts) would need 28,500. From this donor base, Senate candidates must raise 10 percent of the primary grant amount in order to qualify for public subsidies (described below).

Once they pass this threshold, candidates may receive public subsidies designed to approximate total campaign costs. For House candidates, the proposed grant amount is $1,050,000; for Senate contenders, it is $1.25 million plus an additional $250,000 for each of the state's congressional districts. To revisit the example above, the subsidy in North Dakota would be $1.5 million and in California it would be $14.5 million. For both House and Senate races, the subsidy is split for each election phase, with 40 percent of the payment intended for the primary and 60 percent for the general election.

The FENA also contains provisions to encourage the dissemination of public information. Candidates participating in the FENA would also receive media vouchers that they could use for purchasing broadcast advertising at rates 20 percent lower than the lowest broadcast rate. Candidates for the House would receive $100,000 in vouchers, and those for Senate would be eligible for $100,000 per House district in their state. Campaigns could choose to sell the vouchers to the national party committees, which would then use them to buy their own advertising. Participating candidates would also be obligated to participate in one debate with other willing candidates before the primary election and in two debates before the general election. This is similar to a debate requirement in Arizona's Clean Elections law.

In an important departure from Clean Elections systems (and nearly every other public funding scheme in history), the FENA does not include a spending cap. FENA candidates would be free to continue raising money, and small contributions (less than $100 in the aggregate) from in-state donors would receive a five-to-one match from the FENA fund, much as in the New York City CFA. Candidates would stop receiving these contribution matches when they reached three times the primary grant amount. In other words, participating House candidates would receive a grant of $420,000 for the primary and $630,000 for the general election, and would subsequently be able to receive up to $1.26 million in contribution matching grants for about the first $250,000 they raised in increments of $100 or less.

The FENA has attracted well over a hundred co-sponsors in Congress and has also been a fairly popular proposal among reform-oriented interest groups. Common Cause has heralded the FENA as a mechanism to "get our leaders out of the fundraising game and let them do the jobs we've elected them to do."[2] Public Citizen has offered similar support for a FENA system: "Instead of spending time asking for money from lobbyists and corporate special interest groups, candidates for elected office would be able to focus their attention on voters in the communities they represent."[3] Reforms such as the FENA and the New York Campaign Finance Act show promise in some areas and are consistent with the Supreme Court's recent decisions regarding campaign finance. However, it is prudent to consider whether any system would be a remedy for all that ails American democracy.

Toward Effective Reform

For more than a quarter of a century, the fundamental question with regard to public funding has been, Can it make elections better? This book does not provide an all-encompassing answer to that question, but it is fairly clear that there is no perfect campaign finance system. Indeed, the regulatory history of money in politics resembles a Whac-A-Mole game in which reformers address known problems only to see new ones appear—often in unforeseen places. Public election funding cannot turn every election into a nail-biter if districts are drawn to the benefit of one party, nor can it ensure that a candidate is not beholden to wealthy donors or interest groups if those groups may construct super PACs that solicit unlimited contributions and then purchase advertising on the candidate's behalf.

What this book has shown is that public funding can dramatically alter elections under certain circumstances. For instance, Clean Elections systems appear to facilitate high-quality candidacies where they may not have otherwise occurred, and also foster more interaction between candidates and voters. From a normative perspective, it is difficult to argue that publicly focused, well-funded candidacies are bad for democracy. In the same vein, if some combination of increased information or enhanced political efficacy is driving a greater number of people to vote on more of the ballot, the quality of democracy and representation is likely improved when public funding is present. That said, public funding is certainly no savior from the perspective of fiscally conservative candidates, who bear political costs of participation that do not exist for other candidates.

In short, while publicly funded elections may or may not be "better" on balance, the experiences of both the candidates and the voters participating in them are indisputably different than in traditionally financed ones. Before searching for the relationships they *want* to see, reformers should devote considerable effort to understanding how the presence of public election funding is likely to affect the conduct of political campaigns. This book shows that the structure of any future programs will lead to shifting incentives, altered behavior, and in some cases, pervasive gaming among affected candidate populations. Not all of these changes will be clearly positive.

Most everyone wants elections to be fairly conducted, publicly focused, and reasonably competitive, since good representation is likely to follow. However, this book demonstrates that the road between public funding and such elections is not an expressway, and merely believing that subsidies of any size are a panacea does not make it so. In addition to conforming to recent federal court decisions, future campaign finance regulations should weigh all available academic and policy findings in this area. Any future policies will involve some trade-offs as governments weigh the financial costs of public funding schemes against likely participation rates and program effects. Generally, these trade-offs involve considerations of program cost and candidate participation.

A program with larger average subsidies is obviously going to be more costly, but if public funding is designed to foster greater electoral competition, then direct subsidies should be sufficiently large to approximate the cost of a meaningful campaign. Political science has consistently demonstrated that full funding (Mayer et al. 2006; Werner and Mayer 2007; Malhotra 2008) but not partial funding (Jones and Borris 1985; Mayer and Wood 1995) spurs increased competition in legislative elections. Although challengers may find success raising money from ideologically motivated individuals or those whom they know personally in a traditionally financed system (see Francia et al. 2003), they are more likely to be seen as a poor investment by strategic donors since they rarely win. Thus, a system in which public funding pays for only part of the necessary costs of a campaign will not eliminate the traditional funding disparity between challengers and incumbents, because challengers are likely to still have difficulty raising the other half. This is doubly true when we consider that the availability of public funding does not appear to draw more experienced candidates into the political arena, so the comparative advantage that incumbents enjoy in terms of institutional resources, funding lists, and general know-how is likely to continue to give them an edge in the absence of robust subsidies.

As this book has shown, however, that is not the case in the fully funded states: non-incumbent candidates in these states operate at financial parity with their opponents. While it remains to be seen whether the elimination of matching funds via the *McComish* decision will alter this dynamic, matching funds were hardly a prominent feature in Arizona elections when they were legal, and there is little evidence that traditional candidates were purposefully withholding overall spending before the Court made its ruling (Dowling et al. 2012). Moreover, the availability of matching funds is irrelevant for candidates merely looking for a means to attain financial viability that might not have otherwise existed. Full funding—regardless of whether a candidate may be outspent—allows challengers to make a respectable showing despite their institutional disadvantages. Indeed, standard shortcut definitions of candidate quality, which assume that previous elected experience is a strong predictor of the amount of resources that a candidate will command, appear to be much less useful in fully funded environments.

The second aspect that requires balancing is the inclusivity of a given program, as determined by its qualification requirements. Opponents of public funding point out that the downside to allowing candidates to circumvent "market forces" in politics is that those forces often serve a valuable purpose. If candidates must raise money to be successful, then incumbents in particular argue that those who are strong private-source fundraisers are likely leveraging attributes such as community ties and political savvy that would also make them good representatives. An inability to raise money may be the result of a dearth of these attributes. Alternatively, candidates may be unable to secure broad funding support because of ideological extremism that does not appeal to many voters. So reformers are likely to feel a tension between facilitating the campaigns of serious candidates and curbing the entry of frivolous ones. If the qualification threshold is set too high, it will do little to encourage the emergence of new candidates since the system will be much like a traditional one that favors those with experience and connections. However, if the threshold is set too low, then the system runs the risk of being inundated with ideologically extreme or novelty candidates.

There is no clear, uniform answer to this question. Most advocates agree that public funding should be constructed to encourage participation by a wide range of candidates while ensuring that those who accept subsidies will put the money to good use. Given the substantial variation in the look of legislative elections across the country, reformers should consider local conditions and set qualification requirements in such a way as to preserve some element of "market forces" while still persuading good candidates to run, bearing in mind that the definition of a "quality" candidate is somewhat looser where public funding is available. Thus, if the goal of public funding is to encourage a wide range of views, and if the threshold is set appropriately, there is little reason to exclude third-party candidates from participating or to diminish their subsidy amount relative to major-party candidates.

Reformers must also consider whether their favored program should include a spending limit. This will involve weighing the benefits of such a limit against the likelihood of diminished participation in the absence of one; the Fair Elections Now Act is a good example of the considerations that reformers must make in this area. As noted in this book, while partially funded candidates—who still must raise a proportion of their funding from private donors—exhibited no difference in the time they committed to either fundraising or voter interaction, those who accepted

Clean Elections funding spent significantly less time raising money and devoted more time to communicating with voters. This narrative is consistent with the story presented by reform groups about the likely effect of the FENA on how candidates use their time: reduce the necessity of fundraising, and candidates will turn their attention to voters.

The key difference between Clean Elections and FENA is that the latter lacks a statutory spending cap: a FENA candidate would be able to continue raising money—and receiving matching funds—from small donors throughout the campaign. To be fair, in the post-*McComish* public funding world, the absence of a spending cap is the only mechanism to assure candidates that they will have some means of combating a well-funded opponent. However, as long as candidates *may* raise money, it is unrealistic to expect them to stop doing so in the era of the expensive media campaign, and we should anticipate that candidates will respond to the incentives that FENA matching funds provide. In failing to limit spending for participating candidates, the FENA therefore shows little potential to curb fundraising activities or to increase the attention that candidates devote to interaction with the voting public. Even if $1 million is enough for most candidates to wage a visible campaign, the FENA rules create an arms-race mentality in which candidates have an incentive to continue building their funding arsenals. Thus, *McComish* appears to have shaped public funding policies by forcing a choice on reformers: provide participating candidates with some assurance that they can continue to compete with a moneyed opponent or cap spending, eliminate fundraising, and facilitate greater interaction between candidates and voters.

Such a choice exists because, as this book demonstrates, full funding with spending caps has indirect effects on the extent to which candidates engage voters. By essentially eliminating the effort necessary for fundraising, Clean Elections systems have heightened the level of interaction between candidates and voters, since the former rationally choose to spend time seeking votes. These efforts appear to pay off in the form of reduced voter "roll-off": voters in districts where state house candidates accept full public funding are significantly more likely to cast a vote in the state house election, as opposed to voting for the contests at the top of the ballot and leaving the polling place. Either by raising awareness of candidates and their issue positions or by raising perceptions among the electorate about the importance of the office (or a combination of the two), the heightened interaction between candidates and voters during the campaign leads to more voting. Moreover, the change in candidates' propensity to directly engage voters appears to stem from the fact that a high subsidy and spending cap eliminated fundraising from candidates' necessary tasks.

Yet spending caps do not appear to be necessary for encouraging more contact between candidates and citizens; programs can be constructed to directly encourage such behavior. For instance, by explicitly encouraging candidates to seek small donations via a six-to-one-match of contributions under $175, the New York City Campaign Finance Act provides a direct incentive for candidates to broaden their fundraising targets beyond the traditional sources. Indeed, there is evidence that donor pools under the CFA are more representative of the voting public (Malbin et al. 2012). By incentivizing contact with new segments of the electorate, the CFA likely heightens the salience of the election for more private citizens, since by donating they will be literally invested in the race. Other, more straightforward requirements foster the dissemination of more political information to voters. Clean Elections (in Arizona), the CFA, and the FENA all mandate appearance in at least one debate for candidates who accept public funding. Furthermore, in Arizona, participating candidates appear in a "Clean Elections Voter Education Guide" that is distributed statewide and includes personal statements and biographical information.

These features serve as a reminder that programs can be creatively constructed to achieve a wide range of reform objectives. Moreover, this book demonstrates that candidates respond to the incentives that a campaign finance system provides, often in unanticipated ways. Nevertheless, it seems safe to conclude that no public funding system can serve as a panacea for American elections. Especially considering the trade-offs described above, reformers who advance public funding proposals in the future should therefore carefully consider their core objectives and realize that they will likely be forced to prioritize some goals over others. Though public funding may not make elections *better* on all fronts, it is apparent that subsidizing elections makes them vastly *different* from those funded only with private dollars. Whether that difference leads to positive policy outcomes will largely depend on the extent to which reformers account for altered behavior of candidates and voters in publicly funded elections.

APPENDIX I

Description of Data Sources

In order to gain insight into candidate activities and motivation, this book employs a wide range of data from a mixed-methods study. In Chapters 3–6 I analyze elite survey data collected from the major-party lower-house candidate populations in eighteen states during the 2008 election, including all six states offering ubiquitous full (Arizona, Connecticut, and Maine) and partial (Hawaii, Minnesota, and Wisconsin) public financing to legislative candidates in that year. To maximize the possibility of meaningful comparison between publicly and privately (or "traditionally") financed candidates, I also surveyed the candidate populations of twelve additional states with no available public financing for legislative candidates. Criteria for selection as a comparison state include the average cost of a legislative campaign, proximity within Squire's (2007) index of legislative professionalization, average district population, chamber size, electoral timeline, and where possible, geographical location as a proxy for regional culture differences. Thus, I added Alaska, Colorado, Delaware,

Iowa, Michigan, Missouri, Montana, New Mexico, Ohio, Rhode Island, Vermont, and West Virginia to the sampling frame.

Survey instruments (contained in Appendix 2) solicited responses to questions regarding candidate attitudes toward their campaign, the electorate, and their competition. Each candidate was also asked to quantify the amount of time he or she personally devoted to various tasks in ten areas: fundraising, public speeches, field activity, electronic campaigning, media relations, research, strategy, phoning voters, sending mailings, and the courting of interest groups. Finally, the survey allowed for the collection of demographic information about state legislative candidates, information that can be hard to come by; obtaining it allowed for a wide range of factors to be controlled in the subsequent statistical analysis. The dataset therefore provides unprecedented insight into candidate strategy, behavior, and opinion in state legislative contests.

Response rates in surveys of elite candidate populations tend to be low, often less than 40 percent (e.g., Francia and Herrnson 2003; Howell 1982). I made multiple contacts to overcome this issue, devoting particular attention to fully funded candidates, who made up roughly 15 percent of the sampling frame. Initial survey packages were delivered via U.S. mail to candidates' home addresses during the first week of October 2008. Prepaid return envelopes were included, but the cover letter also directed respondents to an identical online version. I also sent electronic invitations to available addresses on October 19, November 11, and December 8, and mailed reminder postcards in mid-November. Electronic mail addresses were obtained for approximately 60 percent of the overall candidate population. Also in mid-November, I assessed the response rate of each state and re-sent full survey packages to nonrespondents in both fully funded and low-responding states. Full packages were re-sent to candidates in Rhode Island, New Mexico, Delaware, and Colorado. While response rates were not problematic in publicly funded states, I re-sent full packages to Hawaii, Connecticut, Wisconsin, and Arizona in an effort to obtain as many responses as possible from those states. I made final contact with remaining nonrespondents in those states by phone in mid-December. Thus, candidates in the sampling frame received up to eight contacts, and there was a higher probability of more contact for publicly funded candidates (especially those accepting full funding). The response window remained open until December 31, 2008.

The overall candidate population contained 2,971 candidates. I received 1,022 responses, for a response rate of 34.4 percent. As noted above, this rate is consistent with previous surveys of elite candidate and/or legislator populations (Poggione 2004; Francia and Herrnson 2003; Howell 1982). State response rates ranged between 23.7 percent in Rhode Island and 49.5 percent in Arizona. Table A.1 contains state-by-state response rates as well as basic characteristics of both the sample and candidate population in the survey frame. The sample contains a higher percentage of fully funded candidates than the population, which is the result of a concentrated effort to illicit responses from those candidates. Women and Democrats also make up a higher proportion of the sample than the population, which should be expected given the high response rates of fully funded candidates in tandem with existing evidence that both Democrats and women are more likely to accept full public funding in state house elections (GAO 2010; Werner and Mayer 2007). To be clear, the effort to oversample candidates who accepted Clean Elections subsidies in Arizona, Connecticut, and Maine almost certainly also raised the proportion of women and Democrats in the sample.

I also employ a range of election data, including fundraising and vote totals. I collected all election data in this book from the office of the secretary of state in each state and, unless otherwise noted, campaign finance data from the appropriate state campaign finance regulatory agencies. Where it is necessary to examine candidate fundraising patterns, I utilize summary financial data on all candidates obtained from the National Institute on Money in State Politics (http://www.followthemoney.org). In all cases, I examine data through the 2008 election. I did not include data from 2010

Table A.1. State-by-State Response Rates

State	Candidate population	Response rate (%)	State	Candidate population	Response rate (%)
Rhode Island	114	23.7	New Mexico	101	36.6
Michigan	207	24.6	Connecticut	239	38.5
Ohio	175	26.9	Maine	288	38.9
Iowa	170	28.2	Montana	183	40.4
West Virginia	151	28.5	Delaware	64	40.6
Missouri	244	29.1	Wisconsin	166	41.0
Vermont	240	31.7	Alaska	69	42.0
Minnesota	266	35.3	Colorado	121	42.1
Hawaii	78	35.9	Arizona	97	49.5

due to uncertainty surrounding the status of matching funds provisions in a number of states as a result of then-pending federal litigation. This is especially true in Arizona, in which matching funds grants were halted for the 2010 election cycle by judicial directive. Connecticut also suspended its matching funds program for the 2010 election.

Finally, throughout this book I report qualitative data derived from sixteen candidate interviews in the wake of the 2006 Arizona legislative election, conducted in person at various locations throughout the state in January 2007. I interviewed candidates of both major parties, for both legislative houses; respondents ranged in electoral success from primary losers to sitting members of the Arizona Legislature. Most conversations were in the range of thirty to sixty minutes in length. I recorded interviews, transcribed responses, and coded for strategic and emotional concerns.

APPENDIX 2

SURVEY INSTRUMENT

Your participation in this study is completely voluntary, and your answers will be kept confidential. You may skip any question you do not feel like answering, without penalty.

Instructions: Please circle your answers when applicable. Survey questions are on both sides of the page.

1) What is your name *(please print legibly)*? *Note:* Your name will never be publicly shared, and you will never be identifiable in our findings. We need your name in order to look at your election results later on.
2) What state and district are you running in?
3) In the 2008 election cycle, you are a(n): 1. Challenger; 2. Incumbent; 3. Candidate for an open seat
4) Including the seat for which you are currently a candidate, have you ever been elected to ANY public office, including, but not limited to: State Legislature, Statewide Office, City Office, County Office, School Board, or Selectperson? 1. Yes; 2. No

5) During the current campaign, are you working either full-time or part-time at another job? *Note:* If you are an incumbent, do not include your responsibilities as a state legislator. 1. Full-Time; 2. Part-Time; 3. Not working at another job

6) Outside of your legislative or campaign duties, what is your occupation?

7) As of today, do you think you will someday run for an even higher office, such as state senate, statewide office, governor, U.S. Congress, or president? 1. Definitely; 2. Probably; 3. Maybe/Unsure; 4. Probably Not; 5. Definitely Not

8) How many of each of the following do you currently count as part of your campaign: Professional Political Consultants_____ Other Paid Staff_____ Volunteers_____

9) In the current election cycle, I *(circle one):* 1. Have accepted or will accept public subsidies under my state's public funding law; 2. Have opted out or will opt out of public money; 3. Am unsure of whether I will accept subsidies; 4. Do not qualify for public subsidies

10) In terms of fundraising in the current election cycle, I *(circle one):* 1. Expect to outraise my main opponent(s); 2. Expect to be outraised by my main opponent(s); 3. Expect levels of funding in my race to be about equal between candidates

11) Would you have entered the race if public election subsidies were not available? 1. Definitely; 2. Probably; 3. Maybe/Unsure; 4. Probably Not; 5. Definitely Not

12) ANSWER THIS QUESTION ONLY IF YOU OPTED OUT OF PUBLIC SUBSIDIES, OR WILL OPT OUT. CHECK ALL THAT APPLY. I chose to opt out of public money because: (a) I feel that to win this race, I must raise more than the subsidy amount; (b) I am confident that if I build a large war chest, it will discourage serious challengers; (c) I am ideologically opposed to using public money for political campaigns; (d) Other (please specify)

13) ANSWER THIS QUESTION ONLY IF YOU OPTED OUT OF PUBLIC SUBSIDIES, OR WILL. CHECK ALL THAT APPLY. I accepted public money because: (a) It allows me to spend less time raising money and more time on other tasks; (b) Without it, I may

not have been able to raise enough money to compete; (c) I wanted to avoid taking money from interest groups; (d) Other (please specify)

14) DURING THE FIRST WEEK OF OCTOBER, what is your best estimate of how many *hours* you, yourself, spent engaged in the following activities? Please complete the table below, listing your NUMBER OF HOURS, and NOT A PERCENTAGE OF TIME. If you are in Arizona or Maine, do not include time spent qualifying for public money as part of the fundraising category.

Task	Number of Hours
Fundraising (AZ, CT, and ME: Not including time spent qualifying for public funds)	
Website Maintenance/Blogging/Email Response/Other Electronic Campaigning	
Door Knocking/Canvassing/Sign Posting/Leafleting/Other Field Activity	
Speaking Engagements/Debates (not including fundraising events)	
Media Activities (Earned Media, Ad Production, Interviews)	
Meeting with Interest Groups/Seeking Endorsements	
Preparing/Sending Mailings Yourself	
Phoning Constituents Yourself	
Researching Policy Issues	
Strategy/Staff Meetings	
Other (please specify)	

15) In terms of my time during the current election cycle, I *(circle):* 1. Feel that I spend/spent too much time raising money in relation to other activities; 2. Feel that my other campaign responsibilities did not allow enough time for fundraising; 3. Feel that the time I spend/ spent raising money is/was just about right

16–21: To what extent do you agree with the following statements? Circle ONE.

16) *When I began this campaign, I underestimated how difficult it would be to raise money.* 1. Strongly Agree; 2. Agree; 3. Neither Agree nor Disagree; 4. Disagree; 5. Strongly Disagree

17) *I have sufficient time, money, and staff to mobilize voters who will support me.* 1. Strongly Agree; 2. Agree; 3. Neither Agree nor Disagree; 4. Disagree; 5. Strongly Disagree

18) *I believe that my race is competitive, and more than one candidate has a realistic chance of winning.* 1. Strongly Agree; 2. Agree; 3. Neither Agree nor Disagree; 4. Disagree; 5. Strongly Disagree

19) *I feel that my message is reaching enough voters.* 1. Strongly Agree; 2. Agree; 3. Neither Agree nor Disagree; 4. Disagree; 5. Strongly Disagree

20) *I believe that the most effective campaign strategy focuses attention on those most likely to vote.* 1. Strongly Agree; 2. Agree; 3. Neither Agree nor Disagree; 4. Disagree; 5. Strongly Disagree

21) *I believe that public funding improves democracy in my state.* 1. Strongly Agree; 2. Agree; 3. Neither Agree nor Disagree; 4. Disagree; 5. Strongly Disagree

22) Overall, how pleased are you with the way your campaign is going in this election? 1. Very Pleased; 2. Pleased; 3. Neither Pleased nor Displeased; 4. Displeased; 5. Strongly Displeased

23) If I you lose this race, will you run for office again? 1. Definitely; 2. Probably; 3. Maybe/Unsure; 4. Probably Not; 5. Definitely Not

24) I am a: 1. Female; 2. Male

25) I am running as a (circle all that apply. You need not be endorsed by your party): 1. Democrat; 2. Republican; 3. Member of another party; 4. Candidate with no party affiliation

26) Of the groups below, which most accurately describes the racial group you identify with the most? 1. African American; 3. Caucasian/White; 5. Native American; 2. Asian; 4. Hispanic/Latino; 6. Bi-racial or Multi-racial; 7. Other *(specify):*

Appendix 3

Methods

The survey and election data described in Appendix 1 offer an important window into the aggregate behavior of legislative candidates. Throughout the text I analyze those data using multivariate statistical methods that are intended to support conclusions about the relationship between two variables while holding other relevant ones constant. I do this in order to exclude those factors as potential confounders that would distort the relationship between the independent and dependent variables of interest to the analysis. At times I also adjust the data to account for the fact that participation in public funding is not a random event, and should be expected to draw candidates in certain circumstances more than others. Unless accounted for, this nonrandomness holds the potential to distort the true relationship between public funding and various outcomes when the candidate serves as the unit of analysis.

Each chapter focuses on a different empirical research question. Since there is considerable range between the dependent variables and units of analysis employed, I use a number of statistical methods in the book. In some cases, I performed some analytical steps before drawing conclusions. More technically inclined readers will therefore no doubt be interested in more details regarding the methods of analysis than are offered in the text.

Chapter 3

Chapter 3 seeks to determine whether public funding affects the manner in which candidates use their time. The central hypothesis of this chapter is that full funding eliminates the need for candidates to spend time raising money, and so they will reinvest that time into other activities designed to garner votes. The candidate survey (see Appendix 2) solicited responses from candidates about how they used their weekly time during the first week of October. The resulting survey data allow for the comparison of activities performed by publicly and traditionally funded candidates. However, statistical inference is complicated by the fact that participation in public funding is optional. Since candidates choose whether to accept subsidies on an individual basis, it stands to reason that certain candidates should be more likely to participate. For this chapter, the lurking problem is that perhaps candidates who would have devoted more time to public interaction—due to ideology, orientation to the political process, or some other reason—are more likely to accept public funding. Or perhaps candidates are more apt to emerge in districts amenable to public interaction activities. In either case, public funding would appear to cause greater public interaction when it was not actually so.

In statistical terms, if candidate participation is nonrandom, then the covariates are unlikely to be balanced between publicly and privately funded candidate groups because the receipt of public election funding necessarily implies that those groups are drawn from different populations. Such imbalance would make inference about public funding difficult with testing of means or even multivariate regression (see Sekhon 2009). Before analyzing the data in a multivariate model, I first seek improved balance between the groups' covariates. A necessary condition for such balance is that observable characteristics have the same distribution in the traditionally and publicly funded groups.

To achieve this balance, I follow the language of experiments in designating a "treatment" group of publicly funded candidates and a "control" group of candidates who raised money exclusively from private sources. I then pre-process the survey data with a genetic matching algorithm intended to improve the balance of the observed covariates between treatment and control groups (on preprocessing, see Ho et al. 2007a, 2007b; on genetic matching and search algorithms, see Sekhon 2006, 2008; Diamond and Sekhon 2006; Mebane and Sekhon 1998; Sekhon and Mebane 1998). The algorithm seeks optimal balance via the construction of matched pairs consisting of one candidate who participated in public funding and one who did not, parsing candidates of one condition whose covariates do not align well with at least one candidate in the opposite condition. Preprocessing in this fashion generally results in a smaller dataset, albeit one in which the observed covariates are more similar between the two groups (Ho et al. 2007a). The software package described in Ho et al. (2007b) supplies postmatching weights that can be used in subsequent analysis of a parsed dataset.

I proceed with an important caveat. As described in Chapter 3, I expect that candidates in partial and full public election funding systems experience markedly different incentives and political conditions. Accordingly, I perform separate matches for the two groups, reflecting my belief that "treatment" is likely to have disparate effects on the behavior of partially and fully funded candidates, since the former continue raising money throughout the campaign but the latter do not. Thus, I construct a separate dataset for each treated group, consisting of all candidates who were subjected to that particular treatment and all candidates who were not. To be clear, the pool of candidates in the control condition is the same for fully and partially funded candidates, but it is not possible for a fully funded candidate to be paired with a partially funded candidate.

The samples from partially and fully funded states contain 96 and 156 publicly funded candidates, respectively, and in both cases the algorithm finds matches for all treated candidates. I delete list-wise 161 cases in which the candidate was not opposed by a major party challenger, 16 cases in which candidates did not complete the time component of the survey, 42 cases in which candidates' reported campaign time exceeded the number of hours in one week, and 5 cases in which candidates did not report their name or district, thus making information about their races irretrievable. Logistic regressions indicate that problematic and missing data are distributed randomly, and I am confident that the exclusion of these cases does not bias the substantive findings.

I allow the matching algorithms to operate on 19 covariates that were unchanged between the point at which the treated candidates opted into public funding and the point at which outcomes were observed. These covariates include measures of candidate employment status, political experience, gender, partisan affiliation, and race, as well as characteristics of the candidate's election and demographic traits of the candidate's district. In addition, I include the propensity score (the probability of receiving treatment given a set of observed covariates) in the algorithm, calculated with a logistic regression model (see Diamond and Sekhon 2006). Ideally, the matching algorithm should improve balance on most of the desired measures.

Tables A.2 and A.3 contain mean levels of relevant covariates for the full and partial funding groups, respectively, both before and after conducting the matches, as well as the postmatching percentage of improvement on a number of balance measures. The three leftmost columns of Table A.2 depict sample mean differences between fully funded and privately funded groups, both before and after matching. Entries in the rightmost columns reflect the percentage of improvement in this difference, as well as the percentage of improvement in empirical quantile measures. Taken together, the entries in Table A.2 raise confidence that matching results in a better-balanced dataset for fully funded candidates. The absolute value of the mean difference is smaller after matching for all but three covariates: the indicator for candidates working full-time, the Hispanic population percentage of the district, and the district's urbanity. The empirical quantile measures also show marked improvement for most covariates postmatching.

The entries in Table A.3 yield similar conclusions about the postmatching balance for partially funded candidates, although the covariates for partially funded candidates are quite similar to the privately financed group even before the match is conducted. Like the fully funded group, the postmatching mean difference for partially funded candidates is larger for three covariates: the indicators for incumbent and full-time employment, and the percentage of the district population with a college degree. However, the postmatching difference in means on all three of these covariates is only about one percentage point. Like those from the matching exercise for fully funded candidates, the empirical quantile measures are also improved postmatching for most covariates in the partial funding

TABLE A.2. Mean Values of Observable Covariates and Balance Assessment, Full Funding

	Means				Percent improvement		
	Treated	Unmatched control	Matched control	Mean diff	eQQ med	eQQ mean	eQQ max
Candidate:							
Challenger	0.38	0.42	0.37	52.69	0.00	100	100
Incumbent	0.35	0.33	0.37	6.11	0.00	100	100
Open-seat	0.27	0.25	0.27	100	0.00	48.79	0.00
Male	0.59	0.67	0.6	85.54	0.00	89.03	0.00
Democrat	0.64	0.56	0.64	100	0.00	45.13	0.00
African American	0.01	0.02	0.01	100	0.00	100	100
Experience	0.63	0.52	0.63	100	0.00	40.25	0.00
Employed part-time	0.28	0.24	0.28	85.91	0.00	34.16	0.00
Employed full-time	0.46	0.47	0.6	-761.34	0.00	-412.12	0.00
District:							
District population	40,374	43,634	37,780	20.44	60.38	44.61	26.5
% Urban	64	64.39	65.71	-337.36	42.84	30.74	8.8
% Black	1.95	3.35	1.94	99.73	53.92	74.33	90.14
% Hispanic	6.01	5.49	4.87	-120.4	-9.21	-17.42	51.09
Household income	70,004	60,712	61,696	10.58	15.66	26.39	-8.55
% College degree	21.4	18.9	20.11	48.56	44.44	30.59	0.00
Household size	2.49	2.53	2.53	3.62	-50.00	-20.65	50.82
Multi-member dist.	0.17	0.13	0.19	37.88	0.00	74.39	0.00
Party vote, 2006	52.18	49.21	51.86	89.19	33.47	31.15	18.79
3rd-party candidate	0.1	0.33	0.12	92.14	0.00	87.87	0.00

TABLE A.3. Mean Values of Observable Covariates and Balance Assessment, Partial Funding

	Means			Percent improvement			
	Treated	Unmatched control	Matched control	Mean diff	eQQ med	eQQ mean	eQQ max
Candidate:							
Challenger	0.54	0.42	0.54	100.00	0.00	26.04	0.00
Incumbent	0.32	0.33	0.33	-42.9	0.00	-62.71	0.00
Open-seat	0.14	0.25	0.13	90.72	0.00	40.83	0.00
Male	0.72	0.67	0.72	100.00	0.00	34.92	0.00
Democrat	0.64	0.56	0.65	86.35	0.00	76.76	0.00
African American	0.02	0.02	0.02	100.00	0.00	-Inf.	-Inf.
Experience	0.49	0.52	0.51	38.49	0.00	-62.71	0.00
Employed part-time	0.29	0.24	0.29	100.00	0.00	34.92	0.00
Employed full-time	0.47	0.47	0.45	-414.98	0.00	-Inf.	-Inf.
District:							
District population	38,557	43,634	39,977	72.04	30.65	27.92	45.6
% Urban	67.00	64.39	65	34.04	-153.96	-103.35	-9.26
% Black	2.85	3.35	2.68	64.97	81.26	32.94	4.62
% Hispanic	2.56	5.49	2.47	96.99	55.39	90.65	80.3
Household income	67,837	60,712	66,549	81.91	64.19	43.41	-66.69
% College degree	19.18	18.90	18.13	-273.19	-120.00	-101.14	-83.33
Household size	2.58	2.53	2.56	67.97	33.33	34.97	81.44
Multi-member dist.	0.00	0.13	0.00	100.00	0.00	100.00	100.00
Party vote, 2006	47.34	49.21	46.13	35.22	42.44	10.87	12.50
3rd-party candidate	0.99	0.33	0.98	98.43	100.00	97.46	0.00

match. In short, for both the fully funded and partially funded candidate groups, I am confident that matching improves balance.

With weights obtained from the matching exercise, I proceed with analysis of the data using a multivariate ordinary least squares (OLS) regression model. Following Francia and Herrnson (2003), the dependent variable is the percentage of weekly time that a candidate devoted to various measures of public interaction (explained in Chapter 3). The independent variable is a dichotomous indicator coded 1 if a candidate accepted full or partial public funding. I also add to each model a dummy variable coded 1 if the candidate has been previously elected to a public office, since experienced candidates are more likely to have an existing base of support and could conceivably need to spend less effort fundraising than political neophytes. Additionally, I include an indicator coded 1 if the candidate is a man. Previous scholarship has found that women state legislators are more likely to seek close interaction with constituents than men (Epstein et al. 2005), and it seems reasonable to conclude that women may exhibit similar tendencies as candidates. Finally, I add the district population and its mean household income (both in tens of thousands), obtained from Lilley et al. (2007). Candidates in more populous districts may find a door-to-door campaign daunting, opting for a media-centric strategy that requires more money (and more fundraising) to execute. Similarly, those in lower-income districts might have to look harder to raise the requisite funds, thus increasing the effort they devote to fundraising.

Alternative Model Using Unmatched Data

Table A.4 shows the coefficients and robust standard errors (clustered by state) for the models described above, using the full survey dataset of unmatched data. The models of partially funded candidates exclude those who accepted full funding and vice versa, so that the referent category in each model is made up solely of traditionally financed candidates. I include these specifications as a robustness check in order to ensure that parsing the dataset with the matching techniques described above did not result in conclusions dramatically different from those rendered by the full set of survey respondents.

The models of unmatched data in Table A.4 yield conclusions quite close to those presented in Chapter 3. Specifically, while the coefficient

TABLE A.4. Candidate Public Interaction Activities, Unmatched Data: OLS Regression Coefficients

	Partial funding				Full funding			
	(1)	(2)	(3)	(4)	(1)	(2)	(3)	(4)
Accepted full funding	–	–	–	–	8.658* (2.248)	10.380* (1.321)	9.937* (1.437)	8.444* (0.796)
Accepted partial funding	0.888 (1.676)	2.236* (0.905)	0.630 (0.983)	1.336* (0.505)	–	–	–	–
Held previous office	0.074 (1.899)	−1.275 (1.085)	−0.619 (1.313)	−1.390 (1.547)	−0.701 (1.640)	−1.663 (0.949)	−0.881 (1.059)	−1.771 (1.202)
Male	2.760 (1.813)	−0.518 (0.923)	−0.298 (1.254)	−0.369 (1.505)	1.788 (1.349)	−0.835 (0.877)	−1.130 (1.249)	−0.574 (1.661)
Dist. population (ten thous.)	−1.425* (0.263)	−0.591* (0.157)	−0.759* (0.141)	−0.508* (0.131)	−1.233* (0.187)	−0.379* (0.125)	−0.526* (0.165)	−0.401* (0.105)
Dist. household income (ten thous.)	0.869 (0.731)	−0.452 (0.253)	−0.285 (0.276)	−0.117 (0.273)	−0.170 (0.480)	−0.291 (0.202)	−0.499* (0.169)	−0.437* (0.166)
Constant	38.790* (5.759)	95.253* (1.985)	83.502* (2.511)	75.600* (2.776)	45.320* (3.508)	93.766* (1.519)	84.480* (1.707)	77.417* (1.864)
N	632	632	632	632	705	705	705	705
R^2	0.059	0.054	0.034	0.015	0.093	0.183	0.104	0.057
Root mean squared error	21.51	10.79	15.24	17.07	21.05	10.14	14.53	16.75
F-statistic	9.484	9.847	11.58	4.503	12.05	56.75	31.07	28.48

Note: Robust standard errors in parentheses, clustered by state. Sampling weights derived from genetic matching.
Dependent variables are the percentage of time (ranging from 0 to 100) devoted to various public interaction indices.
(1) Percentage of time devoted to field activities (canvassing, posting signs, etc.).
(2) Percentage of time devoted to all campaign activities except fundraising.
(3) Percentage of time devoted to all campaign activities except fundraising, research, and staff meetings.
(4) Percentage of time devoted to all campaign activities except fundraising, research, staff meetings, and mail preparation.
*p <.05.

for acceptance of partial funding achieves statistical significance in two of the four models, the positive effects of accepting partial funding on public interaction are substantively small—just over two and one percentage points of weekly time in Models 2 and 4, respectively. In contrast, the effects of full funding are positive and statistically significant in all four models, and are more than four times larger than those in the models of partially funded candidates. Thus, the substantive con-clusions from these alternative models are not different from those in Chapter 3.

Chapter 4

Chapter 4 engages the question of whether more people vote when a pub-licly funded candidate is present. As noted in the chapter, however, voter roll-off, and not turnout, is the appropriate dependent variable for this question. The hypothesis in this chapter is therefore that the percentage of people who vote for the president but who fail to register a preference in state legislative elections will decline when a publicly funded candidate is present. In other words, voter roll-off will diminish.

The unit of analysis in this chapter is the state legislative district. To calculate roll-off, I compiled precinct-level vote totals in all three Clean Elections states for both president and the applicable state legislative of-fice, in all precincts where voters cast ballots for only one house or senate district. I then aggregated these votes to a measure of district-level roll-off, which I express as

$$R = 100\left(1 - \frac{L}{P}\right)$$

where R is ballot roll-off, L is the total number of all votes cast for the ap-plicable state legislative race in a given district, and P is the total number of votes for president in that district. Higher roll-off values are therefore indicative of a greater percentage of voters who cast ballots for the presi-dential election but not the legislative one.

To determine whether public funding indeed decreased roll-off, I em-ploy a quasi-experimental framework, dividing the districts into a "treat-ment" group, in which at least one candidate accepted public funding, and a "control" group, in which no publicly funded candidate was present. The process of group assignment is straightforward in Maine, where at least one candidate accepted public funding in 58 of 151 legislative districts during the 2000 general election. I calculate roll-off only from precincts in which ballots were cast for a single legislative district; approximately 160 precincts were therefore excluded, but well over 500 remain. In 19 state house districts, ballots were counted only from precincts that overlap multiple districts; no usable roll-off figure can be calculated from those districts, leaving 132 Maine House districts in the original sample. Fifty-one of those districts are in the treatment condition.

The construction of a sufficiently large control group is more difficult in Connecticut, where 87 districts saw contested elections in 2008. However, at least one major-party candidate accepted public funding in all but 2 of those districts, yielding a control group too small to support statistical inference. Following Card and Krueger (1994), who examined the effect of minimum wage changes on employment in New Jersey fast-food establishments with a control group of eastern Pennsylvania restaurants, I address this issue by constructing a control group of General Assembly districts from Rhode Island. The Rhode Island House is half the size of the Connecticut House. However, the electoral environment and political climate of Connecticut and Rhode Island are similar in some important areas, including the average spending in a legislative election, proximity within Squire's (2007) index of legislative professionalization, average district population, electoral timeline, and active minor parties. Furthermore, I expect their geographic proximity to mitigate any issues correspondent with cross-state comparisons, such as political culture or regional trends. Paired t-tests confirm that there are no significant differences between the model covariates from Connecticut and Rhode Island districts in their 2004 condition, which improves confidence in Rhode Island as a control state. Since public funding is not available in Rhode Island, I include all Rhode Island assembly districts as potential controls in the Connecticut dataset. I obtained precinct election returns from the websites of the Maine and Rhode Island secretaries of state and a public information request submitted to the Connecticut Office of Legislative Research.

To determine the effect of public funding on roll-off, I first make two comparisons of roll-off levels between the treatment and control district groups in the house and senate elections of each state. I use one-tailed t-tests in all cases. In the first, I look for differences in mean roll-off between treated and control districts in the first election for which Clean Elections subsidies were available. Practical considerations inform the decision to restrict analysis to a single election. Clean Elections became effective for the 2000 election in Arizona and Maine and for the 2008 campaign in Connecticut; in the case of the latter, 2008 is the only year for which roll-off data were available in the Clean Elections era at the time this analysis was conducted. At this writing, 2008 is the only presidential election year since Connecticut has enacted Clean Elections. In both Arizona and Maine, candidate participation rates have become so ubiquitous since 2000 that fewer than five districts would be in the control condition in either state after that year.

I compare same-district roll-off differences between the last election financed solely with private money and the first one during which full public subsidies were available. By "same-district roll-off differences," I mean the roll-off percentage from the last presidential election year before Clean Elections (Election 0) subtracted from the roll-off percentage in the same district in the first election after implementation (Election 1). Accordingly, for each district I compare the difference in roll-off between 1996 and 2000 in Arizona and Maine and between 2004 and 2008 in Connecticut. This approach facilitates a district-level panel analysis, as each election before and after public funding had a contested presidential race at the top of the ballot and there was no intervening redistricting in any case. Gubernatorial elections such as those in 1998 and 2006 generally draw fewer voters; citizens who vote when no presidential candidate is on the ballot may be more knowledgeable or committed, and so roll-off cannot be compared between gubernatorial and presidential election years. A stand-alone analysis of gubernatorial roll-off may seem possible in Maine, which is unique among states in that it redistricts for the third election of every decade. However, gubernatorial candidates were also eligible to accept public funding in 2002, when the public fund released over $1.2 million to the contest for governor. I therefore do not analyze roll-off for the 1998 and 2002 Maine elections.

While basic comparison is informative for preliminary evaluation of whether the presence of a publicly funded candidate reduces roll-off, two factors complicate statistical conclusions about the relationship between Clean Elections and roll-off. The first is the relatively high potential for confounding variables to bias the comparison between groups. For instance, incumbent name recognition or overall spending may also entice voters to cast ballots, which would reduce roll-off. Thus, changes in other variables through time may obscure the true effect of Clean Elections in a comparison of roll-off trends.

Second, with the exception of the lower houses in Connecticut and Maine, none of the legislative houses in the Clean Elections states are made up of more than 36 districts. Arizona's legislature is composed of 30 districts in each house, with 2 members from each district in its House of Representatives; there are 35 members of the Maine Senate and 36 in the Connecticut Senate. Assignment to the treatment or control condition further reduces these numbers. For example, in the first cycle with Clean Elections, there were 3 treated districts in Connecticut Senate and 7 in the Arizona House. To be clear, I believe that an examination of the mean difference-in-differences in roll-off across all states and legislative houses is informative, particularly if such an examination finds consistent patterns. However, I make no claims that such an evaluation is definitive in all instances, due to concerns about omitted variables and small group sizes.

Elections to the lower legislative house of both Connecticut and Maine offer a potential solution to this problem. Both houses have 151 single-member lower-house districts, and the relatively large number of cases in elections to those bodies creates the possibility of calculating difference-in-differences, holding potential confounders constant within a multivariate statistical analysis employing districts as the unit. Since they alone hold realistic opportunities for such a design, I construct OLS models of same-district roll-off difference for the Connecticut and Maine state house elections only. The dependent variable (difference in mean levels of roll-off in districts) is described above. The independent variable of interest for all models is a dichotomous indicator coded 1 if the election was contested by at least one publicly funded candidate; the coefficient for this variable represents the difference-in-difference estimate.

As noted, I expect that factors other than full public funding will affect ballot roll-off trends. For instance, expensive contests spawn more media advertising and direct mail, which should raise awareness of the candidates among the electorate. The presence of either a third-party candidate or an incumbent in a race might also affect roll-off, since incumbent name recognition provides a decision heuristic for some voters (see Lau and Redlawsk 2001) while others may feel that minor parties are more closely aligned with their views. Finally, the percentage of African American voters in the electorate has been shown to be positively correlated with roll-off in a number of state and municipal elections (see Vanderleeuw and Engstrom 1987; Vanderleeuw and Utter 1993; Vanderleeuw and Liu 2002). Particularly for the Connecticut model, which includes data from a 2008 presidential contest that saw the election of an African American president, the racial composition of a district might affect roll-off trends despite being relatively invariant through time.

Probably the most important determinant of changes in roll-off are fluctuations in election contestedness by candidates of major parties. The absence of a major-party challenge is almost certain to increase the proportion of voters who roll off, since partisan voters may prefer making no choice to casting a ballot for a candidate of their nonpreferred party. Moreover, the contestedness of a race in Election 1 (after public funding implementation) is likely to serve as a major determinant of a candidate's public funding status; unopposed candidates will likely perceive little benefit to expending the effort necessary to qualify for Clean Elections funds (rendering theirs a "control" district). To illustrate, of the 35 unopposed Maine candidates for which I obtained roll-off data in 2000, only 6 accepted public subsidies, while at least one Maine candidate ran with Clean Elections funds in 46 percent of districts with contested elections in that year. Participation rates are substantially higher among unopposed candidates in Connecticut, likely due to a lower qualification threshold. It stands to reason that in addition to being less likely to accept public funding, unopposed candidates are also likely to devote much less time to voter interaction in a campaign that they are certain to win. Since "treatment" occurs in a contested election in Election 1, I believe that uncontested elections that occurred in the first cycle after public funding implementation do not provide a reliable counterfactual, and I exclude them from the analysis.

Following these considerations, I calculate panel difference-in-differences with two OLS model specifications from data in Maine as well as Connecticut and Rhode Island to investigate the effect of public funding on voter roll-off between Election 1 (when public funding was available) and Election 0 (when all elections were privately financed). In Specification 1, I model data from all districts in which Election 1 was contested by two major-party candidates, holding the contestedness in Election 0 constant. Specification 2 restricts the analysis to districts in which elections in *both* years were contested, and therefore requires no control for changes to the number of major-party candidates.

The model specifications are:

$$\Delta Y_D = \partial + \beta_1 X_1 + \beta_2 \Delta X_{2D} + \beta_3 \Delta X_{3D}$$
$$+ \beta_4 \Delta X_{4D} + \beta_5 \Delta X_{5D} + \beta 6 X_6 + \varepsilon$$

where

ΔY_D is the difference between roll-off in Election 1 and Election 0 for District D

X_1 is a dummy variable coded 1 for treatment (i.e., at least one candidate in the district accepted public funding) and 0 for control

ΔX_{2D} is the inflation-adjusted difference in total money raised in District D between Election 1 and Election 0

ΔX_{3D} is the difference in the number of minor-party candidates on the ballot in District D between Election 1 and Election 0

ΔX_{4D} is the difference in the number of incumbents running in District D between Election 1 and Election 0

ΔX_{5D} is the difference in major-party contestedness in District D between Election 1 and Election 0 (Specification 1 only)

X_6 is the percentage of African Americans living in the district.

Thus, the β1 coefficient in all models is the difference-in-differences estimator of same-district roll-off changes by treatment condition, holding funding, contestedness, minor-party involvement, incumbency, and racial composition constant. I obtained summary financial information from the website of the National Institute on Money in State Politics, census information on Maine's legislative districts from Barone et al. (1998), and demographic information in Connecticut and Rhode Island from Lilley et al. (2007).

Chapter 5

Chapter 5 includes a logistic regression model intended to describe the determinants of public funding. I model candidates in fully funded and partially funded states separately, given the unique characteristics of each type of system. The dependent variable in these models is a dichotomous indicator coded 1 if a candidate accepted (partial or full) public funding and 0 otherwise. For both models, I also fix effects for state. Independent variables are dummy variables coded 1 if the candidate was unopposed, an incumbent, male, a Democrat, employed full- or part-time, or had been previously elected to an office, and 0 otherwise. Positive, significant values on these coefficients indicate that a candidate in the "one" condition was more likely to accept public funding. Finally, I include a variable for the percentage of total votes cast that the candidate's party received in the district during the 2006 election, scaled between 0 and 100 (the mean of this variable is 53.3 percent). Positive, significant values of this coefficient would suggest that candidates are more likely to accept public funding in districts where their party enjoys greater popularity.

I also model candidate responses to two survey questions measuring the extent to which candidates agreed with statements about their resources, using ordered probit regressions. The first one read, "When I began this campaign, I underestimated how difficult it would be to raise money." The second one was, "I have sufficient time, money, and staff to mobilize voters who will support me." The dependent variable is the candidate's selection from an ordinal five-category Likert scale ranging from "Strongly Disagree" to "Strongly Agree." Responses are scaled from 0 to 4, with "Strongly Disagree" coded as 0 and "Strongly Agree" coded as 4, so that progressively higher values of the dependent variable indicate stronger agreement with the statement.

Because the dependent variables are ordinal, I model them with ordered probit regression models. I restrict the analysis to non-incumbent candidates who faced major-party opposition in the 2008 general election. For each statement, I fit three models, each using a different dataset. The first dataset is made up of the aggregate survey data. The second is the matched dataset for fully funded candidates described above for Chapter 3, and the third is the matched dataset for partially funded candidates (also described above). Since the aggregate data (Model 1 for each question) include both partially and fully funded candidates, I include separate dichotomous indicators as the independent variables of interest, coded 1 if a candidate was in one of those funding conditions and 0 otherwise. The matched datasets (Models 2 and 3) contain only one type each of publicly funded candidate; as such, they employ only one public funding indicator, and the 0 condition in those models represents candidates who accepted no public funding.

With that exception, I employ the same specification across all models, holding constant a range of additional covariates. These include dummy variables coded 1 if the candidate was an incumbent, an open-seat candidate, male, or had been previously elected to an office, and 0 otherwise. Given the coding of the dependent variable, positive, significant values of all dichotomous variables indicate that the candidates in the "one" condition were more progressively likely to agree with a given statement. I also include a variable for the percentage of total votes cast that the candidate's party received in the district during the 2006 election, scaled between 0 and 100. Positive, significant values of this coefficient suggest greater propensity for agreeing with the statement when the candidate's party enjoys greater popularity. Finally, I apply state fixed effects in all models.

Chapter 6

Chapter 6 explores the influence of ideology and/or partisan affiliation on candidates' participation, and how partisan effects might equate to electoral competition. Specifically, I engage the question of whether partisan affiliation is a significant determinant of whether an incumbent will face a publicly funded challenger, using data from all incumbent-contested elections, in all years during which Clean Elections funding was available in each state, through 2008. Reelection-seeking incumbents for the lower legislative houses in Arizona, Connecticut, and Maine serve as the unit of analysis. The initial dataset contains 192 incumbents for Arizona, 132 for Connecticut, and 515 for Maine.

I fit separate logistic regression models for each state. In the models of data from Connecticut and Maine, the dependent variable is a dichotomous indicator of whether the incumbent was challenged by a major-party opponent who accepted full public election subsidies. Given the qualification requirements in Maine, and the fact that the party has won seats in the Maine House, I consider the Green Independent Party of Maine a major party; within the theoretical expectations of this chapter, I group them with Democrats. This adjustment does not affect the substance or significance of results reported in Chapter 6. Since I anticipate that Democratic challengers are more likely to accept public funding, the independent variable of interest is a dichotomous indicator coded 1 if the incumbent was a

Republican. I expect the model to return a significant, positive coefficient on this variable, reflecting higher odds of a publicly funded challenge for Republican incumbents.

That said, there are other factors that might also influence the dependent variable. For instance, challengers are likely to use the incumbent's most recent electoral performance as a shortcut measure of his or her political support in the district, and incumbents who faced close elections in previous years may be viewed as vulnerable. Moreover, it is possible that incumbents who are defending a seat for the first time might be seen as weaker, since they have had less time to gain name recognition and otherwise consolidate the advantages of incumbency. Both of these factors are likely to encourage the emergence of a challenge, which itself should raise the probability of facing a publicly funded challenger. To account for these possibilities, I include as covariates the incumbent's two-party general election victory margin in the previous election as well as a dummy variable coded 1 for the first time an incumbent defended his or her seat and 0 for all reelection campaigns thereafter.

Arizona requires a modified approach. State house elections there are conducted in multimember districts in which the top two vote recipients from each district are elected. Since they may find themselves running in the same district as another incumbent (who may or may not be a member of the same party), and against as many as two opposite-party challengers, Arizona incumbents face a wider range of potential strategic circumstances. To adjust for the differences associated with Arizona's multimember districts, I make the dependent variable for the Arizona model a dichotomous measure of whether the incumbent was challenged by *at least* one publicly funded, non-incumbent member of the opposite party. I also include an additional dummy variable, coded 1 if the incumbent was running as part of a two-member, copartisan incumbent "team," since challengers are likely to view such incumbent units as presenting a more formidable path to victory than running in a district with one incumbent and one open seat.

I fix effects by election cycle in all models. Because the model includes a lagged margin of victory in a given district, the logistic regression models do not include data from 2002 in Arizona or from 2004 in either Arizona or Maine, due to redistricting that occurred in those years. Finally, I cluster standard errors by legislative district; clusters account for redistricting.

NOTES

Introduction

1. Public Radio East, October 9, 2012, "Colbert 'Re-Becoming' the Nation We Always Were," retrieved April 15, 2013, from http://publicradioeast.org/post/colbert-re-becoming-nation-we-always-were.

2. Data from the Center for Responsive Politics, retrieved April 15, 2013, from http://www.opensecrets.org/outsidespending/recips.php?cmte=C00498097&cycle=2012.

3. Remarks by the president in the State of the Union Address, 2010, retrieved April 15, 2013, from http://www.whitehouse.gov/the-press-office/remarks-president-state-union-address.

4. Retrieved January 9, 2013, from http://www.opensecrets.org/pacs/superpacs.php.

5. *Expenditures for Open House Seats, by Election Outcome, 1974–2010,* retrieved April 18, 2012, from http://www.cfinst.org/pdf/vital/VitalStats_t3.pdf.

6. *Campaign Funding Sources for House and Senate Candidates, 1984–2008,* retrieved April 18, 2012, from http://www.cfinst.org/pdf/vital/VitalStats_t8.pdf.

7. Data on federal elections come from the Center for Responsive Politics, "The Money behind the Elections," retrieved January 9, 2013, from http://www.opensecrets.org/bigpicture/index.php. Data from state elections were obtained from the National Institute on Money in State Politics, "National Overview Map," retrieved January 9, 2013, from http://www.followthemoney.org/database/nationalview.phtml.

8. See http://www.gallup.com/poll/149636/Americans-Leaders-Follow-Public-Views-Closely.aspx, retrieved April 18, 2012.

1. Why Public Funding?

1. http://hawaii.gov/campaign/public-financing/public-financing-documents/public-funds-disbursed-in-2008, accessed March 11, 2012.

2. Matching funds "triggers" were deemed unconstitutional by the U.S. Supreme Court in 2011. Arizona's matching funds program had been enjoined in 2010 pending federal litigation. I provide further details below and in Chapter 7. See also Miller 2008; Dowling et al. 2012.

3. In uncontested races the subsidy amounts were $512 and $1,658, respectively. Lower qualification thresholds and subsidies for contested races (compared with Arizona) reflect Maine's much smaller and less professionalized legislative districts (see Squire 2007).

2. Strategic Candidates and Public Funding

1. National Institute on Money in State Politics: http://www.followthemoney.org.

3. Campaign Time

1. I base this claim on data obtained from the National Institute on Money in State Politics, available at http://www.followthemoney.org.

2. One-tailed tests; p-values for Arizona, Connecticut, and Maine are .0000, .0189, and .0000, respectively. Two-tailed tests yield the same conclusions.

3. $p = .0002$.

4. $p = .0000$ in both cases.

5. Statistically significant, one-tailed test; $p = .0000$.

6. $p = .0058$ and .0001, respectively.

7. $p = .0031$ and .2629, respectively.

8. Overall, publicly funded candidates in the matched sample reported higher mean levels of total time spent than traditionally financed candidates: 46.4 to 41.9 weekly hours, respectively. This difference is not statistically significant, however.

4. Voting Behavior

1. One-tailed tests indicate that these differences are statistically significant at $\alpha = .05$ in Connecticut ($p = .0000$) but not in Arizona ($p = .0727$). The small number of districts (30) making up the Arizona House of Representatives poses challenges to inference that employs districts as the unit of analysis; there are 21 districts in the treated group but only 7 in the control condition, and precinct-level data could not be obtained for the remaining two districts. Negative mean roll-off is apparent for Arizona House elections because that state employs two-member districts. Since voters may record up to two choices in those contests, Arizona House elections almost always draw more aggregate votes per precinct than the presidential election.

2. $p = .0075$.

3. $p = .01$ and $p = .038$, respectively.

4. However, the p-values from one-tailed tests are relatively low in Arizona ($p = .0796$), Connecticut ($p = .1244$), and Maine ($p = .0611$).

5. $p = .0000$.

6. $p = .0011$.

7. $p = .0000$ in both cases.

8. $p = .0001$.

5. Candidate Quality

1. $p = .0009$.

2. $p = .1466$.

3. p = .0000; one-tailed tests.

4. One-tailed tests indicate that differences between experienced and non-experienced candidates are statistically significant at α = .05 in traditional states and for candidates who opted out of full funding, but not for candidates who opted out of or participated in partial public funding.

6. Ideology and Partisan Participation

1. I collapse "strongly agree" and "agree" into one category.

7. Clean Elections at the Supreme Court

1. The tables and much of the text in this section originally appeared in Miller (2008). I thank Cambridge University Press for graciously allowing their reproduction here.

2. Data were obtained from the Arizona Citizens' Clean Elections Commission. Data from the 2000 election were unavailable.

3. All excerpts from the 2008 District Court opinion come from *McComish v. Brewer,* No. CV-08-1550-PHX-ROS D. Ariz. Aug. 29, 2008.

4. Amicus Brief of Democracy 21, the Campaign Legal Center, Brennan Center for Justice at NYU School of Law, and Public Citizen, Inc. Retrieved January 18, 2013, from http://www.brennancenter.org/page/-/Democracy/Davis%20v.%20FEC%20Amicus%20Brief%20By%20Brennan%20Center%20et%20al.pdf.

5. All excerpts from the 2010 District Court opinion come from *McComish v. Brewer,* No. CV-08-1550-PHX-ROS D. Ariz Jan. 20, 2010.

6 All excerpts from the 2010 9th Circuit Court of Appeals opinion come from *McComish v. Bennett,* No. 10-15166 9th Cir. May 21, 2010.

7. This and all subsequent quotations from the advocates are taken from the official Supreme Court transcript of the oral argument, available at http://www.supremecourt.gov/oral_arguments/argument_transcripts/10-238.pdf.

8. All excerpts from the 2011 U.S. Supreme Court opinion come from *McComish v. Bennett* 564 U.S. 664 (2011).

9. Data obtained from the Arizona Citizens' Clean Elections Commission; data are not available for 2000 in Arizona, nor are they readily available for Maine or Connecticut.

Conclusion

1. Governor Andrew Cuomo's (D-NY) 2012 State of the State Address: "Building a *New* New York … *with you.*" Transcript available at http://www.governor.ny.gov/assets/documents/Building-a-New-New-York-Book.pdf.

2. Retrieved June 15, 2012, from http://www.commoncause.org/site/apps/advocacy/ActionItem.aspx?c=dkLNK1MQIwG&b=5630197.

3. Retrieved June 15, 2012, from http://www.citizen.org/supportfairelectionsnow.

BIBLIOGRAPHY

Alexander, Brad. 2005. "Good Money and Bad Money: Do Funding Sources Affect Electoral Outcomes?" *Political Research Quarterly* 58(2): 353–358.

Arizona Citizens' Clean Elections Commission. 2011. "2010 Annual Report Including a Summary of the 2010 Arizona Statewide & Legislative Elections." Phoenix.

Barone, Michael, William Lilley III, and Laurence J. DeFranco. 1998. *State Legislative Elections: Voting Patterns and Demographics.* Washington, D.C.: Congressional Quarterly.

Bensel, Richard F. 2004. *The American Ballot Box in the Mid-Nineteenth Century.* New York: Cambridge University Press.

Black, Gordon S. 1972. "A Theory of Political Ambition: Career Choices and the Role of Structural Incentives." *American Political Science Review* 66(1): 144–159.

Blasi, Vincent. 1994. "Free Speech and the Widening Gyre of Fund-Raising: Why Campaign Spending Limits May Not Violate the First Amendment after All." *Columbia Law Review* 94(3): 1281–1325.

Bliss, Lawrence, Pamela Jabar Trinward, Andrew O'Brien, and David Van Wie. 2011. "Brief of Amici Curiae Maine Citizens for Clean Elections, Lawrence Bliss, Pamela Jabar Trinward, Andrew O'Brien, and David Van Wie in Support of Respondents." Amicus Curiae Brief. United States Supreme Court. *Arizona Free Enterprise Club's Freedom Club PAC v. Bennett* (U.S. 10-239) and *McComish v. Bennett* (U.S. 10-239).

Bond, Jon R., Cary Covington, and Richard Fleisher. 1985. "Explaining Challenger Quality in Congressional Elections." *Journal of Politics* 47(2): 510–529.

Brennan, Jason. 2012. *The Ethics of Voting.* Princeton, N.J.: Princeton University Press.

Bronars, Stephen G., and John R. Lott. 1997. "Do Campaign Contributions Alter How a Politician Votes? Or, Do Donors Support Candidates Who Value the Same Thing That They Do?" *Journal of Law and Economics* 40: 317–350.

Brown, Adam R. 2013. "Does Money Buy Votes? The Case of Self-Financed Gubernatorial Candidates, 1998–2008." *Political Behavior* 35(1): 21–41.

Campaign Finance Institute. 2010. "Non-party Spending Doubled in 2010 but Did Not Dictate the Results." Retrieved June 13, 2012, from http://www.cfinst.org/press/PReleases/10-11-05/Non-Party_Spending_Doubled_But_Did_Not_Dictate_Results.aspx.

———. 2011. "State Limits on Contributions to Candidates, 2011–2012 Election Cycle." Retrieved May 8, 2012, from http://www.ncsl.org/Portals/1/documents/legismgt/Limits_to_Candidates_2011-2012.pdf.

Card, David, and Alan B. Krueger. 1994. "Minimum Wages and Employment: A Case Study of the Fast-Food Industry in New Jersey and Pennsylvania." *American Economic Review* 84(4): 772–793.

Carsey, Thomas M., Richard G. Niemi, William D. Berry, Lynda W. Powell, and James M. Snyder Jr. 2008. "State Legislative Elections, 1967–2003: Announcing the Completion of a Cleaned and Updated Dataset." *State Politics and Policy Quarterly* 8(4): 430–443.

Cassie, William, and David Breaux. 1998. "Expenditures and Election Results." In *Campaign Finance in State Legislative Elections,* ed. Joel A. Thompson and Gary F. Moncrief. Washington, D.C.: Congressional Quarterly.

Cassie, William, and Joel A. Thompson. 1998. "Patterns of PAC Contributions to State Legislative Candidates." In *Campaign Finance in State Legislative Elections,* ed. Joel A. Thompson and Gary F. Moncrief. Washington, D.C.: Congressional Quarterly.

Connecticut Secretary of State. 2011. "Secretary of State Merrill Reacts to McComish Case." Press release. Retrieved June 12, 2012, from http://www.sots.ct.gov/sots/lib/sots/releases/2008/6.27.11_merrill_reacts_to_mccomish_decision.pdf.

Connecticut State Elections Enforcement Commission. 2011. "Citizens' Election Program 2010: A Novel Program with Extraordinary Results." Retrieved June 12, 2012, from http://www.ct.gov/seec/lib/seec/publications/2010_citizens_election_program_report_final.pdf.

Corrado, Anthony. 2005. "Money and Politics: A History of Federal Campaign Finance Law." In *The New Campaign Finance Sourcebook,* ed. Anthony Corrado. Washington, D.C.: Brookings Institution Press.

Corrado, Anthony, Thomas Mann, and Norman Ornstein. 2011. "Brief for Amici Curiae Anthony Corrado, Thomas Mann, and Norman Ornstein in Support of Respondents." Amicus Curiae Brief. United States Supreme Court. *Arizona Free Enterprise Club's Freedom Club PAC v. Bennett* (U.S. 10-239) and *McComish v. Bennett* (U.S. 10-239).

Cox, Gary W., and Jonathan N. Katz. 1996. "Why Did the Incumbency Advantage in U.S. House Elections Grow?" *American Journal of Political Science* 40(2): 478–497.

Diamond, Alexis, and Jasjeet S. Sekhon. 2006. "Genetic Matching for Estimating Causal Effects: A General Multivariate Matching Method for Achieving Balance in Observational Studies." Available at http://sekhon.berkeley.edu/papers/GenMatch. pdf. Accessed March 16, 2009.

Donnay, Patrick D., and Graham P. Ramsden. 1995. "Public Financing of Legislative Elections: Lessons from Minnesota." *Legislative Studies Quarterly* 20(3): 351–364.

Dowling, Conor. 2011. "Public Financing and Candidate Participation in Gubernatorial Elections." In *Public Financing in American Elections*, ed. Costas Panagopoulos. Philadelphia: Temple University Press.

Dowling, Conor M., Ryan D. Enos, Anthony Fowler, and Costas Panagopoulos. 2012. "Does Public Financing 'Chill' Political Speech? Exploiting a Court Injunction as a Natural Experiment." *Election Law Journal* 11(3): 302–315.

Downs, Anthony. 1957. *An Economic Theory of Democracy.* New York: Harper and Brothers.

Engstrom, Richard L., and Victoria M. Caridas. 1991. "Voting for Judges: Race and Roll-Off in Judicial Elections." In *Political Participation and American Democracy,* ed. W. Crotty. Westport, Conn.: Greenwood.

Epstein, David, and Peter Zemsky. 1995. "Money Talks: Deterring Quality Challengers in Congressional Elections." *American Political Science Review* 89(2): 295–308.

Epstein, Michael J., Richard G. Niemi, and Lynda W. Powell. 2005. "Do Women and Men State Legislators Differ?" In *Women and Elective Office: Past, Present, and Future,* 2nd edition, ed. Sue Thomas and Clyde Wilcox. New York: Oxford University Press.

Feddersen, Timothy J., and Wolfgang Pesendorfer. 1996. "The Swing Voter's Curse." *American Economic Review* 86(3): 408–424.

Feig, Douglas C. 2007. "Race, Roll-Off, and the Straight-Ticket Option." *Politics and Policy* 35(3): 548–568.

Fellowes, Matthew C., and Patrick J. Wolf. 2004. "Funding Mechanisms and Policy Instruments: How Business Campaign Contributions Influence Congressional Votes." *Political Research Quarterly* 57(2): 315–325.

Francia, Peter, John C. Green, Paul S. Herrnson, Lynda Powell, and Clyde Wilcox. 2003. *The Financiers of Congressional Elections.* New York: Columbia University Press.

Francia, Peter L., and Paul S. Herrnson. 2003. "The Impact of Public Finance Laws on Fundraising in State Legislative Elections." *American Politics Research* 31(5): 520–539.

GAO (Government Accountability Office). 2010. *Campaign Finance Reform: Experiences of Two States That Offer Full Public Funding for Political Candidates.* Washington, D.C.: U.S. Government Accountability Office.

Garrett, R. Sam. 2011. "Back to the Future? The Quest for Public Financing of Congressional Campaigns." In *Public Financing in American Elections,* ed. Costas Panagopoulos. Philadelphia: Temple University Press.

Gerber, Alan S., and Donald P. Green. 2000. "The Effects of Canvassing, Telephone Calls, and Direct Mail on Voter Turnout: A Field Experiment." *American Political Science Review* 94(3): 653–663.

———. 2001. "Do Phone Calls Increase Voter Turnout? A Field Experiment." *Public Opinion Quarterly* 65(1): 75–85.

Goidel, Robert K., and Donald A. Gross. 1996. "Reconsidering the 'Myths and Realities' of Campaign Finance Reform." *Legislative Studies Quarterly* 21(1): 129–149.

Grenzke, Janet. 1989. "Candidate Attributes and PAC Contributions." *Western Politics Quarterly* 42(2): 245–264.

Gross, Donald A., and Robert K. Goidel. 2003. *The States of Campaign Finance Reform.* Columbus: Ohio State University Press.

Hall, Richard L., and Frank W. Wayman. 1990. "Buying Time: Moneyed Interests and the Mobilization of Bias in Congressional Committees." *American Political Science Review* 84(3): 797–820.

Herrnson, Paul S. 2011. *Congressional Elections: Campaigning at Home and in Washington.* 6th edition. Washington, D.C.: CQ Press.

Ho, Daniel E., Kosuke Imai, Gary King, and Elizabeth A. Stuart. 2007a. "Matching as Nonparametric Preprocessing for Reducing Model Dependence in Parametric Causal Inference." *Political Analysis* 15(1): 199–236.

———. 2007b. "Matchit: Nonparametric Preprocessing for Parametric Causal Inference." *Journal of Statistical Software.* Available at http://gking.harvard.edu/matchit/.

Hoffman, Adam. 2005. "The Effects of Campaign Contributions on State Legislators." Ph.D. dissertation, Department of Government and Politics, University of Maryland.

Hogan, Robert. 2004. "Challenger Emergence, Incumbent Success, and Electoral Accountability in State Legislative Elections." *Journal of Politics* 66(4): 1283–1303.

Howell, Susan E. 1982. "Campaign Activities and State Election Outcomes." *Political Behavior* 4(4): 401–417.

Jacobson, Gary. 1980. *Money in Congressional Elections.* New Haven, Conn.: Yale University Press.

———. 1987. "The Marginals Never Vanished: Incumbency and Competition in Elections to the U.S. House of Representatives, 1952–1982." *American Journal of Political Science* 31(1): 126–141.

———. 1989. "Strategic Politicians and the Dynamics of U.S. House Elections, 1946–86." *American Political Science Review* 83(3): 773–793.

———. 1990. "The Effects of Campaign Spending in House Elections: New Evidence for Old Arguments." *American Journal of Political Science* 34(2): 334–362.

———. 2009. *The Politics of Congressional Elections.* 7th edition. New York: Addison Wesley.

Jacobson, Gary C., and Samuel Kernell. 1981. *Strategy and Choice in Congressional Elections.* New Haven, Conn.: Yale University Press.

Jones, Ruth S., and Thomas J. Borris. 1985. "Strategic Contributing in Legislative Campaigns: The Case of Minnesota." *Legislative Studies Quarterly* 10(1): 89–105.

Katyal, Neal Kumar, Tony West, Malcolm Stewart, and William M. Jay. 2011. "Brief for the United States as Amicus Curiae Supporting Respondents." Amicus Curiae Brief. United States Supreme Court. *Arizona Free Enterprise Club's Freedom Club PAC v. Bennett* (U.S. 10-239) and *McComish v. Bennett* (U.S. 10-239).

Kendall, Douglas T., Elizabeth B. Wydra, David H. Gans, and Neil Weare. 2011. "Brief of Constitutional Scholars as Amici Curiae in Support of Respondents." Amicus Curiae Brief. United States Supreme Court. *Arizona Free Enterprise Club's Freedom Club PAC v. Bennett* (U.S. 10-239) and *McComish v. Bennett* (U.S. 10-239).

Knack, Stephen, and Martha Kropf. 2003. "Roll-Off at the Top of the Ballot: Intentional Undervoting in American Presidential Elections." *Politics and Policy* 31(4): 575–594.

Krasno, Jonathan S., and Donald Philip Green. 1988. "Preempting Quality Challengers in House Elections." *Journal of Politics* 50: 920–936.

Kraus, Jeffrey. 2006. "Campaign Finance Reform Reconsidered: New York City's Public Finance Program after Fifteen Years." *Forum* 3(4): 1–27.

———. 2011. "Campaign Finance Reform Reconsidered: New York City's Public Finance Program after Fifteen Years." in *Public Financing in American Elections,* ed. Costas Panagopoulos. Philadelphia: Temple University Press.

La Raja, Raymond. 2008. "Candidate Emergence in State Legislative Elections: Does Public Funding Make a Difference?" Paper presented at the 2008 Temple IPA State Politics and Policy Conference. Retrieved April 1, 2010, from http://www.unc.edu/depts/polisci/statepol/conferences/2008/papers/LaRaja.pdf.

Lau, Richard R., and David P. Redlawsk. 1997. "Voting Correctly." *American Political Science Review* 91(3): 585–598.

———. 2001. "Advantages and Disadvantages of Cognitive Heuristics in Political Decision Making." *American Journal of Political Science* 45(4): 951–971.

Lazarus, Jeffrey. 2008. "Incumbent Vulnerability and Challenger Entry in Statewide Elections." *American Politics Research* 36(1): 108–129.

Lilley, William, Laurence J. DeFranco, Mark F. Bernstein, and Kari L. Ramsby. 2007. *Almanac of State Legislative Elections.* 3rd edition. Washington, D.C.: CQ Press.

Maestas, Cherie D., Sarah Fulton, L. Sandy Maisel, and Walter J. Stone. 2006. "When to Risk It? Institutions, Ambitions, and the Decision to Run for the U.S. House." *American Political Science Review* 100(2): 195–208.

Magleby, David B., and Kelly D. Patterson. 1994. "Trends: Congressional Reform." *Public Opinion Quarterly* 58(3): 419–427.

Maine Ethics Commission. 2011. "Maine Clean Election Act Overview of Participation Rates and Payments, 2000–2010." Augusta.

Maisel, L. Sandy, and Walter J. Stone. 1997. "Determinants of Candidate Emergence in U.S. House Elections: An Exploratory Study." *Legislative Studies Quarterly* 22(1): 79–96.

Malbin, Michael J., Peter W. Brusoe, and Brendan Glavin. 2012. "Small Donors, Big Democracy: New York City's Matching Funds as a Model for the Nation and States." *Election Law Journal* 11(1): 3–20.

Malbin, Michael J., and Thomas Gais. 1998. *The Day after Reform: Sobering Campaign Finance Lessons from the American States.* Washington, D.C.: Brookings Institution Press.

Malbin, Michael J., Norman J. Ornstein, and Thomas J. Mann. 2008. *Vital Statistics on Congress, 2008.* Washington, D.C.: Brookings Institution Press.

Malhotra, Neil. 2008. "The Impact of Public Financing on Electoral Competition: Evidence from Arizona and Maine." *State Politics and Policy Quarterly* 8(3): 263–281.

Masket, Seth, and Michael G. Miller. 2013. "Are Taxpayers Subsidizing Extremism? Public Funding, Parties, and Polarization in Maine and Arizona." Available at https://sites.google.com/site/millerpolsci/docs/Masket-Miller.pdf.

Mayer, Kenneth R., and Timothy Werner. 2007. "Electoral Transitions in Connecticut: The Implementation of Clean Elections in 2008." Paper presented at the 104th Annual Meeting of the American Political Science Association, Boston.

Mayer, Kenneth R., Timothy Werner, and Amanda Williams. 2006. "Do Public Funding Programs Enhance Electoral Competition?" In *The Marketplace of Democracy: Electoral Competition and American Politics,* ed. Michael P. McDonald and John Samples. Washington, D.C.: Brookings Institution Press.

Mayer, Kenneth R., and John M. Wood. 1995. "The Impact of Public Financing on Electoral Competitiveness: Evidence from Wisconsin, 1964–1990." *Legislative Studies Quarterly* 20(1): 69–88.

McDermott, Monika. 2005. "Candidate Occupations and Voter Information Shortcuts." *Journal of Politics* 67(1): 201–219.

McGhee, Eric, and Raymond La Raja. 2008. "Campaign Finance: Timing and Its Torments." Paper presented at the annual meeting of the MPSA Annual National Conference, Chicago. Available at http://convention2.allacademic.com/one/mpsa/mpsa08/index.php?click_key=3&PHPSESSID=jfr793banss8oa54puulapf5b3. Accessed October 13, 2008.

McNulty, John E. 2005. "Phone-Based GOTV—What's on the Line? Field Experiments with Varied Partisan Components, 2002–2003." *Annals of the American Academy of Political and Social Science* 601(1): 41–65.

Mebane, Walter R., and Jasjeet S. Sekhon. 1998. "Genetic Optimization Using Derivatives (GENOUD)." Available at http://sekhon.polisci.berkeley.edu/rgenoud/. Accessed March 16, 2009.

Miller, Michael G. 2008. "Gaming Arizona: Public Money and Shifting Candidate Strategies." *PS: Political Science and Politics* 41(3): 527–532.

———. 2011a. "After the GAO Report: What Do We Know about Public Election Funding?" *Election Law Journal: Rules, Politics, and Policy* 10(3): 273–290.

———. 2011b. "Public Money, Candidate Time, and Electoral Outcomes in State Legislative Elections." In *Public Financing in American Elections,* ed. Costas Panagopoulos. Philadelphia: Temple University Press.

Miller, Michael G., and Costas Panagopoulos. 2011. "Public Financing, Attitudes toward Government and Politics, and Efficacy." In *Public Financing in American Elections,* ed. Costas Panagopoulos. Philadelphia: Temple University Press.

Miller, Thomas J., Mark E. Schantz, and Meghan Lee Gavin. 2011. "Brief of the States of Iowa, Connecticut, Maryland, New Mexico, and Vermont as Amici Curiae in Support of Respondents." Amicus Curiae Brief. United States Supreme Court. *Arizona Free Enterprise Club's Freedom Club PAC v. Bennett* (U.S. 10-239) and *McComish v. Bennett* (U.S. 10-239).

Milyo, Jeffrey, David M. Primo, and Matthew Jacobsmeier. 2011. "Does Public Financing of State Election Campaigns Increase Voter Turnout?" In *Public Financing in American Elections,* ed. Costas Panagopoulos. Philadelphia: Temple University Press.

Mutch, Robert E. 2001. "Three Centuries of Campaign Finance Law." In *A User's Guide to Campaign Finance Reform,* ed. Gerald C. Lubenow. Lanham, Md.: Rowman and Littlefield.

NALEO (National Association of Latino Elected and Appointed Officials). 2008. *How Much Help? Public Financing and Latino Candidates.* Washington, D.C.: NALEO Educational Fund.

Nelson, Candice J., and David Magleby. 1990. *The Money Chase: Congressional Campaign Finance Reform.* Washington, D.C.: Brookings Institution Press.

Nichols, Mike. 2009. "Anatomy of a Failed Idea." *Wisconsin Interest* 18(3).

Nickerson, David W. 2005. "Partisan Mobilization Using Volunteer Phone Banks and Door Hangers." *Annals of the American Academy of Political and Social Science* 601(1): 10–27.

———. 2006. "Volunteer Phone Calls Can Increase Turnout: Evidence from Eight Field Experiments." *American Politics Research* 34(3): 271–292.

———. 2007. "Quality Is Job One: Professional and Volunteer Voter Mobilization Calls." *American Journal of Political Science* 51(2): 269–282.

Nickerson, David W., Ryan D. Friedrichs, and David C. King. 2006. "Partisan Mobilization Campaigns in the Field: Results from a Statewide Turnout Experiment in Michigan." *Political Research Quarterly* 59(1): 85–97.

Niven, David. 2001. "The Limits of Mobilization: Turnout Evidence from State House Primaries." *Political Behavior* 23(4): 335–350.

———. 2002. "The Mobilization Calendar: The Time-Dependent Effects of Personal Contact on Turnout." *American Politics Research* 30(3): 307–322.

Panagopoulos, Costas. 2009. "Partisan and Nonpartisan Message Content and Voter Mobilization: Field Experimental Evidence." *Political Research Quarterly* 62(1): 70–76.

———. 2011. "Introduction." In *Public Financing in American Elections,* ed. Costas Panagopoulos. Philadelphia: Temple University Press.

Panagopoulos, Costas, Ryan D. Enos, Conor Dowling, and Anthony Fowler. 2011. "Brief for Amici Curiae Costas Panagopoulos, Ph.D., Ryan D. Enos, Ph.D., Conor M. Dowling, Ph.D., and Anthony Fowler in Support of Respondents." Amicus Curiae Brief. United States Supreme Court. *Arizona Free Enterprise Club's Freedom Club PAC v. Bennett* (U.S. 10-239) and *McComish v. Bennett* (U.S. 10-239).

Poggione, Sarah. 2004. "Exploring Gender Differences in State Legislators' Policy Preferences." *Political Research Quarterly* 57(2): 305–314.

Powell, Lynda. 2012. *The Influence of Campaign Contributions in State Legislatures.* Ann Arbor: University of Michigan Press.

Primo, David. 2002. "Public Opinion and Campaign Finance." *Independent Review* 7(2): 207–219.

Primo, David M., and Jeffrey Milyo. 2006. "Campaign Finance Laws and Political Efficacy: Evidence from the States." *Election Law Journal: Rules, Politics, and Policy* 5(1): 23–39.

Pritchard, Anita. 1992. "Strategic Considerations in the Decision to Challenge a State Legislative Incumbent." *Legislative Studies Quarterly* 17: 381–393.

Riker, William H., and Peter C. Ordeshook. 1968. "A Theory of the Calculus of Voting." *American Political Science Review* 62(1): 25–42.

Roosevelt, Theodore. 1907. "President's Seventh Annual Message to Congress." Retrieved November 9, 2012, from http://millercenter.org/president/speeches/detail/3779.

Rosenstone, Steven J., and John Marc Hansen. 1993. *Mobilization, Participation, and Democracy in America.* New York: Macmillan.

Sabato, Larry J. 1989. *Paying for Elections: The Campaign Finance Thicket.* New York: Priority Press.

Schier, Steven E. 2000. *By Invitation Only: The Rise of Exclusive Politics in the United States.* Pittsburgh: University of Pittsburgh Press.

Schultz, David. 2002. "Special Interest Money in Minnesota State Politics." In *Money, Politics, and Campaign Finance Reform Law in the States,* ed. David Schultz. Durham, N.C.: Carolina Academic Press.

Sekhon, Jasjeet S. 2006. "Alternative Balance Metrics for Bias Reduction in Matching Methods for Causal Inference." Available at http://sekhon.berkeley.edu/papers/SekhonBalanceMetrics.pdf. Accessed March 16, 2009.

———. 2008. "Multivariate and Propensity Score Matching Software with Automated Balance Optimization: The Matching Package for R." Available at http://sekhon.berkeley.edu/papers/MatchingJSS.pdf. Accessed March 16, 2009.

———. 2009. "Opiates for the Matches: Matching Methods for Causal Inference." Available at http://sekhon.berkeley.edu/papers/opiates.pdf. Accessed March 16, 2009.

Sekhon, Jasjeet S., and Walter R. Mebane. 1998. "Genetic Optimization Using Derivatives." *Political Analysis* 7(1): 187–210.

Sorauf, Frank J. 1992. *Inside Campaign Finance: Myths and Realities.* New Haven, Conn.: Yale University Press.

Squire, Peverill. 2007. "Measuring State Legislative Professionalism: The Squire Index Revisited." *State Politics and Policy Quarterly* 7(2): 211–227.

Steen, Jennifer A. 2006. *Self-Financed Candidates in Congressional Elections.* Ann Arbor: University of Michigan Press.

Stone, Walter J., L. Sandy Maisel, and Cherie D. Maestas. 2004. "Quality Counts: Extending the Strategic Politician Model of Incumbent Deterrence." *American Journal of Political Science* 48(3): 479–495.

Thielemann, Gregory S., and Donald R. Dixon. 1994. "Explaining Contributions: Rational Contributors and the Elections for the 71st Texas House." *Legislative Studies Quarterly* 19(4): 495–506.

Thompson, Joel A., William Cassie, and Malcolm E. Jewell. 1994. "A Sacred Cow or Just a Lot of Bull? Party and PAC Money in State Legislative Elections." *Political Research Quarterly* 47(1): 223–237.

Vanderleeuw, James M., and Richard L. Engstrom. 1987. "Race, Referendums, and Roll-Off." *Journal of Politics* 49(4): 1081–1092.

Vanderleeuw, James M., and Baodong Liu. 2002. "Political Empowerment, Mobilization, and Black Voter Roll-Off." *Urban Affairs Review* 37(3): 380–396.

Vanderleeuw, James M., and Glenn H. Utter. 1993. "Voter Roll-Off and the Electoral Context: A Test of Two Theses." *Social Science Quarterly* 74(3): 664–673.

Van Dunk, Emily. 1997. "Challenger Quality in State Legislative Elections." *Political Research Quarterly* 50(4): 793–807.

Wattenberg, Martin P., Ian McAllister, and Anthony Salvanto. 2000. "How Voting Is Like Taking an SAT Test: An Analysis of American Voter Roll-Off." *American Politics Research* 28(2): 234–250.

Wawro, Gregory. 2001. "A Panel Probit Analysis of Campaign Contributions and Roll-Call Votes." *American Journal of Political Science* 45(3): 563–579.

Werner, Timothy, and Kenneth R. Mayer. 2007. "Public Election Funding, Competition, and Candidate Gender." *PS: Political Science and Politics* 40: 661–667.

Wertheimer, Fred, and Susan Weiss Manes. 1994. "Campaign Finance Reform: A Key to Restoring the Health of Our Democracy." *Columbia Law Review* 94(4): 1126–1159.

Wilcox, Clyde. 2001. "Contributing as Political Participation." In *A User's Guide to Campaign Finance Reform,* ed. Gerald Lubenow. Lanham, Md.: Rowman and Littlefield.

Wilson, Megan. 2012. "Stephen Colbert Shuts Down His Super PAC." *The Hill,* November 13. Retrieved April 15, 2013, from http://thehill.com/blogs/ballot-box/fundraising/267535-colbert-shuts-down-his-super-pac.

Witko, Christopher. 2006. "PACs, Issue Context, and Congressional Decisionmaking." *Political Research Quarterly* 59(2): 283–295.

Woolley, Peter, and Tim Vercellotti. 2007. "Public Attitudes toward the Clean Elections Initiative." Retrieved August 15, 2009, from http://eagletonpoll.rutgers.edu/polls/CE_FinalReport_11_07.pdf.

INDEX

Page numbers followed by letters *f* and *t* refer to figures and tables, respectively.

ideology, and public funding programs: cost
calculus regarding, 35–36, 45, 108–9,
116–17; likelihood of participating in,
10–11; opposition vs. strategic advantage,
116–17; opting-out of, 108–17, 111*t,*
122–23; radicalism among participants
in, 94
incumbents: command of resources among,
101*t,* 102; fundraising comfort level
among, 100, 101*t;* inherent advantages
of, 2, 3, 18–19, 36, 81, 83; likelihood
of facing publicly funded challenger,
partisan dynamics in, 119*f,* 120–22,
121*t,* 123; odds of winning, 80; PACs
and, 2; reduced importance of public
funding for, 38; spending gap between
challengers and, 5, 18–19, 81, 83, 150;
and voter roll-off, 76, 76*t*
information dissemination: candidates' role
in, 70; Clean Elections and, 153
Iowa, on matching funds provision, 137

Jay, William, 139
Jones, Ruth S., 82
Jones, Walter, Jr., 146

Kagan, Elena, 140
Kennedy, John F., 15–16
Kraus, Jeffrey, 146

labor unions, campaign funding by, 15
La Raja, Raymond, 19, 89, 117
Larson, John, 146
Latino candidates, public election funding
and, 6

Maine: costs of running for legislative office
in, 31; funding levels of traditional vs.
publicly funded candidates in, 103–4, 104*f;*
on matching funds provision, 137; voter
roll-off trends in, 71–75, 72*f,* 74*f,* 76*t,* 77
Maine public election funding program, 4,
21, 22*t,* 24–25; 2010 election campaign,
141; candidates opting out of, 110;
and candidates' time allocations, vs.

traditional campaigns, 54, 55*f;* and
electoral competition, 82–83, 85–87, 86*f;*
and incumbent-challenged elections,
partisan dynamics in, 119*f,* 120–22, 121*t,*
123; and overall campaign spending, 5;
partisan gap in participation in, 118,
119*f;* primary goal of, 68; qualification
requirements for, 34
Malbin, Michael, J., 7, 19, 49, 143, 146, 153
Malhotra, Neil, 7, 37, 83, 123, 150
market forces: Republicans' belief in,
112–13, 122; traditional campaign
finance and, 10
Maryland: on matching funds provision,
137; public election funding program
in, 21
mass media: and campaign spending,
explosion in, 16, 49; and candidate
visibility, 15; Fair Elections Now Act
(FENA) on, 147
matching funds, 125–32; Fair Elections
Now Act (FENA) and, 148, 152; First
Amendment challenge to, 124–25,
132–40; importance to participating
candidates, 125, 126*t;* loss of, and future
of public funding, 140–41, 144, 150;
in New York City program, 144–45;
participating candidates on, 127, 129–30;
and shift in spending calculus, 126–30,
131–32; timing of allocation of, 127–32,
131*t;* traditional candidates on, 126–29
Maurer, William, 138
Mayer, Kenneth R., 6, 58, 82, 83
McComish, John, 132
McComish v. Bennett, 11, 124–25, 136–40;
and future of public funding, 140–41,
143–44, 152
McComish v. Brewer, 132, 133, 134–36
Merrill, Denise, 141
Michigan, public election funding program
in, 21
Millionaire's Amendment, 133–34;
matching funds provisions compared to,
134, 138, 140
Milyo, Jeffrey, 68